COFFEE AND PEASANTS IN GUATEMALA

J.C. CAMBRANES

COFFEE AND PEASANTS

THE ORIGINS OF THE MODERN PLANTATION ECONOMY IN GUATEMALA, 1853-1897

Distributed in the U.S.A. & Canada by

CIRMA / Plumsock Mesoamerican Studies
Box 38
South Woodstock, Vermont 05071
U.S.A.

Original title: "Café y Campesinos en Guatemala, 1853-1897."
Universidad de San Carlos de Guatemala, 1985.

© 1985, Julio Castellanos Cambranes
English version revised by Carla Clason-Höök.
Cover: Designgrupp – Comunidad
ISBN 91 85894 09 5

The English edition was possible thanks to the finantial support
of the Plumsock Fundation of Indianapolis, Indiana, USA, and
the Swedish Agency for Research and Cooperation with Developing Countries (SAREC), Stockholm, Sweden.

GULF OF MEXICO

GUATEMALA HONDURAS

EL
SALVADOR

NICARAGUA

COSTA
RICA

PACIFIC OCEAN

PANAMA

The development of coffee growing in Guatemala

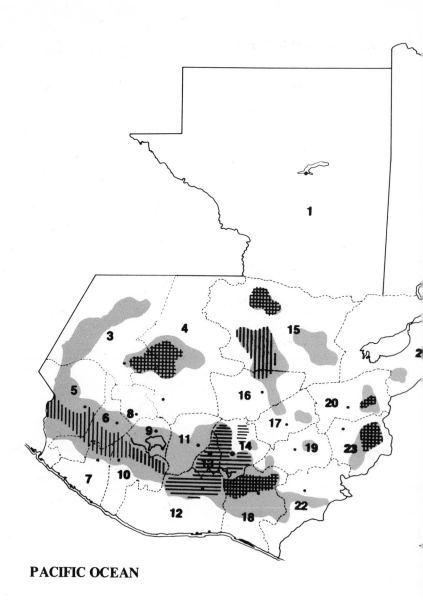

PACIFIC OCEAN

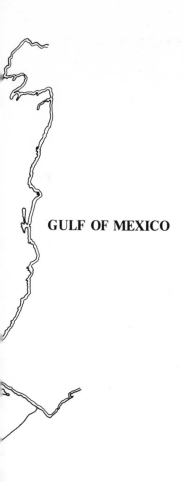

GULF OF MEXICO

1 El Petén
2 Belice
3 Huehuetenango
4 El Quiché
5 San Marcos
6 Quetzaltenango
7 Retalhuleu
8 Totonicapán
9 Sololá
10 Suchitepéquez
11 Chimaltenango
12 Escuintla
13 Sacatepéquez
14 Guatemala
15 Alta Verapaz
16 Baja Verapaz
17 El Progreso
18 Santa Rosa
19 Jalapa
20 Zacapa
21 Izabal
22 Jutiapa
23 Chiquimula

▤ Since 1835
▥ Since 1850
▦ Since 1870
■ Since 1900

0 30 50   Km
10 20 30   Miles

CONTENTS

INTRODUCTION

In 1979, a proposal for a research project on present day agricultural production systems in Guatemala was submitted to the Board of Directors of the Faculty of Agronomy at the University of San Carlos, Guatemala. The proposal was accepted and, from August of that year until May 1980, I worked on the project in the newly inaugurated Institute for Agronomic Research (IIA) of the aforementioned Faculty.

In the proposal I had pointed out the notable inequality with characterizes regional agricultural development in Guatemala and the need for special attention to be given to the creation and expansion of coffee growing in that contry. This is important in order to improve our understanding of the present relationship and the interdependence which exists between modern and traditional techniques, the cornerstone of the agrosystems under investigation.

With the help of diligent research assistants, I managed to compile extensive material from the Archivo General de Centroamérica and the Registro de la Propiedad Inmueble, in Guatemala City. As Director of Publications on Economic History from

15

the Ministry of Finance, I had access to classified material from
the State Property Department within that same Ministry. Here
is stored all information concerning the expropriation of plantations and other property belonging to German nationals in
Guatemala in 1943. The interest which this project awoke in
the late licenciado Julio Segura Trujillo, then Secretary General of Economic Planning of the Guatemalan government, not
only facilitated my periodical visits to many former German fincas (coffee plantation), which today are either State owned or
peasant cooperatives and where the entry of unofficial visitors
is not allowed, but gave me the opportunity of doing some research in the confidential archives of the Instituto de Transformación Agraria (INTA), where many of the private files on exp-
ropiated fincas are kept.

On the fincas I was able to freely conduct interviews with
administrators, foremen, shop personnel, workers and family
members. In some of the fincas valuable documents concerning
the entreprenurial activities of the owners were discovered. A
Fullbright Scholarship permitted me to work for nine months,
from September 1980 to May 1981, in the archives of the late
Edwin Paul Dieseldorff, German agricultural entrepreneur from
Alta Verapaz, which are currently at Tulane University Library, New Orleans.

As I became increasingly familiar with the content of E.P. Dieseldorff's comercial and personal correspondence, I was able to
verify, correct and expand the information I had already compiled on the modern plantation economy in Guatemalan agriculture. The correspondence examined contained more than one
million items covering the period from 1889 to 1940, the organization of E.P Dieseldorff's agricultural concerns (one of many
of its kind in Guatemala at the time), and his rapport with the
Guatemalan government for over fifty years. Research carried
out in the German archives at Merseburg and Potsdam permitted me to compile interesting data on the influx of German capital into Guatemala and the role which the Germans played in
the development of coffee growing in the country.

Given the bulk of first hand information compiled on coffee
production and its impact on the socio-economic life of the count-

ry, what was meant to be an introduction on the subject of agricultural production, turned out to be the first volume of this work. As a result, I have divided the study into three parts so as to permit the reader to fully comprehend the history of agricultural development in Guatemala over the last one hundred and fifty years and its effects on the social and political structure which has prevailed in the country from the time the *finqueros* (landlords) came to power in 1871 to the present day.

The first part, presented herein, is concerned almost exclusively with the immediate antecedents and general conditions surrounding the introduction of coffee growing in Guatemala. The title I have chosen — "Coffee and Peasants", attempts to underline not only the economic and political impact of commercial coffee production on the life of the peasant communities, but my particular interest in presenting the members of those communities as protagonists of Guatemalan history.

The historical development of Guatemala, from the time of the conquest to the present day, has been largely characterized by the high degree of societal divisions; a product of the permanent dictatorship of minority groups which, through the repressive apparatus of the State, have perpetuated the unequal distribution of wealth and the exploitation of indian peasants and mestizo labour. The authoritarian character of the Colonial Feudal State, introduced by the Spaniards in 1524, and of the National State, created by the *"founding fathers of the Nation"* in 1821, has subjugated the workers of this country for centuries and has given rise to an equally perpetual class struggle which has led to the semi-destruction of indigenous peasant communities, the alienation of wage labour, increased racial discrimination, terrible living conditions for the greater part of the population and the ever-increasing use of terror as a means of domination by those in whose hands power rests: the landlord and the bureaucratic-military bourgeoisie. For these reasons, it is only possible to understand our contemporary history by becoming acquainted with the history of the Guatemalan peasantry and with the ways in which the agricultural bourgeoisie seized thousands of caballerias[*] of communal property,

---

[*] A caballeria = Agrarian measure of 96 acres

made slaves out of rural labourers, introduced coffee growing and consequently reinforced an economic and political system founded during the period of Spanish colonial domination.

This volume marks an attempt at documenting the events of Guatemalan agricultural history over the course of the latter half of the nineteenth-century, as recounted by its leading protagonists: the peasantry, the agricultural entrepreneurs and the State authorities themselves. To achieve this end, it was necessary to transcribe lengthy but fascinating reports and memoranda addressed to Ministries of the Interior, dictators in office and the German Chancery, from *corregidores* to *jefes politicos* (local government representatives), members of the peasant communities, agricultural entrepreneurs and German diplomats posted in Guatemala. This should permit the reader to formulate an objective picture of the intimate connection between the development of commercial agriculture and the creation of a coffee State; between the consolidation of the bourgeoisie in power and the expropriation of communal land; between the instauration of slavery and the impoverishment of the peasantry; and between the adoption of a dictatorial model for agricultural development by the finqueros and the accumulation of capital in Guatemala.

As pointed out by an historian in a recent study awaiting publication (Jesús Maria Añoveros: *"Estructura Agraria y Poder Politico en Guatemala: La Reforma Agraria de Arbenz"* — unpublished doctoral thesis submitted to the Department of American History, Universidad Complutense de Madrid: 1982, 561 pp. —), the history of Guatemala is marked by *"political power which has always been wielded by the economically priviledged class, due to the agrarian structure which developed in the country."* (p. 25). Consequently, only the destruction of the monopoly on the land and its redistribution among those who work it, will bring about the beginning of true change in our agricultural development. Any tranformation in the agrarian structure which calls for the centralization of land ownership would be equivalent to the establishment of a new dictatorship and the subjugation of the peasantry to a new breed of oppression no less abhorrent than that which they have had to tolerate to date.

*   *   *

While this study on coffee and peasantry in Guatemala was a joint effort, I would like to clarify that I alone am responsible for the contents and opinions expressed herein. However, I must add that this first volume could not have been completed without the able assistance of my colleagues Carlos Lemus Estrada, Iris Amanda Ruiz, Roberto Ganddini (research assistants); Elvira Busch and Mariela Miranda (typing assistants).

I would also like to thank Dr. Antonio Sandoval, Dean of the Faculty of Agronomy at the University of San Carlos, Carlos Orlando Arjona, and Oscar René-Leiva, Directors of the Insitute for Agronomic Research, for their support and understanding; and Evelin Castellanos, Julio César Pinto Soria, Roberto Cabrera, Edelberto Torres-Rivas and Marco Tulio Pinelo for their kind encouragement. I am eternally indebted to my North American colleagues and historians Chris Lutz, Steve Webre, Ralph Lee Woodward Jr. and Bill Nañez, who not only suggested that I apply for the Fullbright Scholarship, but recommended me for that scholarship, guided my research at the University of Tulane and made my stay in New Orleans so pleasant. Lastly, I would like to express my gratitude to my Swedish friends Magnus Mörner, Weine Karlsson, Director of the Institute for Latin American Studies of the University of Stockholm, and Roland Anrup for having given me the opportunity to work in their beautiful country, affording me living proof of the meaning of the word solidarity.

CHAPTER I

COLONIAL HERITAGE AND AGRICULTURE

The legacy bequeathed to Guatemala by Spanish colonists at the time of its political independence — September 15, 1821 — not only included mass poverty and material backwardness but, more significantly, a highly stratified class structure which had as its material base an agrarian economy entirely subordinated to the interests of a small group of Spaniards and *criollos* (Spanish descendants), strict supporters of the colonial system of feudal domination, exporters of agricultural products and importers of consumer goods manufactured in Europe.

This legacy also included a Conservative agrarian legislation and the custom among the affluent of acquiring large expanses of land for social prestige and hoarding earnings generated from trade and agriculture. As pointed out by the Guatemalan historian, Ignacio Solís, during the colonial period it was common for the wealthy to keep their capital completely idle, which meant that it

"gave its holders no pleasure other than the intimate satisfaction of knowing that they posessed treasures

21

> *whose value was estimated as being astronomical by the*
> *population, whose natural tendency was to exaggerate."*[1]

The division of agriculture

As early as the sixteenth-century and immediately following the Conquest, the Spaniards showed a particular interest in Guatemalan products. The *encomenderos* (early conquerors who became powerful lords) exacted commodity tribute from the Indians in the form of cacao which they later sold to merchants who undertook to deliver it to Mexico. From the 16th Century until just before Independence, the cultivation of *xiquilite* (Indigofera tinctoria), a blue dye known as indigo, largely demanded by the European textile industry, was also a source of enrichment for many merchants.[2] The colonists did little to diversify agriculture and improve the traditional system of tilling the soil. This factor contributed to the slow development of agricultural production and the extremely limited use of modern agricultural technology. In keeping with Spanish interests, agriculture was divided into two principal sectors: the commercial sector which comprised of medium- and large-scale landowners, interested in cacao, indigo and sugar cane, and the sector made up of the bulk of Indian and *mestizo* (mixture of Indian and Spanish) peasants dedicated to growing foodstuffs on small plots of land either made available to them by the Spanish authorities or simply snatched from the mountains. As a consequence, while only a minority of foreigners and their offspring worked the land for lucrative purposes, the majority of peasants did so to alleviate their hunger and as a means of paying the tribute exacted from them.

1. Ignacio Solís, *"Memorias de la Casa de la Moneda de Guatemala y del desarrollo económico del país. Contiene datos sobre la riqueza mineralógica de América Central".* (Publication of the Ministry of Finance, 6 volumes, Guatemala, 1978-1979, volume II), p 576.

2. Robert S. Smith, *"La producción y el comercio del añil en el Reino de Guatemala".* Article published in Jorge Luján Muññoz (ed.): *"Economía de Guatemala, 1750-1940. Antología de lecturas y materiales."* (Publication of the Faculty of Humanities, University of San Carlos, Guatemala, 2 volumes). Guatemala, 1980, volume I, pp. 215-287.

The cultivation of the indigo plant

At the end of the eighteenth-century the indigo traded by the merchants residing in Guatemala City faced growing competition from the international market. This was due not only to the poor quality of the Central American variety and its high price on the foreign market due to heavy taxes imposed by the colonial authorities, but also to the fact that Dutch, French and English colonists were flooding the European market with this commodity. In Guatemala it was soon discovered that the Dutch were shipping 400,000 pounds of indigo annually to Amsterdam from their Asian colonies.[3] The annual average of indigo produced in Central America from 1772 to 1781 was 697,200 pounds and between 1783 and 1892, 972,189 pounds.[4] In addition, between 1793 and 1796, close to 3,000,000 pounds of indigo, earmarked for Spain, were shipped from Caracas as Venezuela experienced an upward swing in its production of the product. As a result, at the beginning of the nineteenth-century, four harvests of Central American _xiquilite_, that is, approximately 3,424,000 pounds of indigo, were lying in storage in the ports of Havana, Veracruz and Honduras with Guatemalan merchants not knowing how to place it into the already saturated international market.[5]

Coffee as a cash crop

The economic crisis which threatened indigo producers and merchants in the Kingdom of Guatemala at the end of the eighteenth-century prompted liberal-minded members of the _Sociedad Económica de Amigos del País_ — a colonial institution comprising of prominent landowners, merchants and intellectuals residing in the country — , to recommend that an end be put to the _"single-crop policy"_ and that immediate efforts be made to experiment with other crops demanded on the inter-

---

3. Ibid., p. 258.
4. Manuel Rubio Sánchez, _"Historia del Añil o Xiquilite en Centro América"._ (Publication of the Ministry of Education, 2 volumes.) San Salvador, El Salvador: 1976, Vol. I, p 104.
5. Robert S. Smith, op. cit., p. 258.

national market.[6] In 1803, it was decided that those landowners who succeeded in diversifying agricultural production in the country should be exempt from paying taxes and tithes for a period of ten years. In order to assist *xiquilite* growers, the colonial government decided to make this product entirely tax-deductible. This same practice was later applied to cacao, sugar, cotton and coffee producers.[7] This is the first mention in Guatemala of coffee as a tradeable commodity on the international market. However, while evidence attests to the fact that coffee was already being grown in the country, all available data seem to suggest that there was no large-scale coffee production, despite the demand for this product in Europe at the time.

Coffee was first grown as a cash crop in the fifteenth-century in the Arabian colony of Harar in Abyssinia.[8] By the middle of the eighteenth-century, it was already a popular beverage in Europe. French colonists invested millions of Francs in growing coffee in their Caribbean colonies, and by 1753 succeeded in producing 70,000 quintals (1 quintal = a one hundred weight) in Martinique, and 2,948 in Guadeloupe. In 1789, the French produced 662,000 quintals of coffee in Haiti and this led to the introduction and development of coffee growing in Cuba.[9] In a document dated 1811 which summed up the economic crisis plaguing Guatemala at the time, influential merchants living in the country noted the success Cuba was enjoying with its coffee production. They suggested that Guatemala do likewise for speculative reasons, and condemned the medieval practice of leaving arable land idle:

> *"Everyone is well aware of the contribution which coffee has made over the past twenty years to Cuba's agriculture and commerce. Just prior to this period, coffee was imported from Puerto Rico for consumers in Havana, and just last year, 1810 to be precise, Cuba produced 399,601 arrobas (weight of about 25 lbs.).*

6. Ramón A. Salazar, *"Historia de Veintiún Años"* (Guatemala, 1928.), p. 261.
7. Ignacio Solis, op. cit. volume IV, p. 928.
8. William H. Ukers, *"All About Coffee"* (New York; 1922), p. 197.
9. Francisco Pérez de la Riva, *"El Café Historia de su cultivo y explotación en Cuba"* (La Habana, 1944), pp. 8 and 22.

> *Every day it is becoming increasingly apparent that the*
> *wealth of this nation lies in these vast terrains which*
> *invite us to devote our time and our energy to their*
> *cultivation. Yet, they lie abandoned, untilled, land*
> *turned to scrub, shelter for wild animals and reptiles,*
> *while no man rich or poor heeds the call."[10]*

Coffee reached Guatemala and Costa Rica in the eighteenth century. Initially it was grown as an ornamental plant on an experimental basis. During the first half of the nineteenth-century, roasted and ground coffee was sold by apothecaries and street vendors as a remedy for inebriation. It appears, however, that the sale of imported coffee was also quite widespread, perhaps because of its superior blend and taste.[11]

The cultivation of cochineal

For a variety of reasons, Guatemala, unlike Costa Rica, did not grow coffee exclusively as a cash crop until the middle of the nineteenth-century. Firstly, little was known of the conditions and methods required for large-scale production and processing. Secondly, coffee required an outlay of capital which the average landowner was not prepared to make, for fear of failure. On the other hand, for centuries Guatemalans had been growing *xiquilite* and were well-versed in the marketing of indigo as a dye. It is most likely that this had some bearing on the decision to embark on the production of cochineal, source of a red

10. *Apuntamientos sobre agricultura y el comercio del Reyno de Guatemala.* In: *Economia de Guatemala,* op. cit. vol. I, p. 64.
11. Juan J. Rodríguez, *"Desde cuándo se cultivó el café en Guatemala?"* Article published in *La Republica,* Guatemala: July 31, 1900. In 1802 and 1803, the *Gaceta de Guatemala* reported that coffee was being shipped to Cádiz, from the ports of Veracruz and Omoa, respectively. However, according to a study on the coffee trade, carried out in our country, *"there have never been any documents"* to attest that coffee had been grown in Guatemala. See Manuel Rubio Sánchez, *"Historia del Comercio del Café en Guatemala. Siglos XVIII y XIX".* Article published in *Anales de la Sociedad de Geografia e Historia de Guatemala",* vol. L, Jan-Dec 1977, Part I, pp. 174-175. Robert A. Naylor, in his unpublished study entitled *"British Commercial Relations with Central America, 1821-1851"* (Tulane University, New Orleans 1958) states that in 1834, 1835 and 1849, small quantities of coffee from Jamaica were introduced to Central America. He also points out that by 1835 Central American coffee was being exported to England for the equivalent of 3,596 Sterling Pounds (see pp. 315, 319 and 331).

dye also widely used and in great demand by the European textile industry. Furthermore, the agroexporters interested in the production of cochineal inhabited a region well-suited to the cultivation of *nopal* (Opuntia ficus indica), a class of cactus used to nurture the insects from which the cochineal is extracted.

Cochineal was first produced for commercial purposes during a period marked by Guatemala's Independence and the civil wars which ensued — a difficult period for the more conservative members of the ruling class. Much of the land belonging to the Conservatives was confiscated by the Liberal sector which was vying for political hegemony. Funds which could have been allocated for the country's agricultural development either left the country in the hands of wealthy emigrants of Spanish descent or were used to defray the costs of financing military expenditures during that turbulent period. However, the *laissez-faire* policy, adopted in the country after its independence, lured English and German merchants to Guatemala who, in no time, proved to be particularly enterprising and ultimately responsible for the creation of modern plantations which, over the course of the nineteenth-century would supplant the *estates* of the Spanish colonial period. By making ever-increasing investments in agricultural ventures, newcomers to the country set an example for the local affluent community and succeeded, as such, in creating a new and more stable base for commercial agriculture. As I pointed out in an earlier publication, the direct result of the arrival of the foreigner who brought financial resources to the country, was the appearance of a sector inclined towards the development of capitalist agricultural production, unlike the landowner interested in the promotion of the extensive and low productivity agriculture characteristic of the period of Spanish rule in Guatemala[12] With the increase in the number of modern plantations from the middle of the nineteenth-century, the Guatemalan economy became increasingly more capitalistic in nature. The notion of wealth for

---

12. J.C. Cambranes, *"Aspectos del desarrollo economico y social de Guatemala, a la luz de fuentes historicas alemanes, 1868-1885".* (Publication of the Institute for Economic and Social Research — IIES — , University of San Carlos, Guatemala, 1975).

wealth's sake, or rather, the accumulation of land left idle and equally unproductive capital hoarded just for the sake of prestige, started losing the social significance it had during the Spanish colonial period. This occurred despite resistance from the traditional landowner who, in the eyes of the foreign entrepreneur, did nothing but impede development. According to a Swiss national, interested in the acquisition of land well-suited for intensive agriculture,

> *"the owner of this property abides by the same*
> *philosophy as the majority of the landowners in this*
> *country, and this philosophy impedes progress. They*
> *don't cultivate their land, but at the same time they're*
> *not prepared to sell it to other more enterprising persons,*
> *foreigners in particular. Land such as this could,*
> *because of its proximity to the Capital, be extremely*
> *valuable if it were properly cultivated".*[13]

Consequently, from the time of Independence onward, the driving force behind Guatemala's growing national economy, was the individual willing to invest his money in agriculture, organizing and developing a modern plantation economy. This driving force was specially the foreign or Guatemalan entrepreneur who converted his money into capital by reorganizing agricultural production, making it ripe for the production of goods destined for the international market, taking advantage of soil and climatic conditions, implementing scientific techniques for extensive crop cultivation, optimally combined with supervised labour-intensive methods which facilitated the systematic exploitation of rural labour, the principal factor of production.

Cochineal gained importance in Guatemala and replaced indigo as the chief and almost sole export crop from the 1820s until the 1860s. However, the innovation of chemical dyes in Europe and their implementation in the textile industry shortly thereafter, in addition to domestic factors in Guatemala, led to a decline in its production level. Nevertheless, in 1851 the producti-

---

13. Gustav Bernouilli, *"Reise in der Republik Guatemala".* Article published in *Petermann's Geographische Mitteilungen",* 1874, vol. 20, Book VIII, p. 281.

on of dyestuffs generated employment for many people and bolstered the circulation of money which affected vast sectors of the society, above and beyond constituting the base of the national economy.[14] Land, cheap labour and capital investment were the key components of the emerging economic institution referred to as the modern plantation economy which would, in time, shape the political and social organization of Guatemala from the latter half of the 19th century to the present, after tying the destiny of the country to foreign neo-colonialism.

It has often been said that one of the characteristics of cochineal production is that the product, also known as *grana*, flourishes both on large and small areas of land, which makes it a rather *"democratic"* crop. This says nothing about the reality of the conditions under which *grana* production was first developed in Guatemala. In fact, in Amatitlan, Antigua and parts of Oriente, small, medium and large-sized *nopal* plantations were cropping up and many families subsisted from growing cochineal at home.[15] However, the majority of small and medium-sized producers tended to sell their crops in advance to exporters who, together with the large plantation owners, constituted the largest single group to benefit from *grana* production. As pointed out by one observer:

> *"Most plantation owners do not have sufficient capital of their own. For that reason, they are obliged to borrow, at interest rates which range from 12% to 24%, and often find themselves forced to sell their product below the market price even before the actual harvest. As a result, the entrepreneur is left with little or no money and then finds himself, sometimes even before the harvest, having to ask for payment for next year's harvest. It is easy to see how the landowner was almost always in debt and how a single year's loss was capable of ruining him entirely."[16]*

14. Ignacio Solís, op. cit., vol. IV, p. 635.
15. Ibid., p. 629.
16. Gustav Bernouilli, *"Briefe aus Guatemala"*. Article published in *"Petermann's Geographische Mitteilungen"*, 1870, vol. 16, Book XII, p. 438.

Unfavourable weather conditions almost always meant disaster for small and medium-sized cochineal producers. An unexpected downpour or a sudden drop in temperature could easily destroy an entire harvest and bring about severe material loss. For these reasons, cochineal production has always been the vocation of the privileged class; of men such as Carl Friedrich Rudolph Klee, German merchant and agro-exporter who, for more than thirty years, capriciously manipulated _grana_ prices in Guatemala[17], or foreign and native _hacendado_ (owner of a colonial style estate) who, in the second half of the nineteenth-century, would become coffee growers. A foreign investor, interested in growing cotton on the Southern Plain of Guatemala similarly stated in 1861:

> _"The advantage of cotton is that, unlike cochineal, it can be produced in large or small quantities, by any and everyone, rich or poor. This is not the case with cochineal, coffee or sugar which require such financing that they are almost the birthright of the capitalists alone."_[18]

In addition to the small and medium-sized landowners for whom cochineal production meant constantly having to rely on usurious and commercial capital, there were thousands of families working as _colonos_ (tenant farmer) tied to the plantations where _nopal_ was cultivated, and seasonal rural labourers employed by the landowners during the harvest. Solís speaks of

> _"persons of both sexes, Indians and ladinos (persons of mixed Spanish and Indian ancestry) alike, even children, gainfully employed in that agroindustry..."_[19]

for whom cochineal production meant forced labour, indebtedness to a plantation owner for money advanced as wages for ser-

---

17. Deutches Zentralarchiv Merseburg (hereinafter referred to as DZA Merseburg), Auswärtiges Amt (AA), Rep. 14, No. 534, Hesse to AA., July 1, 1852.
18. General Archives of Centroamerica (hereinafter referred to as AGCA), BI, Ministry of the Interior (MGJ), folder No. 28590, Joaquin de la Torre addressing the Minister of the Interior (MG), April 21 1862.
19. Ignacio Solís, op. cit., vol. IV, p. 629.

vices to be rendered on the plantation. And when their work was not sufficient as to satisfy the debt, they easily became indebted for life and perpetually tied to the *estate*. Thus, by stating that

"the Guatemalans had placed all their hopes of wealth and economic well-being in the production of cochineal",[20]

which was often the case, the Guatemalan *agricultor* (cultivator) is clearly being identified with the entrepreneur and the agro-exporter, and Guatemala, with the *plantation*. Thus, our country became one inmense plantation, beginning in the first half of the 19th century with the production of cochineal; coffee and sugar cane, during the second half of the nineteenth-century; and bananas, cotton, cardamom and a small number of other products, throughout the twentieth-century. The country became the property of a handful of native oligarchs and foreign capitalists who, after having set up a political dictatorship, succeeded in monopolizing the factors of production and the international commercialization of agricultural production, while fostering the pauperization and economic and social oppression of the vast majority of the Guatemalan population and the country's underdevelopment.

Guatemala's legacy of underdevelopment has its roots in the chronic disparity in the distribution of profits derived from agricultural products destined for the international market, and, in particular, in the nature of the State and the socio-political organization which the coffee economy created in 1871.

It has been demonstrated that it is erroneous to associate the plantation, as an economic institution, with the slavery, misery, single-cropping, foreign dependency and backwardness of a people.[21] However, not enough light has been shed on the fact that while the plantation economy is and has been the cornerstone of economic development in Guatemala, development has not taken place because the capital generated from agriculture for the export market, instead of being used to accelerate the

---

20. Ibid.
21. See Frank C. Innes, *"Plantations as Institutions Under Stress in the Caribbean Today: A Historical Geographic Approach"*. Article published in: "NS/Canadian Journal of Latin American Studies", vol. VI, No. 12, 1981, pp. 81-87.

development process in our country, has only served to create and consolidate capitalism and a ruling class which is the protégé of the State.

The industrial countries linked the agricultural economies of colonial and semi-colonial countries, such as Guatemala, to their own interests through the modern plantation system, the international market, and _"trade and friendship"_ treaties. While the developed countries have become increasingly wealthy at the expense of those countries dependent on the export of raw materials and foodstufs, the latter have not been able to establish a solid base to finance the diversification of their economies and their development, due to their continual decapitalization. On the other hand, even though coffee growing became the economic pursuit which most contributed to the transformation of the social and political life of the country since the second half of the nineteenth-century, rural labourers have hardly earned enough to subsist. Meanwhile, plantation owners, high ranking State officials, and the vast national network of servants of the established order, have improved their standard of living and consumption levels, importing tremendous quantities of sumptuous goods and further contributing to the country's decapitalization. Under these circumstances the need to change the nature of the plantation system introduced in the nineteenth-century becomes imperative. Changes are needed which would allow for new and more dynamic ways of controlling the ownership and exploitation of land, for the development of agricultural production, for domestic consumption and export, for a public investment policy, for external trade, and for the redistribution of income among all those persons involved in the production process in Guatemala.

CHAPTER II

THE MEN AND THE EPOCH

In the middle of the 19th century, the Guatemalan economy centred on agriculture. More than three fourths of the population, roughly 900,000 persons[1], were either directly or indirectly dependent on the land: peasants, plantation owners, labourers, cattle-raisers, nopal and sugar cane producers, merchants and moneylenders involved in agricultural export production (cochineal, hides, etc.), rural artisans who manufactured clothing and items for domestic use, small merchants who sold these goods in the markets of Guatemala City and other large towns throughout the country, and personnel engaged on the large *haciendas* (administrators, foremen, muleteers and carters, etc).

The character of the Conservative State

Political power lay in the hands of Rafael Carrera, former peasant guerilla leader turned dictator in 1839, and of prominent

1. Karl von Scherzer, *"Las tribus indias de Guatemala"* (trad. by Evelin Paap). Article published in *Mesoamérica,* Journal of the Center for Regional Research on Mesoamerica — CIRMA — , Antigua Guatemala, vol. 1, January-June of 1980, p. 254.

members of the native oligarchy, of colonial descent, whose spokesman was the well-known landowner, politician, academician and fervent believer, Juan José Aycinena.[2] These traditionalists were staunch advocates of the fusion of Church and State. They did not wish to associate with foreigners or free trade and agricultural development based on the notion of commercial agriculture, but longed *"to return to the past"*, to a long lost life of tranquility, shrouded in incense and religious canticles, sheltered by the laws and customs of colonial society. A foreigner visiting the country in 1854 noted that Aycinena had succeeded in monopolizing control of the country's civil administration and tried to make Guatemala a Protectorate of the Spanish Crown, to turn it into a theocratic State and to eradicate the growing influence of foreign merchants and entrepreneurs.[3] The Church, the most powerful of all institutions of the period, was represented by a variety of Catholic congregations which, with Carrera's rise to power, had recovered their political power and their land, which had been expropriated during the anticlerical campaigns waged by the Liberals between 1825 and 1837. In the countryside, the Church made its presence felt with more than 100 parishes in 17 departments throughout the country; and also through its large rural landholdings, its tithes and its loans to landowners and sugar cane and nopal producers. Despite the boom in cochineal production, the old Spanish institutions still enjoyed a powerful and influential role in the socioeconomic life of the country. The *Consulado de Comercio*, for example, which resembled a Chamber of Commerce, grouped together most of the agro-exporters and importers of Spanish origin who were responsible for commercial legislation and promoted independent external trade and the expansion and improvement of domestic and international communication systems. These merchants saw their schemes vanish into thin air due to their limited funds, their dependency on merchants from the English enclave of Belize, who served as commercial middlemen

2. David L. Chandler, *"Juan José de Aycinena. Conservador Idealista de Guatemala del Siglo Diecinueve".* Unpublished doctoral dissertation, Tulane University, New Orleans, 1972.
3. DZA Merseburg, A A., Rep 120, CXIII, 16a, No. 8, Hesse to Manteufel, August 30, 1854.

between England and Central America[4], and growing competition from foreign merchants who arrived immediately after Independence and acted as local representatives for large commercial concerns or manufacturers of consumer goods in the European metropolises. Another institution which dates back to the Spanish colonial period, is the _Sociedad Económica de Amigos del País_, whose membership was largely composed of conservative landowners, politicians and intellectuals. The production and commercialization of cochineal not only generated wealth for a group of foreign merchants and investors, but developed increasing bourgeois attitudes among the land owners, members of the prominent _"criollo"_ families. A result of this activity was the adoption of a development program by a sector of the oligarchy, which conceived the country's progress in terms of the promotion of commercial agriculture and colonization by Europeans,

> _"because in the same way intermarriage begets the perfect individual, the introduction of a well-selected foreign element can lead to the rapid development of a civilization"_.[5]

Most high-ranking State officials belonged to the _Consulado de Comercio_ and the _Sociedad Económica_. The advocates of development were a small minority and their influence did not make itself felt until the 1860's when coffee growing started to gain importance. Rank and file bureaucrats lived off revenue derived from taxes levied on foreign imports (maritime sales tax) and earnings from State monopolies, generated from the sale of tobacco and liquor. Laws and provisions were enforced by rural and urban civil authorities, in keeping with patterns of political control characteristic of the period of Spanish domination. At the departmental level, corregidores represented the President of the Republic, while priests represented high Church dignitaries residing in the Capital of Guatemala.

---

4. Robert A. Naylor, op. cit., p. 79
5. Ignacio Solis, op. cit., vol. III A, p. 835.

The native peasantry

The peasantry was the backbone of the entire conservative order; however, it did not constitute a homogeneous class. President Carrera, with the wise counsel of Aycinena, made it appear as if he were interested in the lot of the peasant masses, whom, according to one foreigner,

> "loved him like a demigod, like the Archangel Raphael; a sentiment largely induced by the clergy".[6]

The vast majority of peasants were free men who lived in their communities and grew foodstuffs (corn, beans, wheat, sugar cane etc.), cotton, etc., and who on a small scale, raised cattle, pigs, sheep and fowl for consumption and sale in the markets of nearby villages and the City of Guatemala. Many communities owned large tracts of land, generally fallow, while others remained without sufficient land for their able-bodied members. The poor distribution of communal farming property prompted some communities to attempt a take-over of their neighbours' land. There were constant conflicts between communities and often those peasants involved in territorial disputes lost their lives as a result. Disparities in the Indian communities of the mid-nineteenth century were a carry-over of the inequalities of the colonial period. It is common knowledge that for the Guatemalan people, the Conquest meant enslavement and extermination if they dared to resist subjugation and serfdom. Tens of thousands of Indians were massacred by Spanish Conquistadors, and thousands more succumbed to diseases and infirmities "imported" from Europe or as a result of outrages committed by foreigners. The Spanish Crown declared all occupied land property of the King of Spain and this land was distributed amongst the Conquistadors. In 1538, Spain instructed Francisco Marroquín, recently appointed Bishop of Guatemala, to see that the Indians grouped together and settled in towns and villages where they could be politically controlled and more readily subjec-

---

6. Gustav Bernouilli, "Briefe aus Guatemala". Article published in "Petermann's Geographische Mitteilungen, 1869, vol. 15, Book XI, p. 427.

ted to taxation and forced labour.[7] Marroquin carried out these orders only after cajoling and deceiving the natives (he even went so far as to hire a musician from Mexico to dazzle them), who sought refuge in the mountains, caves and ravines. This policy of forcing the Indians, accustomed to living dispersed and on their own, to live in towns and villages, Spanish style, prevailed throughout the period of colonial domination; however,

> _"economic desolation and the inability to pay tribute obliged the Indians to flee their communities (...) and settle in regions beyond colonial control, in isolated valleys, hillsides, etc., which mean avoiding having to pay tribute, but, above all, avoiding having to perform forced labour on the large plantations. Another decisive factor which prompted this exodus was the search for new land, superior in quality to that which had been assigned to them by colonial law".[8]_

Several factors led to the Crown's ultimate recognition of some of the natives rights, the main one being that it understood that it was not only necessary to avoid the extermination of a people which supplied them with tax money and labour, but that this same population hid in terrain not readily accessible to the colonist and in depopulated zones controlled by the Spaniards.

---

7. Richard Konetzke, _"Colección de Documentos para la Historia de la Formación Social de Hispanoamérica, 1493-1810"._ (Publication of the Consejo Superior de Investigaciones Científicas. Madrid, 1953, Royal Letter Patent, _"Al Gobernador de la Provincia de Guatemala sobre lo de juntarse los indios para ser industriados"._) Valladolid, 26 February 1538. Volume I, p. 183.

8. Julio César Pinto Soria, _"Estructura agraria y asentamientos en la Capitanía General de Guatemala. Algunos apuntes históricos"._ (Publication of the Center for Urban and Regional Studies (CEUR) of the University of San Carlos), Guatemala, July 1980, p. 13. According to Jesús María García Añoveros, the _reducciones_ proved to be "the only efficient means of converting the Indians who were dispersed in the mountains and ravines"; and of "keeping track of them" so as to be able to exact tribute from them in addition to controlling the work force"; furthermore, it was virtually the only way of "exercising some control over them". See: "La realidad Social dela Diócesis de Guatemala". Article published in "Mesoamérica", Antigua, Guatemala, vol. I, 1980, p. 115.

The landless

The minority of rural labourers was made up of the legion of *mestizos* known in Guatemala as *"ladinos"*. Most of them did not have legal access to land during the colonial period and were rejected just as much by the colonial authorities as by the Indian communities. These individuals came to constitute a mass of landless men condemned to slave labour on Spanish-owned plantations, where they settled as tenant farmers. Prior to and after Independence, many *ladinos* disappeared into the mountains establishing settlements far from government representatives, in an attempt to lead an independent existence. Once discovered, they were subjected to the same demeaning policy as the native population and were reduced to criminals and potential enemies of public order who had to be kept under surveillance at all times. In 1861 the *corregidor* of Escuintla observed that this department had become

> *"a refuge for many undesirables because of its wide open spaces which do not permit local authorities to keep an eye on them or maintain order".*[9]

Faced with this situation, Gregorio Solares, the *corregidor* quoted above, a prominent landowner and influential military man, drew up a list of 33 *"completely isolated"* settlements located in the department under his jurisdiction, where unknown and suspicious *"characters"* resided. They were subsequently captured and transferred *"under the supreme vigilance of the authorities"*, to towns in the departments of Amatitlán and Suchitepéquez, where they could work on the nopal and sugar cane plantations.[10] Some years later, the *corregidor* of this same

---

9. A.C.G.A., Bl, M.G.J., folder No. 28584, from Gregorio Solares to the Minister of the Interior, October 2, 1861.
10. Ibid. In 1847, the Minister of the Interior ordered the *corregidores* in each Department to issue an edict which would place landless men, whom they viewed as potential revolutionaries, under the control of the authorities. The edicts had to contain the following articles:
> "1. Persons without work shall not be permitted to remain in the Department. A person who is not self-employed must have an employer for whom he works at the standard wage.
> 2. Those persons who desire to change employers must procure a ▸

department, also a landowner and member of a prominent local family, wrote to the Minister of the Interior that he had repeatedly ordered his subordinates to prohibit

> _"the dispersion in the mountains of those persons who are so-inclined, and to see to it that they live together on_ haciendas _or villages, where they can be surveilled not only by local authorities but by the landowners themselves, who are more than interested in seeing order maintained and their tenants conducting themselves in an orderly fashion"._[11]

Independence: a political manoeuvre

This obsession of the rural authorities to maintain public order and establish towns adjacent to the _haciendas_, made up of people living independently and somewhat removed from the economic and political hub of the country, is easier to understand if one bears in mind that much like the colonial period, nineteenth century authorities were often large-scale landowners who

▸ certificate from their first employer attesting to their good conduct and present same to the prospective employer.

3. Those looking for work for the first time or under any other circumstances which make it impossible to comply with the foregoing article, must obtain certification from the Mayor of their town or village who shall not issue a certificate of any kind to persons whom he does not know or to persons involved in legal action, nor shall he charge for any such certificate.

4. It is strictly forbidden to hire a person without similar certification from the Mayor of his town or his former employer. Violation of this regulation can mean a fine of between five and twenty pesos. It is also forbidden to take on a person with a debt outstanding until such time as this debt is settled.

5. Any person without work or without an employer who requires his services, is subject to arrest by the local authorities. Vagrants shall be subject to performing public works. Young men shall be taught a trade but shall always remain under the vigilance of the Mayors.

6. Violation of any one of these orders is punishable by law and the transgressor is subject to a fine of between five and twenty _pesos_, depending on the circumstances. A.G.C.A., B1, M.G.J., folder No. 28539, expediente No. 13, Circular letter from the Minister of the Interior to the _corregidores_, August 13, 1847.

11. Ibid., folder No. 28605, from Luis Arrivillaga to the Minister of the Interior, June 14, 1866.

considered the labour force to be of considerable economic significance. The truth is that Independence was a veritable political ploy orchestrated by the *criollos* who managed to preserve the economic and social structure of the period of Spanish rule. For that reason, this political event, celebrated annually in Guatemala by the oligarchy and by State institutions, represented a veritable farse for the masses inhabiting the countryside. A limited number of *criollo* families succeeded in retaining the spoils of the Conquest: the best land for producing cochineal, raising cattle, establishing sugar cane plantations, etc., while native and *mestizo* peasants were left without any arable land. During the period of colonial domination, the appropriation of land to the different communities was effected on the basis of political and economic considerations and accordingly

> *"there was never any correlation whatsoever between the number of Indians from a given village and the amount of land assigned to them. Naturally, the land granted to each Indian family was inadequate. This situation became even more acute when the Indian population began to grow and socio-economic laws of the colonial period came into play which led to the systematic monopolization of the land in the hands of a parasitic minority".[12]*

Mestizo tenant farmers working on the plantations of the large landowners were forced to hand over anywhere from 50% to 75% of the cereal they produced, and lived constantly indebted to their employers. Three hundred and fifteen of every 1,000 persons died before the age of five. In the Department of Amatitlán, one of the two most important cochinealproducing regions, 506 children, more than half of every thousand born, died at an early age.

> *"The mortality rate is higher in Amatitlán than in any other part of the Republic", wrote a prominent Guatemalan politician in 1863. "This phenomenon is due to the agglomeration of thousands of wage*

12. Julio César Pinto Soria, op. cit., p. 11.

_labourers gathering there, spurred on by the higher
wages being paid in nopal and cochineal production;
wages which, as a rule, are squandered on excesses. The
unhealthy climate characteristic of the areas around the
lagoon of Amatitlán also contributes to the mortality rate."[13]_

The fact is that sanitary conditions in the country were devastating. In 1863, there were scarcely 33 physicians, most of whom lived in the Capital, which was the home of only 12% of the entire population.[14] More than 90% of the peasant population never received any medical attention. In brief, Guatemalan society under the Conservative dictatorship was a society of oppressed peasants who, under wretched living conditions, grew corn, beans, wheat, cotton, etc., in quantities incapable of meeting the country's needs. The nobility impeded the rise of the bourgeoisie as a class. Any opposition whatsoever to the dictatorship from enlightened members of the petite bourgeoisie (intellectuals and artisans), or the ruling class itself, could mean imprisonment, exile, even execution. With living conditions being what they were, it was not surprising that many peasants preferred to live on the fringe of society, and in the absence of national integrity certain traits inherent in the peasantry became even more imbedded. The concentration of agricultural export production in the center of the country meant that many peasant communities not only managed to hold on to the land they had acquired from the Spanish colonial authorities, but to develop economically, by restructuring their former cultural and religious institutions which dated back to the pre-Columbian era. Their isolation not only permitted them to do away with vices introduced by the colonists, designed to deprave them and make them more vulnerable, but to increase their agricultural productivity on the basis of their tradition of communal labour. This occurred chiefly in those regions not readily accessible to Conservative authorities. A European visiting one of these communities noted with astonishment their high organizational level.

---

13. Pío Casal, _"Reseña de la situación de Guatemala"._ Guatemala, 1981, p. 30.
14. Ibid.

He discovered that no one drank liquor or played cards. Instead of finding the *"savages"* he had been warned about in the Capital, he encountered *"industrious and hard-working men"* who could produce in a given year 45,000 quintals of corn, 5,000 quintals of black beans, 32,000 quintals of wheat, 1,500 quintals of potatoes, and 20,000 pounds of fleece.[15] A lesson should be learnt from these peasant communities and the enthusiasm, spirit of cooperation and fraternity with which they worked the land.

Production relations in the Indian communities permitted the peasants to meet their basic needs as long as they were able to remain removed from the sway of the powerful ruling class which enjoyed political hegemony in the country.

The peasant communities were familiar with rotation crops and plots. The men cultivated individual plots granted to them by the community in usufruct and would alternate crops when these plots were depleted. They did likewise with the land which they worked jointly for the community fund. Peasants and their families divided the plots assigned to them into

> *"four parts, in order to alternate between corn, black beans, cotton, etc., in three of the four, and have the remaining part to grow such items as sugar cane, Guinea grass, plaintain and the like".[16]*

The great storm

Due to the agricultural conditions prevailing in Guatemala in the middle of the nineteenth-century, the stormy weather which decimated the country in 1852, causing deaths and extensive material damage, was catastrophic. It all began on 19 October with colossal waves off the Pacific coast and incessant driving rain throughout the country.[17] In Amatitlán, the country's largest cochineal-producing region, it rained non-stop

---

15. Karl von Scherzer, op. cit., p. 261.
16. A.G.C.A., B1, M.G.J., folder No. 28576, Municipality of Sacatepéquez to the *corregidor* of the Department May 17, 1858.
17. Ibid., folder No. 28555, from Luis Avila to the Minister of the Interior, October 24, 1852.

from 21 October to 3 November and destroyed all the nopal plantations. The destruction was such that the *corregidor* deemed it impossible to *"arrive at an approximate calculation of the damages sustained".* According to him, the landowners had even lost *"all hope of recovery".*[18]

> *"Only yesterday it finally stopped raining in this Capital",* wrote the corregidor of Amatitlán to his superiors, *"leaving cochineal plantations totally destroyed. Other villages in that district have suffered similar damage and according to reports which have come in, most of the fields sown with black beans and corn were ruined. Although I've been seeing to it that the roads are repaired, all efforts have been in vain, since today's rain only destroys yesterday's reparations..."*[19]

In other rich cochineal-producing areas such as Antigua, Salamá and Chiquimula, the havoc wreaked meant that *"not even half of the expected cochineal crop was saved"*[20] and *"immeasurable quantities of grain and nopal have been lost".*[21] In the rest of the country, terrible floods destroyed sugar cane, corn, beans and other crops. Thousands of heads of cattle, pigs and fowl drowned and losses in *pesos* were estimated to be in the hundreds of thousands. Overflowing rivers *"swept away everything in their path", "washing away sturdy foundations",* causing *"hillocks to cave in"* and consequently *"leveled settlements, killed animals and destroyed sown fields".*[22] The extent of the damage was such that the Central Government was on the brink of bankruptcy in 1852 and 1853.[23] Following this natural disaster, the price of food, livestock and farm implements rose substantially. In the countryside hunger and disease ran rampant and thro-

18. Ibid., from José A. Piloña to the Minister of the Interior, October 23, 1852.
19. Ibid., José M. Palomo to the Minister of the Interior, November 4, 1852.
20. Ibid., October 27, 1852.
21. Ibid., from Vicente Cerna to the Minister of the Interior, November 12, 1852.
22. Ibid., folder No. 28555 includes reports on this disaster sent to the Ministry of the Interior from almost all of the departments in the Republic.
23. Ignacio Solís, op. cit., vol. III B, p. 921.

ughout the country *"funds were lacking"*.[24] It was then that the *Sociedad Económica* and the Conservative Government decided to systematically promote the diversification of crops, coffee in particular, following the example of Costa Rica which, at that point in time, was already exporting more than 70,000 quintals of coffee to England annually for the equivalent of 120,000 Sterling pounds, a sum which exceeded what was being paid on the international market for Guatemalan cochineal.[25]

_____

24. A.G.C.A., Bl, M.G.J., folder No. 28559, dossier No. 116, from Domingo Machuca to the Minister of the Interior, October 5, 1853.
25. Robert A. Naylor, op. cit., p. 252.

CHAPTER III

COFFEE: THE FACTORS OF PRODUCTION

Guatemala's transition from the pre-capitalist society inherited from the Spanish colonial period, to the predominantly capitalist society we know today, was a trying and difficult process which lasted more than a century. After analyzing historical documents and the circumstances under which coffee growing first came about and was developed in the country, I have reached the conclusion that the emerging agricultural bourgeoisie in Guatemala during the first half of the nineteenth century knew how to take advantage of the arrival of foreign entrepreneurs interested in introducing modern technology and investing the necessary capital in commercial agriculture. With the help of the State, which was fashioned after its own interests, the ruling class developed a vigorous plantation economy largely centered on coffee growing. As I mentioned earlier, the economic power of the Spaniards became increasingly debilitated because of the flight of capital and the civil wars which followed independence. However, with the growing and successful production of cochineal, the coffers of many landowners and merchants began to fill up once again. This created objective conditions for Guatemala to begin to develop certain traits cha-

45

racteristic of the modern production and commercialization of agricultural products, and to witness the appearance, on the economic and political scene, of the incipient Guatemalan bourgeoisie — offshoot of an obsolete colonial oligarchy. The production of cochineal, followed by that of coffee, mobilizedcommercial, usurious and financial capital, in quantities of which were unheard of before that time. Foreign merchants and investors set up agro-industries of a capitalist nature which served as a model for this ruling class of colonial descent which would ultimately turn into a veritable agricultural bourgeoisie. According to Solís, cochineal production *"attracted enormous quantities of gold from various countries to our market, a fair part of which went to the Mint"*.[1] Millions of *pesos* entered the country either to be invested in agricultural ventures or as payment for exports.[2] Favourable climatic conditions afforded the entrepreneur the opportunity of rapidly multiplying the money he had invested in cochineal. An 1846 study on cochineal production in Guatemala, published in number 38 of the official *"Gazette"*, reported that every *peso* invested annually, yielded 3.48 *pesos* when the product was sold to the exporter.[3] The exporter, in turn, earned in excess of that.

The rise of commercial coffee growing

The latter half of the nineteenth century was of extreme significance to Guatemala's plantation economy. It marked the beginning and gradual development of coffee growing as part of the expansionary process of the international division of labour which turned the developed countries of Europe, such as England, France and Germany, and the United States, into large manufacturers and traders of industrial products, particularly machinery, and the countries of Latin America and the rest of the world, into suppliers of raw materials and foodstuffs. These foodstuffs were viewed, as early as the sixteenth-century, as *"colonial products"*, because they came from areas inhabited

---

1. Ignacio Solís, op. cit., vol III A, p. 635.
2. Gustav Bernouilli, "Briefe aus...": 1870, vol. 16, Book XII, p. 438,
3. See article by Ignacio Solís in work previously cited, vol. III A, p. 636-638.

by European colonists (Portuguese, Spanish, French, English and Dutch), all devoted to the commercialization of these products. Coffee had always been considered a _"colonial product"_, and coffee growing in Guatemala added a welcome stabilizing touch to agricultural export production, following the fluctuations experienced in cochineal production. In time, coffee, unlike cochineal which is only produced in certain regions, was being grown in all the departments of Guatemala and, as a result, agricultural export production was no longer as isolated a phenomenon as it had been up to then. In Guatemala, this also gave way to what has appropriately and technically been referred to by Luis Eduardo Nieto Arteta, in the case of Colombia, as _"the geographical development of an agricultural economy"_.[4] With the advent of coffee growing in Guatemala, vast areas of the country which had once been neglected by Spanish colonists were incorporated into the economic life of the country and the overcame their limitations and traditional tendencies toward isolation, thus allowing for the creation of more ideal conditions for the development of a national economy. The foregoing can be viewed as the positive aspects of coffee growing. The fact that coffee growing also encouraged large-scale colonization and contributed to the levelling, occupation and incorporation of land, which was once virgin or fallow, into the agricultural process, was also a sign of progress. All the regions where coffee growing was developed became densely populated within a very short period of time. New towns were built, some of which became relatively large in size and together with others, already in existence, formed actual cities: Retalhuleu, Coatepeque, Cobán, Mazatenango and others.

Coffee growing necessitated the creation and organization of an entire infrastructure capable of promoting trade and speeding up the transport and loading of coffee and other products which were being exported in smaller quantities. Banks were opened, new and improved roads were constructed, new ports were built, steamers sailed inland rivers, railway tracks were laid linking both oceans and connecting important coffee pro-

---

4. Luis Eduardo Nieto Arteta, _"El café en la sociedad colombiana"_, Bogota, Colombia, 1975, p. 19.

ducing centers with loading docks. Furthermore, thousands of people found work in new jobs concerned with the maintenance and expansion of this infrastructure. These factors, together with the rise in the purchasing power of the population, facilitated the gradual expansion and further development of what was once a feeble domestic market. Business establishments created in the Capital, opened branches and agencies in inland cities. In some of these cities, new commercial enterprises were set up as centers for the distribution of manufactures, closely connected to the coffee fincas which sprang up in the different regions as new agricultural units, or where colonial haciendas once stood.

A new type of latifundia

To date, one of the key aspects of the rural character of Guatemalan society has been the persistent image of the *latifundia,* supreme symbol of the power base of the ruling class. Since Independence, the lay *latifundia* has remained intact, despite Liberal attacks on the clerical *latifundia* in which property belonging to the Church was confiscated and sold at ridiculously low prices. The *latifundia* provided material grounds for reinforcing *"debt slavery"* in the countryside, an institution which represented the greatest barrier to economic and social development in Guatemala. Not only did the *latifundia,* vestige of the period of Spanish rule, survive our political secession from Spain, but it was also revitalized by the production of cochineal and coffee, after assuming the role of a capitalist agricultural unit with modern organization of export production. A new breed of *latifundia* emerged with the appearance of the coffee and sugar cane *finca,* which, as pointed out earlier, supplanted the colonial *hacienda,* and the *finquero,* as an agricultural entrepreneur, replaced the traditional *hacendado.* The *finca* and the *finquero* were two fundamental factors in coffee production and agricultural development in Guatemala as of the last half of the nineteenth-century. They constituted a new economic order more in keeping with the times in terms of world-scale capitalist expansion. It is on the *finca* that modern entrepreneurial organization and spirit spawned an agricultural product which would be put on the European and North American market, contribute to the greater development of international capital and the process of capital accumulation in our country. It was in this manner that the development of coffee production and of an agricultural bourgeoisie, represented by the new class of landowner, the *finquero*, evolved simultaneously. For that very reason it is important to understand the emergence of the *finquero*, the socio-economic and political framework in which he first appeared, the obstacles which confronted him and the manner in which he eliminated those obstacles until he succeeded on June 30, 1871, in wresting political power from those conservative forces opposing him.

The peasantry's double plunderage

The appearance of the agricultural entrepreneur on the economic and political scene marked a new era of suffering in the history of the Guatemalan peasantry. The urban and rural bourgeoisie, strongly supported by foreign capital and entrepreneurs, plundered property belonging to the natives, and exploited labour force in order to meet the demands of a plantation economy. The plunder of both land and labour constituted the base of capital development in Guatemala from the middle of the nineteeth century.

The expropriation of land and exploitation af native labour did not only take place with the advent of coffee growing in Guatemala. It is well known that the Conquest of America was waged by feudal lords and merchants from the Iberian Peninsula, whose only aspiration was to extract mineral wealth from the New World. In those countries without large quantities of gold and silver, such as Guatemala and El Salvador, land and forced labour, furnished by the native population, constituted the spoils of the Conquest. As early as 1512, Ferdinand V, *"the Catholic"*, wrote in a royal letter patent that the wealth of the Indies, the Islands and the Mainland, was *"the good use of Indians"*.[5] This same king is also known to have reported that *"the*

---

5. Richard Konetzke, *"Colección de Documentos..."* Royal Patent Letter: "Que ninguno pueda tener más de trescientos indios de repartimiento", Burgos, February 22, 1512. Vol. I, p. 34.

riches of these parts (America) are the Indians".[6]

The first thing the Spaniards did once they were settled in Guatemala was to demand *encomiendas* of natives, whom they forced to pay tribute in foodstuffs (corn, black beans, wheat, salt, honey, fish), cash crops (cacao, sarsaparilla) and money, and render personal services which included planting and sowing and constructing houses, public building, churches and roads. Thousands of workers died during this period of forced labour. By the middle of the sixteenth-century, 84 *encomenderos* had placed thousands of peasants under their control subjecting them to pay tribute and to put in intense work days.[7] By the end of the sixteenth-century, 200 families of *encomenderos* had already distributed most of the half million population then living in the Kingdom of Guatemala, which was made up of what today are the Mexican State of Chiapas and the Central American Republics of Guatemala, El Salvador, Honduras, Nicaragua and Costa Rica.[8] When an *encomendero* died his widow and offspring continued to receive tribute from the natives, in conformity with a colonial policy whereby the eldest son was designated statutory heir of the *encomienda*. This practice prevailed until the middle of the eighteenth-century.[9]

The outrages committed by the *encomenderos* against the Guatemalan population, which included inexorable slavery and exploitation, were sanctioned by the Spanish authorities, as they

─────────────────────

6. *Ibid., Royal Patent Letter, "Sobre los indios de la Isla de San Juan",* p. 37. *"In the absence of precious metals, land was a powerful incentive for soldiers and colonizers who voyaged to the Indies. For that reason, authority vested in the captain of the expedition permitted him to divy up land among his soldiers and personnel. However this authority was often abused and the Indians were robbed of their possesions, especially their land...",* Jose Maria Ots Capdequi, *"Manual de Derecho Español en las Indias y del Derecho propiamente Indiano",* Buenos Aires 1935, p. 163. Cited by Clodoveo Torres Moss in his essay entitled: *"La Propiedad Agraria en el Reino de Guatemala durante el Siglo XVI. La tierra, estimulo en las empresas de descubrimiento y conquista".* In *"El Imparcial",* May 28, 1982.
7.Francisco de Solano, *"Los Mayas del Siglo XVIII, Pervivencia y Transformación de la Sociedad Indigena guatemalteca, durante la Administración Borbónica."* Ediciones Cultura Hispánica, Madrid, 1974, p. 83.
8. Author's personal estimation.
9. Severo Martínez Peláez, *"La Patria del Criollo. Ensayo de Interpretación de realidad colonial guatemalteca",* Editorial Universitaria Centroamericana, Sixth edition, San José, Costa Rica, 1979, p. 83.

were deemed to be the determining factor in the colonial socio-economic and political system. The tribute which the natives had to pay to the King of Spain was ceded by the latter, as _"enco-miendas"_, to the principal captains, soldiers and functionaries — instruments of Spanish power in America — , in gratitude for services rendered to the Crown and in return for the _enco-mendero's_ readiness to serve as an instrument of terror and repression amongst those members of the agrarian community who dared to defy the established order. With the knowledge that they in fact were official representatives of Spanish colonialism, the _encomenderos_ pressured the native population with the purpose of sizing their property. In 1549, the King of Spain ordered the President of the _Audiencia de los Confines_ (colonial tribunals) to prohibit the _encomenderos_ from forcing the native authorities of the communities to sell them their land. The following was pointed out in a Royal Decree dated 29 April of that same year: _"It is said that they make the indian chiefs sell their land, paying them what they will, and that the indians suffer as a result of this"._[10]

In another Decree dated 9 October of the same year, he ordered the same functionary to appoint a _"man of scruples"_ to visit the areas where the communities despoiled by the _encomenderos_ were, and force them to return _"to the indians that land which they had taken from them in exchange for a shirt or an arroba of wine"._[11]

However, the Crown's willingness to accept the encroachment of the land through the so-called _"composición de tierras"_* led to increased tension in the countryside and to an open battle over land tenure. For the purpose of avoiding further social strife and plundering of communal property by the _encomenderos_, the Crown forbade them to live in the villages. The _encomenderos_ however, made a mockery of the Royal Decrees. The King of Spain was very far away and colonial bureaucrats often operated on the basis of their own interests. Most of the people in charge of enforcing colonial legislation in the rural areas, the _Corregi-_

10. Richard Konetzke, _"Colección de Documentos..."_. Royal Letter Patent: _"Al Presidente de la Audiencia de los Confines que los encomenderos no tomen a los indios sus tierras y prados"._ Valladoilid, April 29, 1549, volume I, p. 258.

11. Clodoveo Torres Moss, op. cit.

dores and the *Alcaldes Mayores* (mayors) were either *encomenderos* or large-scale landowners. It is stated in a document of the period that these colonial authorities *"not only refuse to give land to the Indians so that they might build their own villages, but when they do, they take it away from them by violent means, selling their children as slaves and bringing their women to their homes to serve them, either spinning, weaving or tilling, without remuneration, whereupon they annihilate entire villages which missionaries had worked so hard to create..."*[12]

The mestizos and the land

The land distribution process of the sixteenth and seventeenth-centuries did not take into account the *mestizos*, whose numbers increased over the years of Spanish domination in Guatemala. A Guatemalan historian has concluded that the agrarian blockade against the *mestizos became a principle of the economic policy adopted by the colonial authorities*.[13] This probably occurred during the first two centuries of Spanish rule, due to the fact that all the fertile land located near the natives villages was monopolized by Europeans. Officially, however, the *mestizos* were, by virtue of a Royal Decree dated October 15, 1754, permitted to purchase or sell land.[14] In 1804 Guatemala was reported as having more than 4,000 families of small-scale *mestizo* landowners.[15]

In fact, for persons of limited economic means, like the vast majority of small-scale *mestizo* farmers, it was relatively complicated to become the absolute owner of a piece of land since this meant getting involved in long drawn out bureaucratic procedures, and often in court action. Moreover, those persons purchasing land had to effect payment before receiving confirma-

---

12. Julio César Pinto Soria, op. cit., p. 42.
* *Composicion de tierras:* This transaction became generalized in Guatemala from 1591 onward. The Spanish Crown gave colonists a limited amount of land. However, the Crown recognized land taken illegally in order to receive extra payments through taxation of more land.
13. Severo Martinez Peláez, op. cit., p. 159.
14. José María Ots Capdequí, *"El régimen de la tierra en la América española durante el período colonial".* University of Santo Domingo, 1946, pp. 105-117.
15. Julio César Pinto Soria, op. cit., p. 10.

tion of their title deeds. For these reasons, most _mestizos_ found themselves obliged to work the fallow land belonging to European landowners and their offspring, known as _criollos_, as tenant farmers. The _mestizos_ were also taken on as foremen and trustworthy employees on the _haciendas_ of the colonists where the greater part of the labour force was made up of natives. J.C. Pinto has indicated that there were close to 10,000 tenant farmers in Guatemala at the beginning of the nineteenth century.[16] In the Guatemalan _Gazette_ of November 11, 1799, a _criollo_ spoke of these small-scale farmers as _"the ones who put food on our tables, wander hither and thither, thrown out here, rejected there, always scrounging for someone who will rent them a smittering of land in exchange for their slave labour"_.[17] In 1810, near the end of the period of Spanish domination. Guatemala, prominent members of the _Consulado de Comercio_ were forced to admit that the standard of living of the Guatemalan peasants was much like _"that of the earth's first inhabitants"_.[18] Small-scale _mestizo_ farmers grew their corn, wheat and vegetables _"on plots of land which were insecure even if they were their own"_. In addition to paying commodity, tribute to Spanish authorities, the peasants were subjected to

> _"forced labour, and sent in groups by the Alcaldes Mayores to the haciendas of those who solicited their services. They were forced to render those services as provided for by law; to carry on their backs and shoulders loads belonging to the Alcaldes themselves, the Priests and the other members of the white race, from one place to another; to construct buildings, temples and houses, under the supervision of architects and masons; and lastly, to perform all those painstaking servile tasks which are reserved for these people throughout the Kingdom of Guatemala. They are,_

---

16. Ibid.
17. Ibid.
18. _"Apuntamientos sobre la agricultura y el comercio del Reyno de Guatemala"_. Article published in: _"Economia de Guatemala en los siglos XVIII y XIX"_. Jorge Luján Muñoz (edit.), Guatemala, 1974, p. 34.

> *without exception, the repose of the other classes, they are the ones who put food on our tables, attending to our needs, affording us a life of luxury, while they, who are so frugal in their eating habits, barely eat enough to sustain themselves. And if the Indian men are said to work hard then it can be said that the women work even harder; even the Indian children are employed; as soon as they have taken their first steps, they accompany their mothers up the mountains in search of kindlewood and are immediately walking long distances with their fathers, carrying their share of the load on their backs".[19]*

The progressive sector of the ruling class.

The Spanish colonist and the *criollos* did not always have the means or the inclination to use their vast landholdings and the manpower at their disposal for productive purposes. In addition to their interest in large-scale cattle-raising and sugar cane production for the confection of brown sugar, known as *panela,* for the domestic market, the profits generated from the indigo trade and the importation of European manufactured goods, were not re-invested to expand capital. At the beginning of the nineteenth-century, the incipient agrarian bourgeoisie was no more than a small sector of the ruling class, with an eye to development. From 1821 onward, following their appearance on the political scene as Liberals, they were known chiefly for trying to promote the development of the national economy through European colonization, free trade and the use of financial resources procured from foreign loans. Despite the fact that many Liberals were *mestizos* from the urban middle class, they were largely influenced by the landowners and merchants who filled their ranks and by the same prejudices which the Conservatives harboured against the masses — whom they considered to be primitive, decadent and racially inferior — which accoun-

---

19. Ibid.

ted for their failure in attempting to give Guatemala a new political and economic direction. As Pinto Soria points out, the historical limitations of Central American liberalism prevented it from _"implementing effective social measures which in one way or another would improve the lot of the exploited masses"_, and as such, _"gain their sympathy and support"_.[20]

The degree of revolutionary inconsequence exhibited by the liberal sector of the ruling class became evident in 1829, when the Legislative Assembly of Guatemala decided to enact laws which favoured the development of commercial agriculture. At that time, both the Liberals and the Conservatives who belonged to this Constituent Assembly believed in the restoration of forced labour, prevalent during the colonial period and officially abolished at the end of 1829 because they were convenient for them as landowners.[21] Based on the old myth that Guatemalan agriculture was neglected because of the laziness of the peasant, a statute of March 17, 1830 was sanctioned whereby all those persons without property and members of peasant communities were forced to work on _haciendas_ and small farms. This statute granted the _hacendados_ the right to solicit from the mayors of the different villages the men they required to do farm work. If a worker became indebted to a landowner, he could not leave the _hacienda_ until such time as his debt was settled. In this way the powerful once more succeeded in institutionalizing the system of _mandamientos_ and _peonaje_* to guarantee themselves a semi-slavelike labour force on their land.[22] The chief victims of this law governing the contracting of labour and forced labour were all those communities situated within reach of the _hacendados_. In 1839 the landowners ordered the mayors of each municipality to keep a small book which would list the names of those peasants, according to their respective jurisdiction, "suitable for doing farm work".[23] As a result, thousands

20. Julio César Pinto Soria, _"Guatemala en la Década de la Independencia"_, Editorial Universitaria, Guatemala, 1978, p. 49.
21. Ibid., p. 13.
* Peonaje: System by which a man was forced to work until he payed off his debts to the landowner.
22. Ignacio Solís, op. cit., vol. III A, p. 809
23. A.G.C.A., BI, M.G.J., folder No. 28621, Miguel García Zelaya to the Minister of the Interior, November 18, 1871.

of peasants were forced to work for landowners who, often failed to pay their employees the wages they had promised, humiliating and mistreating them.

> *"We have been the victims of out and out treachery",*
> *complained dozens of peasants from Acatenango and*
> *Santa Lucía Cotzumalguapa, before the Court of First*
> *Instance in Escuintla: "Hired to work for a real*
> *(colonial coinage) a day, plus meals, on the hacienda*
> *'Apopaya', we are given ten ears of corn a day, our*
> *contracts run out after a year, they pay us monthly at*
> *less than the agreed rate... We wait on tables and*
> *perform odd jobs and often, there is so much work that*
> *two or three days do not suffice to get the job done. So*
> *with three times the normal work load and under the*
> *infernal sun of the Southern Plain, we struggle to*
> *sustain our families whom we can't even afford to clothe.*
> *Should we fall sick, we don't even have a penny for*
> *medication. Every year the balance of accounts*
> *increases. This squelches all hopes of being able to pay*
> *our debts. We work eighty, sometimes ninety days. They*
> *pay us for thirty. For that work we receive 20 reales and*
> *each one of us is only given 30 rations of corn.*
> *Naturally, to meet our needs during the fifty or sixty*
> *days we work without pay and without corn, we have to*
> *ask for an advance which they give us at a rate of 2 to*
> *1, automatically doubling our debt. This is Don Manuel*
> *Galvez Garcia's way of turning us into eternal slaves*
> *subject to the most rash imprisonment and vile attacks."*[24]

Agrarian legislation

The Conservative State claimed to regard the native as *"the good savage",* worthy of protection and tutelage. To this end, a *"Fiscal Protector de Indios"* was appointed, whose task was to

---

24. Ibid., folder No. 28604, Memo sent to the Court of First Instance, Escuintla, March 12, 1862.

oversee the welfare of the natives. In 1869, one of these persons
so appointed stated that in Guatemala it should not be compulsory to

> _"pay a day's wages to a man who doesn't want to work
> and is capable of earning a living by other honest
> means". "The authorities haven't the right to compel the
> people to work as wage labourers. It would be tyrannical
> to force a person to work constantly and deprive him of
> the rest to which he is entitled, if he choses to work only
> part of the year in order to be able to rest for the rema-
> inder."_[25]

The laws of the middle of the nineteenth century, like those
during the period of Spanish domination, favoured the landow-
ning sector. For example, when the peasants refused to perform
forced labour, henchmen employed by the _hacendados_ would
come to their homes in the middle of the night, take them cap-
tive, tie them up and cart them off to jails on the _haciendas_. On
other occasions, the landowners,

> _"for lack of being able to find men to work the land,
> obliged the Governor to accept money so that he with the
> help of calpules (communal chiefs) and assistants would
> distribute it amongst the villagers and force them to
> accept it in return for certain mecates de trabajo.*_ _But they
> refuse. However, forced in this way they accept the workload
> assigned to them. As demonstrated each one has his land
> to work and when a man fails to show up at work as he has
> been obliged to do, either because his family needs him or
> for any other reason, then the Governor and the ladino alcal-
> des not only throw him in jail but the calpules and the assis-
> tants as well"._[26]

According to one Conservative, this procedure was at odds with
State policy which supposedly protected the interests of the rural

---

25. Ibid., folder No. 28621, _Fiscal Protector de Indios_ to the Minister of the Interior, February 24, 1869.
26. Ibid.

masses following the model of patriarchal domination characteristic of the colonial period.

> *"This is something worthy of admiration in our Republic and which should particularly attract the attention of the Government", commented the same functionary, "because this arbitrary procedure can become quite critical, particularly when the Indians are tricked into believing that these mandamientos are Government orders. This is not very credible because these people are not authorized to persecute them. On the contrary, they are supposed to be interested in their well being, like any good family man would be."*[27]

Members of the peasant communities of Santo Tomás and Magdalena Milpas Altas, in the Corregimiento of Sacatepéquez, complained in 1861 to Rafael Carrera, about the forced labour they were compelled to perform by nopal producers in the region.

The peasants claimed that they were forced to go to Antigua, Amatitlán and other cochineal-producing areas and were paid one *real* for tasks which were impossible to complete in a single work day.

> *"Today we weren't even able to get through with the cleaning and time is marching on", wrote the peasants to Carrera in their petition, asking that he help them by "excusing them from the mandamiento work so that they might get their own work done and meet their own needs."*[28]

Advances for rural labourers

The scarcity of manpower in the countryside reactivated the antiquated system of *mandamientos.* This system of forced labour

---

27. Ibid.
* Mecate de trabajo: measure of work, approximately $20m^2$.
28. Ibid., folder No. 28586, From the people of Santo Tomás and Magdalena to the President of the Republic, June 24, 1861.

in turn provoked the peasantry's reluctance to serve the landowners. To break this vicious circle, many landowners showed that they were prepared to give generous advances to the workers. What they succeeded in doing was to *"corner"* them into performing farm work. However, the practice of giving money advances only added to the friction between the landowners interested in commercial agricultural production and the peasantry who was being forced to work. Because of the money advances which were paid as wages for services due, many of the labourers tended to make a mockery of the *hacendados* and cochineal producers by not showing up at work on the agreed date. In 1847, the Conservative Government blamed the landowners for losses incurred as a result of these advances of wages. However, in order to prevent the workers from committing such fraudulent acts, the Government stipulated that the landowners verify the personal history of the beneficiary of the advance before giving it to him, since many were believed to be malevolent *"convicts"* and *"outlaws".* Public edicts prohibited the hiring of persons without a letter of recommendation from a former employer. This document had to certify that the bearer had no outstanding debts with his former *"amo"* (employer). The landowner who failed to comply with this order had to pay a minimum fine of five *pesos.*[29] Whether these orders issued by the Conservative Government were respected or not, they nevertheless attest to the presence of forces within the ruling clique interested in controlling the labour force and guaranteeing the landowners the workers they required. By the middle of the nineteenth century, these forces had gained economic strength as a result of intensive cochineal production.

The fall in the demand for cochineal in the 1860s and the resulting downward trend in its market price, prompted wealthy plantation owners to reinvest their capital in coffee cultivation which, by that time, had already expanded in the country since it promised greater and more secure returns. In 1868, Fredrick Augener, Consul of the Confederation of Northern Germany in

---

29. Ibid., folder No. 28539, expediente No. 13, Circular from the Minister of the Interior to the *Corregidores* of the different Departments. August 13, 1847.

Guatemala, and one of the most prominent agro-exporters and merchants in the region, wrote to Bismarck, stating that in 1868,

> *"to date, cochineal has been the largest export crop in this country, currently yielding 14,000 one hundred and fifty pound bales, at 90 to 100 pesos a bale. Lately, people have been getting increasingly involved in coffee growing, and cochineal production has fallen by the wayside. The decision to invest in coffee seems to be a wise choice for the country since profits from cochineal are very unreliable and its production often brings colossal losses for plantation owners".[30]*

In 1888, a German diplomat informed his Chancellor in a message from Guatemala, that cochineal production *"no longer brought any returns to the producer, because of its low price in London. He pointed out however, that many cochineal producers had*

> *"persevered so as to be in a position to expand rapidly should the situation permit".[31]*

D2A Potzdam, A.A.; folder no. 52810 Augener to Bismarck; January 13, 1968.
31. Ibid., folder No. 12436, Bergen to Bülow, November 8, 1888.

CHAPTER IV

THE BEGINNINGS OF THE COFFEE TRADE

The story of the first decades of commercial coffee growing in Guatemala has been largely exalted by traditional historians, as one of a generation of energetic and enterprising men who, confronted with serious obstacles, managed, in twenty years, to create a solid base for what in our time would constitute the country's *"greatest source of generative wealth"*.[1] But these accounts only tell half the story, having never taken into consideration the major productive force in the country: the peasantry. The peasants built roads, cleared jungles, planted coffee, constructed *beneficios* (coffee processing plant) established coffee plantations, laid railroad tracks and installed a telegraph network, and all of this for a pittance.

After 1835, coffee was promoted as a cash crop which would benefit large and small producers alike, as it had in Costa Rica.[2] But initially, because it was a new crop in the country,

1. Ignacio Solís, op. cit., vol. III B, p. 927.
2. Unless otherwise specified, references to coffee growing in Costa Rica and El Salvador are taken from Ciro F. Santana Cardoso, "Historia económica del café en Centroamérica (Siglo XIX): Estudio comparativo". Article published in: *"Estudios Sociales Centroamericanos,* San Jose, Costa Rica, Jan-Apr. 1975, Year IV, No. 10, pp. 9-55.

experiments were confined to Escuintla and the vicinity of the Capital of Guatemala. However, the few successful yields obtained by the middle of the nineteenth-century allowed for the collection of seeds for future nurseries and a small quantity of coffee was already exported by 1852.[3] In 1853, immediately following the great storm, coffee growing was once again promoted and the Government offered a bonus of 25 *pesos* to every coffee grower with 1,000 plants ripe for picking and 2 *pesos* for every quintal of coffee exported. The former bonus was offered until 1859, while the one for exports remained in force until 1863. This appeal to develop coffee growing issued by agroexporters through the *Sociedad Económica*, the *Consulado de Comercio* and by means of governmental measures and provisions, was heeded by the *corregidores*, even though some of them lived in regions where ecological and topographical conditions did not lend themselves to coffee growing. According to a Guatemalan historian, the Conservative Government introduced imported *"equipment to shell and clean the coffee. This equipment, which was to serve as a model, was set up in the most important developing production centers".*[4] Nonetheless, coffee plantations established in Escuintla and the central region of the country still had to deal with the inexperience of the coffee growers in 1855. One of these growers, a prominent member of the *Sociedad Económica*, mentioned in a memorandum addressed to the *Consejo de Estado* on March 21, 1855 that,

> *"the coffee in the Departments of Escuintla, Sacatepéquez, the district of Amatitlán and elsewhere, is not planted in an orderly fashion. The way in which it is picked and cleaned is equally inappropriate and an unnecessary amount of time and energy is being wasted because no one knows how to operate the equipment and no one is being trained to do so..."*[5]

The arrival of experts in the field, Costa Ricans in particular,

3. Ignacio Solís, op. cit., vol. III B, p. 929.
4. Ibid., p. 934.
5. A.G.C.A., M.G.J., folder No. 28566, Memorandum from Manuel Larrave to the *Consejo de Estado*, March 21, 1855.

coupled with experiments conducted by foreign entrepreneurs on their own property, helped to gradually overcome the problems first encountered. The Du Teil brothers, on the basis of the French experience in Haiti, experimented with coffee on their terrain on the Southern Plain. It is said that they received and studied _"reports on the subject sent to them by other coffee producing nations".[6]_ Saturnino Tinoco, a _"wealthy capitalist"_ from Costa Rica, also became the owner of a coffee plantation frequently visited by other affluent landowners interested in acquiring a better understanding of the crop. Apparently Tinoco devoted a fair amount of his time to passing on the knowledge and expertise he had acquired to these potential coffee growers.[7]

First attempts by the Liberal Government under Mariano Gálvez and the Conservative Government of Rafael Carrera to democratize the commercial production of coffee, by handing over idle land to landless men and the promotion of the crop in the native communities, were well received by these small-scale producers. In response to the promotion of coffee growing, many communities devoted themselves to planting coffee and establishing medium-sized plantations, conscious of the fact that in this way they would become more solvent economically and increase their chances of not falling prey to the forced labour imposed by the landowners.

As early as 1853, the _corregidor_ of Escuintla informed his superiors that

> _"the people of Escuintla are very compentent when it comes to farming and planting. Of the entire village, three leagues in circumference have been used for farming, plants and fruit trees, and there is also coffee which could very well become an export crop".[8]_

On March 13 1853 the _corregidor_ of Suchitepéquez wrote that

> "all the residents of this village have undertaken to plant coffee and other crops suitable for export".[9]

6. Ignacio Solís, op. cit., vol. III B, p. 942.
7. Ibid., p. 943.
8. A.G.C.A., B1, M.G.J., folder No. 28560, José M. Mollinedo to the Minister of the Interior, March 19, 1853.
9. Ibid., folder No. 28559, expediente No. 111, Manuel Fuentes to the Minister of the Interior, May 13, 1853.

In 1859 the *corregidor* of Verapaz spoke of the enthusiasm with which the communities of Cobán, San Pedro Carchá and San Cristobal had planted coffee and later prepared for transplants.[10] Three years later that same *corregidor* wrote that

> *"in San Pedro Carchá I had the pleasure of seeing the magnificent progress in the community's coffee plantation which already boasts over 25,000 plants perfectly placed, maintained and tended to, as well as a large nursery. Instructions have already been issued concerning transplants and the necessary steps have already been taken. That means that by the end of the year the number of trees planted will rise to 40 or 50,000."[11]*

The contradictions of coffee cultivation

The effect that coffee growing had on some regions well suited for its propagation was contradictory. On the one hand it proved that the communities did in fact welcome innovation and progress — as long as they could continue to work with dignity, were not subject to restrictions on the production of a crop destined for the external market and as long as production was carried out according to means of organization that satisfied their wishes as independent producers. However, once it was discovered that the regions inhabited by the peasants were blessed with the type of soil best suited for coffee growing, these same regions were invaded by small, medium and large-scale landowners interested in making an instant profit, at the expense of the peasantry. In this way, sleepy villages with few inhabitants were turned overnight into important centers of agricultural production and trade, and old lifestyles and work habits were never the same. Escuintla is a perfect example of such a phenomenon. At the end of 1857, the *corregidor* wrote that,

> *"only a few years back Escuintla was a village where*

---

10. Ibid., folder No. 28577, Juan E. Valdéz to the Minister of the Interior, July 15, 1859.
11. Ibid., folder No. 28588, Juan E. Valdéz to the Minister of the Interior, September 6, 1862.

even the most basic items were lacking, which meant
that the people who came on holidays had to bring
along the brooms they needed to sweep the floors of their
huts, the only type of dwelling at the time. In the
environs, there were approximately 30 mills, two or three
operated by water, others by hand or activated by oxen in
sheds made of blades of cane in which only brown
sugar was made, since in those days producing refined
sugar was unheard of. The roads were no more than
paths where one had difficulty walking, and the man
who managed to walk from this village to the Capital
city in one day became notorious... Today there are 5
sugar mills in the vicinity producing sugar as good as
the sugar from Ahuachapán. There are also mills which
produce brown sugar, and in addition to that which is
required for distillation, a considerable quantity is being
exported abroad, and this incentive is causing many
people to plant sugar cane. There are two coffee farms.
Each one has 30,000 plants and each one is bearing
fruit. There are other plantations, although less
productive, and a lot more land is being prepared to
transplant seedlings when the rainy season begins. So it
looks like Escuintla, should have a regular harvest,
within two years. There is also an increasing number of
pastures in the area, and in some villages of this
department there is land planted with Guinea grass for
the cattle to graze on, and there is a demand for land
for coffee and sugar plantations. The value of the land
has gone up tremendously over the past two years. The
number of carts has increased because they facilitate the
transport of goods to the port and other destinations.
But it is vital to exercise certain control, otherwise,
regardless of the money invested to repair roads, they
will never be maintained regularly because of the
limited intelligence of the carters. Even the Indians, who
have always been considered slow-witted, have improved
their lot and in no time at all have distinguished
themselves from the ladinos. As far as food goes, they
have bread and coffee for breakfast every day, meat and

65

*cheese for lunch and dinner, and it is rare to find an
Indian who lights his home with a torch. Most of them
use candles".[12]*

The conflict which resulted from the Conservative Government's order which promoted coffee growing in the native communities and permitted persons living outside the communities to settle there and establish private coffee farms, became clear in 1856 when the community members of Petapa, interested in getting involved in coffee growing, tenaciously opposed the *corregidor's* plan to hand over part of their land to a Spanish entrepreneur by the name of José Mariano Arrechea. On this occasion, the *corregidor* believed that the requests for communal property on which to grow coffee ought to be met: a) because it is *"in the interest of the Republic and will be profitable;"* b) *"because it will keep the people busy and productive";* and c) *"because, in addition to investing money, the people will learn a lot about coffee growing".*[13] These same Conservative authorities who unofficially sanctioned the spoliation of the communities, also believed that coffee growing would be *"advantageous for the people",* and repeatedly advised the various municipalities, by means of circular letters, to care for the coffee planted in the communities.

*"Most of those people still have land designated for that
purpose", recounted a prominent member of the
Conservative oligarchy to the Minister of the Interior,
"and it is very likely that the residents will follow suit,
which means that in a short period of time the people
will have an area for speculation which should prove to
be quite lucrative..."[14]*

---

12. Ibid., folder No. 28575, José Mollinedo to the Minister of the Interior, December 31, 1857.
13. Ibid., folder No. 28568, Gregorio Solares to the Minister of the Interior, April 4, 1856.
14. Ibid., folder No. 28604, J. Aycinena to the Minister of the Interior, April 17, 1858.

In fact, the coffee development project implemented in the communities was poorly administered from the start because it allowed private parties to settle as life tenants on land belonging to the peasants.

The occupation of communal lands

The practice which allowed people to use and enjoy the fruits of communal property as tenant farmers, in return for an annual tax of 3% on the value of the land, was legalized on August 5, 1835.[15] From 1839 onward, the Conservatives who had come to power continued to observe this liberal statute. However, to give the impression that they were abiding by the people's wishes, the Conservatives stipulated that all land transfers be approved by the communal authorities, who did not appear to be at all interested in giving up part of their land for life tenancy, although in some instances, out of economic necessity, they were prepared to do so. The communities, however, protected their land religiously and viewed any fragmentation of it by State authorities as an assault on their interests. On one occasion, Rafael Carrera seized 57 _caballerias_ from the community of Santa Lucía Cotzumalguapa and sold them to _criollo_ Manuel María Herrera. Upon the dictator's death, the peasants declared the sale illegal and tried to recover the property.[16]

One of the chief arguments brandished by the communities in order to avoid having to rent their property, stated that private individuals tended to put their livestock out to graze on land cultivated by the peasants. This inevitably led to countless lawsuits [17]

> "The Indians of Chipilapa hereby swere that we are the lawful owners of that parcel of land, granted to us in the year 1818, as attested to by a deed issued on that date", claimed community members to Rafael Carrera in 1853, "however,

---

15. Ibid., folder No. 28575, José M. Flores to the Minister of the Interior, October 23, 1858.
16. Ibid., folder No. 28600, _Juez Preventivo_ to the _corregidor_ of Suchitepéquez, September 10, 1865.
17. Ibid., folder No. 28577, Manuel Tzoc to President Rafael Carrera, December 9, 1859.

we do not have the benefit of enjoying that land as if it were ours. Since locusts infested our crops, and the plague struck our families, the most vital grains, such as corn, which is our only asset and sole source of nourishment, is still lacking in these parts, and, as a result we are going hungry. There is no other explanation other than the lack of certainty where our crops are concerned. We struggle to plant and care for our crops but they are ruined overnight by cattle trampling over them; cattle deliberately set out to pasture on our land or on the boundaries, where the tenant farmers settle for the purposes of taking over. It is this type of injustice which prevails among the hacendados *which is ruining us."[18]*

Other communities registered similar complaints. The community of Escuintla, for example, informed Rafael Carrera in their petition of March 19, 1853 that they were continual victims of *"immeasurable losses and damage",* because *"newcomers"* permitted their cattle to graze on their cornfields.

"Former corregidores", wrote members of the community, "due to the destruction caused by the cattle, issued edicts essentially designed to avoid damage of this nature. They saw to it that the cattle were kept at a distance and as such eliminated grounds for dispute and imposed heavy penalties on the cattle ranchers who let this occur. This was done during Spanish rule, and it was not all that long ago that corregidor Arriola issued, with the approval of the Supreme Government, an edict which was carried out with the most laudable enthusiasm. He enforced the withdrawal of cattle to within 4 leagues from our settlements, in accordance with Statute 20, heading 3, book 6 of the Recopilación de Indias. But Mr. Arriola is no longer corregidor of this district and since his departure, our woes have started all over again..."[19]

---

18. Ibid., folder No. 28575, Community of Chipilapa to President Rafael Carrera, January 24, 1853.
19. Ibid., folder No. 28560, expediente No. 7, Community of Escuintla to President Rafael Carrera, March 19, 1853.

The pro-development sector of the oligarchy believed it was necessary to seize that land ideal for coffee growing from peasants and distribute it amongst private individuals.

> _"The Indians have always objected to seeing the land they don't cultivate given to others who do", wrote a corregidor and wealthy hacendado to the Minister of the Interior in 1858, "and it is my wish and I've achieved as much, as to develop a new source of wealth, such as coffee. The more farmers there are, the more employment there will be for those people who, for lack of work, turn to the bottle."_[20]

"What do all these villages derive from their territorial assets?", the _corregidor_ of Retalhuleu asked himself in 1863. "What is the purpose of agricultural expansion and progress?" "What benefits do they provide for the municipalities of these villages which lack the basic essentials for their development?" He himself replied:

> _"As far as the ejidos (common public land) are concerned, these chief sources of wealth are quite extensive in many of the Indian villages which only grow corn and beans which today, and in the future, will only take up a very small part of that expanse. For example, San Felipe, which has 38 caballerias, 11 7/8 cuerdas and 172 1/2 square varas, (yard) only has coffee sown on 1,101 manzanas and 2 cuerdas; San Francisco Zapotitlán, which has 22 caballerias of ejidos, does not have coffee or sugar fincas, and those that are there, notable for their size, are found on landed property. The village of Samayac, which has 69 caballerias 114 cuerdas, and that of San Pablo, with its 15 caballerias, are in temperate climates, and like San Felipe and San Francisco, have vast fertile and well-irrigated plateaus and valleys where coffee could be cultivated and reap excellent results."_[21]

20. Ibid., folder No. 28576, Gregorio Solares to the Minister of the Interior, March 4, 1858.
21. Ibid., folder No. 28593, Nazario Toledo to the Minister of the Interior, March 21, 1863.

In other words, the more aggressive and dynamic sector of the ruling class believed that in order for coffee growing to develop in Guatemala it was necessary to expropriate communal property and sacrifice the interest of the majority of the population for those of a more enterprising and ambitious minority.

> *"Agriculture in this Department will never prosper as it should", assured the aforementioned corregidor. "The avarice of the Indians and the softness of the ladinos won't permit it."*[22]

In some regions such as Verapaz, the occupation of communal property was openly promoted and it was even stipulated that all *ladinos* who chose to devote their time to growing coffee would be exempt from doing military service.[23] Communal authorities, were mostly subject to economic pressure and those who lacked the necessary funds to pay their taxes were advised to rent a part of their land which supposedly would be profitable. An attempt was made at minimizing the damage caused to community members by cattle grazing on their sown fields and appealing to their sense of greed by luring them with the idea that those who leased their land would establish valuable *fincas* which would not only increase the price of the property but also turn it into an important work centre for the community.

> *"The tax on cattle pastures is meant to benefit the community", pointed out the Minister of the Interior to the corregidor of Suchitepéquez in 1861, so that he would pass that on to the community members of his jurisdiction: "That is also the purpose of planting coffee which will increase the value of their property and create lucrative employment for the village itself."*[24]

The occupation of land belonging to the communities by per-

---

22. Ibid.
23. Ibid., folder No. 28588, Juan E. Valdéz to the Minister of the Interior, September 6, 1862.
24. Ibid., folder No. 28584, Minister of the Interior to the *Corregidor* of Suchitepéquez, October 26, 1861.

sons unknown to those parts implied a substantial change in the traditional economic and social life of the peasants. The community lived as subsistence farmers, with only some surplus destined for market. The peasant was interested in procuring food and satisfying his most basic needs. He did so by cultivating only a small part of the vast expanses of communal property often made up of dense forest. This land was the mainstay and the refuge of a population which had been cruelly decimated and repressed during the period of Spanish domination. Memories of the humiliation, the abuses, the excesses and the exploitation of that abominable period were still fresh in the minds of the peasants. People remembered when villages which managed to survive infirmities and infant malnutrition were overburdened with forced labour which bound their inhabitants to a lifetime of ignominious servitude from the time they were old enough to be put to work. After Independence, many communities found themselves with vast areas of land in their possession. The inhabitants who no longer were slaves of Spanish colonists, tried to begin their lives anew, with dignity, and forget how they had been mistreated during the colonial period. Thus, the arrival of foreign colonists who appeared dissatisfied with the simple privilege of using the portions of land leased to them by the communities at the request of the Conservative authorities, and who tried by any means to take possession of _all_ communal property to grow coffee and other lucrative crops, naturally sparked repulsion and fervent resistance.

Peasant violence

As a result of the reasons stated above, the first _ladinos_ to arrive to Suchitepéquez with the intention of growing coffee had to deal with the open hostility of the peasants which often led to personal aggression and the destruction of coffee seedbeds. In this connection, the _corregidor_ of Suchitepéquez wrote to the Minister of the Interior in 1858 that,

> _"the Indians are not prepared to give up their land and have suggested as much both with words and deeds and even though it might seem appropriate to distribute the_

71

> *land so that agriculture might prosper, this ought to be*
> *done gradually, and coupled with the participation of*
> *the Indians. To proceed otherwise would be to encourage*
> *a series of complaints, protests and friction".*[25]

In 1858, the Minister of the Interior instructed the departmental *corregidores* regarding how to lease communal property and levy the tax *"referred to in the statute of August 5, 1835".* An annual tax of 2 *reales* was to be charged for every 100 *varas* of irrigable land, 1 and a half *reales* for fertile land, 1 *real* for barren land and half a *real* was to be paid by cattle raisers for grazing rights for every animal over one year old.[26]

The outcome of the agrarian measures taken by those members of the Conservative Government keen on development was increased violence in the countryside. In response to the invasion of communal property by *ladinos* who were in the habit of moving boundary stones during the night and continually taking possession of more and more land, the peasants often destroyed coffee plantations. Reports from *corregidores* and other rank and file rural authorities make constant mention of *"disorder in the villages",* and of *"Indians who have begun to violently destroy coffee nurseries".* Reference is also made to *"insults and threats to some of the coffee growers in the vicinity"* and to *demands for them to vacate the property",* and to secret plans among the members of the different communities to *"assault the ladino who plants without permission from the municipalities".*[27] In a particular document I found that in 1863 the illegal cultivation of coffee on communal property was so widespread that community members of the southwestern part of Guatemala had become *"archenemies"* of coffee growing.[28]

> *"More than one thousand Indians from a place called*
> *El Palmar in the jurisdiction of Quezaltenango have joi-*

---

25. Ibid., folder No. 28575, José M. Flores to the Minister of the Interior, October 23, 1858.
26. Ibid.
27. Ibid., folder No. 28593, *Corregidor* of Suchitepéquez to the Minister of the Interior, August 8, 1863.
28. Ibid., Joaquín Faye to the Minister of the Interior, August 22, 1863.

*ned forces with those from San Felipe and have taken
part in these assaults", wrote the* corregidor *of Retalhuleu
to the Minister of the Interior on September 8, 1863, "and
witnessing the State of affairs, I ordered that the cultivation
of coffee be suspended as well as the granting of property
for this purpose, but the Indians of San Felipe nonetheless
insist on destroying the coffee plantations."*[29]

A government collaborator by the name of Pedro Ajú, informed the Minister of the Interior, at the beginning of 1864, that
the communities of San Felipe, San Antonio, Samayac, Santo
Domingo, Cuyotenango, San Sebastian and El Palmar were
planning

*"to meet, in order to destroy the coffee plantations in
Palmar, starting in the village of San Felipe and
continuing on to any and every place where coffee is
grown".*[30]

The communities believed that all the problems which came
about as a result of coffee growing were due to the distribution
of communal property to persons who used it for speculative purposes. On some occasions, the *ladinos* would bribe corrupt community authorities who, in turn, would rent them *"previously
leased land",* without prior authorization from the peasants. As
a matter of fact, according to community members of San Felipe, Pedro Ajú, as Governor of a community, was known to accept
bribes from *ladinos, "forgetting that the main objective of his mission was to protect his own kind."*

The peasants claimed that Ajú

*"has deliberately used his administrative power to harm
us, as shown by the resolute and rash way he protects
coffee, to the detriment of the cereals and grains which
are essential for those of us who see agriculture
exclusively as a means of subsistence and not as a way*

---

29. Ibid., Joaquín Faye to the Minister of the Interior, September 8, 1863.
30. Ibid., folder No. 28595, Pedro Ajú to the Minister of the Interior, January 22, 1864.

73

> *of generating huge sums of capital. We are not
> underestimating the usefulness of coffee, nor are we
> opposed to it, as long as it is done in a way other than
> the way it has been done to date and it not affect our
> property and our means of subsistence".[31]*

The communities requested that all the land granted to the *ladinos* be measured once again and that they pay the compulsory tax without delay. In this way, the communities demonstrated that they were ready to accept that coffee be grown within their territorial boundaries by those persons who had initiated coffee growing in 1863, but not by those who had invaded their property after that date. In addition, they demanded that the Conservative Government guarantee them title to the land that they had leased, as well as that land *"already in their possession"* and their agrarian rights *"against any encroachment or measure"* which could be *"detrimental"* to their property. They also asked Government authorities to guarantee the communities and their leaders the liberty of exercising their rights which were often threatened and violated; that payments made by the tenants go into a community fund to be administered by the communities; the removal of the Governor of San Felipe, *"a person from Patzún by the name of Pedro Ajú"* and of the political commissioner *"for all the conveniences caused"*. The community members aked that Juan Sop, *"resident of this village"*, be appointed Governor and *"that they not be chastized, oppressed or harassed without just cause"*.

> *"Coffee growing was first developed in this region nearly
> nine years ago", the community of San Felipe told Rafael
> Carrera in a memorandum of February 27, 1864, "and
> that date markes the beginning of our struggle with the
> coffee entrepreneurs, which is due to their hostile way of
> dealing with our interests which date back to that time.
> Everyone is well aware of the ploys used by the coffee
> growers to seize almost all of our land (...) We cannot
> help but deplore the fact that these coffee growing*

---

31. Ibid., Community of San Felipe to the President of the Republic, February 15, 1864.

> _gentlemen want to treat us like the European colonists_
> _treated the Indians or natives in the country we know_
> _today as the great Republic of North America. Those_
> _gentlemen and ourselves have the sacred links which_
> _make us members of one nation, ruled by one_
> _Government and by one set of laws. Could it be that they_
> _want to use this factor and historic precedent against us_
> _because we lack large sums of capital for lucrative_
> _ventures, art and industry or that they want to take our_
> _only element of vitality from us, throw us out of our_
> _homes and off our land and turn us and future_
> _generations into a nomadic and wandering people,_
> _without a fixed domicile and without the ties and the_
> _obligations which home and property engender? This is_
> _neither just nor reasonable and even the most fervent_
> _coffee producer must admit it and do justice..."_[32]

The "pioneers" of private coffee cultivation

Ignacio Solís was a descendant of landowners of colonial origin, and what he wrote about coffee at the end of the nineteenth-century faithfully reflects the picture that the agrarian bourgeoisie painted for us of the beginning of coffee growing in Guatemala:

> _"In Cobán, Verapaz, the unforgettable Julio Rossignon,_
> _shareholder of Messrs. Rosa and Bouret, a Parisian_
> _publishing house, set up an immense coffee plantation,_
> _the largest of its kind in the district during that period._
> _Everything seemed to spell success for Mr. Rossignon,_
> _given his experience in agriculture, the quality of the soil_
> _and the luxuriance of the plants. But this was not the_
> _case. There was excessive foliage, a limited yield and a_
> _short season. It was too damp and, in addition to the_
> _torrential rainstorms, there were daily showers which_
> _kept the earth and the air consistently moist. The_

32. Ibid., folder No. 28607, Community of San Felipe to the President of the Republic, February 27, 1864.

> *deforestation in the mountains of Alta Verapaz and*
> *neighbouring districts has somewhat modified the*
> *climate in a way which favours coffee growing, so that it*
> *has expanded ever since, thanks, to a great degree, to the*
> *migration of foreign entrepreneurs, attracted by the*
> *deserved reputation of the richness of that soil made*
> *famous by the press. But we musn't forget the*
> *contribution made by Julio Rossignon's intelligence and*
> *tenacity".*[33]

In fact, Rossignon was nothing more than a French adventurer who came to Guatemala during the first half of the nineteenth-century, as a spearhead of foreign capital, later to become involved in commercial agriculture. Rossignon had studied botany in his own country, however, his knowledge of coffee growing was more theoretical than practical. He was one of the first foreigners to come to Alta Verapaz. At the expense of the peasantry, he tried, although unsuccessfully, to amass a fast fortune. Other European entrepreneurs who came to know him, would remember him as an example not to be followed if one wanted to *"succeed"* in the coffee business. A notorious wastrel and partygoer, he spent more time seducing young peasant girls than working.[34] According to communal authorities in Cobán in 1862.

> *"after having bought land in this same city, the*
> *foreigners have also taken much more and it has*
> *reached a point where we cannot even plant a kernel of*
> *corn because they have taken the best land. In a spot*
> *called Chiben Corral, they've taken away from us*
> *approximately 500* cuerdas *and won't permit us to*
> *remove even a single stick for our fences. Julio*
> *Rossignon bought some land in a place called Saclac*
> *and in addition to what he bought, took over other*
> *parcels of land that did not belong to him. And what's*

33. Ignacio Solís, op. cit., vol. III B, p. 945.
34. Franz Sarg, "Alte Erinnerungen an der Alta Verapaz". Article published in: *Frey,* Stuttgart, 1939, p. 23.

_worse, if a cow should happen to wander onto his
property by mistake, he would be already reaching for
his gun to blow it to bits..."[35]_

In Alta Verapaz, many foreigners, taking advantage of the privileges extended by State authorities to lease communal property, began to take possession of vast tracts of land sown by the peasants. The penetration of _ladinos_ was also particularly encouraged by the local authorities who, in addition to giving them land suited for coffee growing, tended to give them money loans in order to cover initial expenses. These loans could be paid back many years later because of continual extensions granted by the authorities. The money came from community chests and it is very likely that it was taken without the consent of the community members and that much corruption took place when the funds were managed by them.[36]

In addition to the land and money which belonged to the communities, _ladinos_ and foreigners received a generous quantity of seedlings free from the authorities. As early as June 2, 1859, the _corregidor_ of Verapaz informed the Minister of the Interior that he had visited several communities in his district and that,

_"the seedlings for transplant during the coming year,
which I personally saw, are so great in number that they
could easily be used for several fincas or even for
providing many entrepreneurs interested in devoting
themselves to planting this rare and valuable crop".[37]_

Some _corregidores_ energetically promoted the creation of seedbeds and nurseries in the communities to better serve the interests of the _ladinos_ and foreigners who had settled in the heart of the country. _Corregidores_ and high-ranking officials believed that the peasants should devote themselves exclusively to growing corn and other foodstuffs and leave the coffee growing to

---

35. A.G.C.A., BI, M.G.J., folder No. 28579, Seven Authorities from Verapaz to the President of the Republic, October 7, 1861.
36. Ibid., folder No. 28588, Juan E. Valdéz to the Minister of the Interior, June 26, 1862.
37. Ibid., folder No. 28580, Juan E. Valdéz to the Minister of the Interior, June 2, 1859.

the foreigners. According to the *corregidor* of Verapaz in 1866, the foreigners had a *"negligible amount of land as compared with the residents".*[38] By this he insinuated that it was necessary to further promote the distribution of communal property. Many *corregidores* tried to give the impression that the peasant communities willingly gave up part of their property to foreigners, due to the fact that a large part of the ruling class was opposed to the enrichment and expansion of the economic base of the incipient agrarian bourgeoisie and their cohorts, the foreign investors. Furthermore, in some regions, such as Alta Verapaz, the *corregidor,* despite the fact that the foreigners had already managed to seize several hundred *caballerías* of communal property in 1866, attempted to play down the numbers, stating that the municipalities had only leased land to *"five or six entrepreneurs",* and *"only small portions of land that don't even make up a caballería".*

> *"I explained with insistence"* (to the community), *wrote the* corregidor *to the Minister of the Interior,* "that the corporation was absolutely free to grant or deny land without the least amount of interference from the corregimiento, *unless it was a question of the lieutenant's (second to the* corregidor) *approval of land transfers that the municipalities might make voluntarily."*[39]

From complaints registered by the peasant communities, we can see that they were coerced by the *corregidores* into handing over their land to be leased, after the entrepreneurs interested in land suited for coffee growing received authorization from these *corregidores,* in exchange for a sum of money, to take possession of the land they wanted. There was corruption at every level among Conservative authorities. By means of graft one could easily obtain authorization to monopolize and expropriate peasant property.

---

38. Ibid., folder No. 28604, Juan E. Valdéz to the Minister of the Interior, September 14, 1866.
39. Ibid.

In a Memorandum addressed to President Vicente Cerna, suc-
cesor of Rafael Carrera, members of the community of San Cristobal Cajcoj, Alta Verapaz, wrote that Carrera had instructed
them to only lease property to those persons born in the community.

> "They're tyrannizing us and taking away our best land
> which we cultivate and use for our cattle to graze on",
> claimed the peasants of San Cristobal Cajcoj: "They've
> already taken several plots of land from us and forced
> us to remove our animals and keep them on a tiny spot,
> and we know they want to seize the land where close to
> sixty peasants from this village grow corn, also many
> foreigners are coming to settle here..."[40]

The plan for agrarian expropriation

In order for foreign capital to make headway in Guatemalan
agriculture, the resistance of the peasants had to be broken. For
the most part, the presence of the communities on land which
was already cleared and suitable for coffee growing, represented a real obstacle for speculators, private farmers and foreign
entrepreneurs interested in that property. Only through different forms of persuasion, coercion and deceit, were Conservative authorities and entrepreneurs able to make the peasants lease their land to life tenants. In Alta Verapaz and other regions,
community members owned land with boundaries which were
often imprecise or delineated by mountains, rivers and streams
which were extremely difficult to negotiate. In Verapaz the initial occupation of land by foreigners in the communities only
came about by forcing the peasants to retreat into the mountains. They tricked them into moving off land which they had already worked and clearing other terrain which would later be used
for coffee production. Following this policy, local authorities, rep-
resenting the interests of the entrepreneurs, told the commu-

---

40. Ibid., Residents of San Cristobal Cajcoj to the President of the Republic,
August 20, 1866.

nities that the Central Government wanted them to cultivate in the mountains and for that reason they should move to villages more and more removed from the spots where foreign coffee growers had settled. On one occasion, these authorities even availed themselves of the influence of a local priest within his parish, to get their message across in his Sunday sermon.

> *"For some days now they have tried to make us believe that Your Excellency has ordered that we be removed from our native soil", declared the community of San Pedro Carchá to President Vicente Cerna, in a petition written on May 21, 1867, "forcing us to scatter throughout the villages of Cajabón, San Agustín, Panzós and San Juan and making us abandon our sown fields. And even under these conditions we have started working on land that even we are not familiar with. To keep this strange programme going, they have made us believe, through sermons delivered by Father Basilio Cordero, that they have received instructions from the Supreme Government to force us to leave our homes."[41]*

When the Minister of the Interior requested information concerning this so-called *"abuse of authority"*, the authorities of Alta Verapaz replied that much time had passed since

> *"the many Indians from the village of Carchá had left for the dual purpose of planting their crops and living nearby, settling in Panzós, Lanquin and Cahabón. The mayor of Carchá has not thrown out anyone, nor has he forced anyone to settle elsewhere", stated the corregidor's lieutenant. "It's all a lie. All those who have gone to Cahabón and Lanquin to live in the vicinity, have done so voluntarily".[42]*

---

41. Ibid., folder No. 28610, Community of San Pedro Carchá to the President of the Republic, May 21, 1867.
42. Ibid., Zenón Orellana to Juan E. Valdéz, August 23, 1867.

The *corregidor,* however, has assured his superiors that *"no one had forced the Indians to stay in Lanquín, Cahabón and Panzós; quite the contrary, they seem quite pleased to be there..."*[43] However, the peasant communities were not all that satisfied. In a complaint addressed to Cerna on July 9, 1867, the inhabitants of San Pedro Carchá stated that

> *"after having had our houses and our ranchos, which are the fruit of our labour, taken away from us, we have once more been informed by the authorities that Your Excellency has been authorized to do so. And although Your Excellency has ordered that a temple be built for us in the mountains, we are fully aware that this is not true. The Commissioner of Panzós has forced us to plant coffee in the mountains where we grow corn. This appears to be nothing more than an attempt to exterminate us..."*[44]

Communal property was also gradually invaded in the western regions of the country, notably Quezaltenango and San Marcos. In these departments, wheat, corn and other subsistence crops were traditionally grown. After the 1850s however, it was discovered that in these departments there were also regions where the land was ideal for growing coffee. Many *ladinos* and foreigners, with the support of local authorities, headed that way. In Quezaltenango, a region known by the name of Costa Cuca was

> *"particulary rich in natural elements, ideal for farming, which leads us to believe that there is something good in store for our working class, since there is no longer any doubt about the abundance of the crops or their superior quality, as shown by the productive plantation of Manuel Fuentes Franco. Following his example, many*

---

43. Ibid., Juan E. Valdéz to the Minister of the Interior, November 4, 1867.
44. Ibid., folder No. 28583, Francisco García to the Minister of the Interior, May 1, 1861.

> *people seeking employment have headed for this area*
> *with visions of planting and growing coffee".*[45]

The *corregidor* of San Marcos pointed out in May of 1861 that *"the chief source of wealth in those highland villages was wheat, corn, beans and potatoes",* and that coffee growing was becoming more widespread in San Marcos, although most of the trees planted still had not borne fruit.[46] Three years later, however, in a report addressed to the Minister of the Interior, another *Corregidor* from the same department spoke of the

> *"satisfactory results derived from agricultural*
> *production, particulary coffee production which should*
> *improve even more by the end of the year because so*
> *much planting is going on in different adaptable*
> *climates and with enthusiasm bordering on delirium".*[47]

In Occidente an attempt was also made at persuading, through devious means, all those Indian communities unwilling to lease their property to do so. Often, the *corregidor* of a given department would call together the *Principales,* or most respected members of the community, and assure them that the municipalities would not lose their title to the land they leased, that rents would generate generous earnings for the community fund and that coffee would bring wealth to the country. According to the authorities, this wealth would be distributed among the community members who worked for the coffee entrepreneurs.[48] They even told the peasants that the President himself had leased his land in order to contribute to the development of coffee growing in the country. In San Marcos, the municipality of San Pablo, believing this to be true, addressed Rafael Carrera on March 28, 1864, and told him that ever since

---

45. Ibid., folder No. 28606, Residents of Quezaltenango to the President of the Republic, July 9, 1867.
46. Ibid., folder No. 28585, Francisco García to the Minister of the Interior, May 1, 1861.
47. Ibid., folder No. 28595, Miguel Zelaya to the Minister of the Interior, April 14, 1864.
48. Ibid., folder No. 28597, Miguel Zelaya to the Minister of the Interior, May 17, 1864.

it was discovered that the Government was encouraging the municipalities to lease part of their porperty, the people of San Pedro

> _"tried to observe these dispositions because many people had taken land and kept it uncultivated and others had sold the deeds which they claim belonged to their parents (...) The municipality, in fulfilment of the statute governing this issue and in observance of the charitable intentions of the Supreme Government, gave up its land so that a coffee plantation might be established there. And many of us have heard that the President himself has handed his land over for coffee production..."_[49]

As indicated by the members of the community of San Pablo, the land which people most wanted to lease was often uncultivated and there was a lot of speculation on the sale of rights to use and enjoy the land. This practice prevailed throughout Guatemala. A _corregidor_ referred to this practice in 1867 as _detrimental to agriculture and municipal resources"_, and with the knowledge that the _Fiscal del Gobierno_ was drafting a regulation concerning the concession of communal property to individuals interested in coffe growing, he suggested that it was _"essential to repress the establishment of any such regulation"._

> _"Often, poor individuals, clearly without the means to set up a coffee plantation, try to lease land and offer to cultivate it. Then, once the land is theirs to use and enjoy, they abandon it and devote themselves to another variety of speculation, so as to create resources to be able to plant. They spend considerable time doing this, at least four or five years, and during that period, the land remains uncultivated and rent is not paid regularly."_[50]

Other anomalies associated with the handing over of commu-

---

49. Ibid., Municipality of San Pablo to the President of the Republic, March 28, 1864.
50. Ibid., folder No. 28612, Gabriel Cárdenas to the Minister of the Interior, June 15, 1867.

nal property to private parties were pointed out in 1866 by this same *corregidor* of Suchitepéquez, who was determined to curb the excesses which characterized the agrarian redistribution project promoted by the Conservatives. These anomalies reflect the monopolistic tendencies amongst persons who recognized the increasing commercial value of the land which was well on its way to becoming a veritable commodity with the development of coffee production.

> *"As a precautionary and repressive measure to contain the blind ambition to acquire land in that village (San Felipe Retalhuleu, JCC)", wrote the corregidor to the Minister of the Interior, "it has been decided that no petitioner shall receive more than two hundred cuerdas. But there is no lack of ill-intentioned and crafty people ready to break the law, while seeking its protection, who have claimed and acquired this area in ways which appear to be legal. Thus, after possessing the permissible 200 cuerdas, they send a third party out to acquire many more for them. Hereyou can see an obvious case of fraud and mockery of the municipality's intention to avoid the reconcentration of land in the hands of the few and an attack toward the superior authority of the Department, on the grounds that, as representative of the Government, he ought to adequately protect agriculture."[51]*

The main contradiction of Conservative agrarian policy

The Conservative Government permitted agrarian redistribution in Guatemala by fostering the handing over of land to private parties, which by law belonged to the peasant communities. This policy was prompted by demands made as a result of economic development in the country; the need to promote cash crops such as coffee, as espoused by the *Consulado de Comercio* and the *Sociedad Economia;* the thirst for land belonging

---

51. Ibid., folder No. 28607, Gabriel Cárdenas to the Minister of the Interior, January 25, 1866.

to the rural poor, most of whom were _ladinos_ or peasants from small communities without enough land for distribution among all the members; pressure from members of the ruling class who were interested in communal property suitable for coffee growing; and pressure from foreign capitalists, who promoted changes in land tenure legislation inherited from the period of Spanish domination.

A key and characteristic contradiction in the agrarian redistribution plan promoted by the Conservatives, was that land leased to life tenants by the communities did not become the private property of the parties who took possession of it. They did, however, retain the right to bequeath the land to their offspring, sublet it, even sell their acquired right to use and enjoy the fruits of it, but the land continued to be the legal property of the municipalities which had leased them in return for a negligible annual tax. In this way, a large percentage of _finqueros_, some of whom came to be prominent coffee growers, were simple tenant farmers on communal property during the Conservative period. For example, a _finca_ called "Monte Limar", as early as 1864, produced 1,000 quintals of coffee for export, while the community of San Pablo, owner of the land where _"Monte Limar"_ was situated, and which only produced a mere 11 quintals of coffee during that same year, became private property in 1880.[52] Even J. Rufino Barrios, _caudillo_ (leader) of the _finqueros_ from Occidente and one of the fathers of the Guatemalan agrarian bourgeoisie, who in 1864 produced 5 quintals of _coffe_,[53] did not become the rightful owner of the _finca "San José el Porvenir",_ also located on property belonging to the community of San Pablo, until 1879.[54] _"Chocolá",_ the renowned _finca_ belonging to the Spaniard José Guardiola, and located in the Department of Suchitepéquez, became private property in 1874.[55] And these are only few examples...

52. Index to the _Expedientes_ which to date correspond to the Archivo de la Escribanía del Gobierno and Sección de Tierras. Guatemala, 1944, Department of San Marcos, paquete No. 7, 1880/1881, p. 236.
53. A.G.C.A., B1, M.G.J., folder No. 28596, Municipality of Santa Lucia Malacatán to the Minister of the Interior, January 22, 1864.
54. Index to the _Expedientes..,_ op. cit., Department of San Marcos, paquete No. 6, p. 235.
55. Ibid., Department of Suchitepéquez, paquete No. 7, p. 194.

CHAPTER V

THE CHARACTER OF THE NEW RURAL PROPERTY

Prior to 1821, all landowners in Guatemala had been beneficiaries of the Spanish Crown after the latter had plundered land belonging to the pre-Columbian peoples of Guatemala. Independence was followed by a new wave of usurpation, looting, and the buying and selling of land which permitted the expansion of the economic base of those groups who had acquired their power by monopolizing agricultural property. However, the landowner who appears during the period of Spanish domination must not be mistaken for the landowner-entrepreneur of the national period. Any references to the origins of the *latifundia* system in Guatemala must specify the type of *latifundia* under discussion, so as not to confuse the *criollo* or Spanish *hacendado* of the colonial period with the German *finquero* of the nineteenth-century, for whom owning property was nothing more than an agricultural venture of a capitalist nature. For that reason, and in view of the documentation I have compiled, it is reasonable to conclude that Guatemala has known various manifestations of land concentration, every one of which was a function of the country's agricultural development and the prevailing economic and political situation. It is not my intention to identify these different manifestations and periods, but to demonstrate that while the *latifundia* system which emerged during the period of Spanish colonization was endemically feudal in nature, the system of the latter half of the nineteenth-century was inherently capitalistic. With the passage of time, land was concentrated in the hands of foreigners, and in particular Germans. In 1943, all German property was confiscated and thousands of *caballerias* belonging to hundreds of lucrative coffee farms, sugar plantations and cattle ranches established by German nationals were passed into the hands of the State or of high officials who later backed the bourgeoisie which virtually controlled the State. The concentration of farm property in the hands of the bourgeoisie has still not reached its final phase in Guatemala, due to internal struggles for power and political hegemony within the different sectors of the ruling class and high ranking bureaucrats, enriched by the excercise of this power.

In the mid-nineteenth century, as recorded in the files of the *Archivo de la Escribania del Gobierno,* more than 70% of the country's best land was controlled by some 1,000 peasant communities distributed throughout the 17 departments of the Republic of Guatemala.[1] As indicated by a Conservative official in 1866, many of these communities did not have title deeds.[2] Whenever a dispute over land would arise, the members of the community would make it perfectly clear that the land had been theirs *"since time immemorial",* and that its boundaries were well protected. They did not permit their neighbours to trespass on *"a single inch of property"* which did not belong to them, and when this occurred, endless court action ensued.[3]

The peasantry constituted the social base of the Conservative dictatorship. Clerical politicians, such as Juan José Aycinena and Francisco Pavón, knew how to use Rafael Carrera's pea-

---

1. Pío Casal, op. cit., p. 20.
2. A.G.C.A., B1, M.G.J., folder No. 28604, J. Domingo Segura to Minister of the Interior, September 28, 1868.
3. Ibid., folder No. 28628, dossier No. 231, Municipality of Guanagazápa, the Indians of the town to the President of the Republic, January 14, 1871.

sant background to their advantage, and in the different disputes over land which came about, they tried to take a neutral stand and not disfavour the Indian communities, always trying to show compassion for the needs of the peasantry. In fact, the Conservative dictatorship only masked the growing differences within Guatemalan society, the internal struggle for power within the ruling class, and the class struggle existing in the country. Together with conflicts of an economic nature (contradictions existing between the Conservative oligarchy and the advocates of development, who favoured the establishment of agricultural enterprise in the country; the merchants of colonial origin and the newly arrived foreigners; and the private landowners, the agricultural entrepreneurs and the rural labour force engaged on the plantations) there were also glaring political and social differences which were evident from the ideas upheld by factions opposing the ruling class and by the ever-widening gap between the rich and the poor. This social distinction was closely linked to existing racial discrimination of colonial origin. The economic backdrop of this scenario featured a new breed of landowner who felt he had to undermine the insti-tution of communal ownership of property.

For the above mentioned reasons, the sympathy displayed by the Conservatives — the most reactionary and arrogant clique of the ruling class —, and Rafael Carrera himself — instrument of the Conservatives —, with respect to the demands and complaints made by the rural population, was more apparent than real.

The Government knew that the peasantry had to be treated with kid gloves, particulary because of its tendency to solve territorial disputes by taking up arms, as Carrera's own movement had done. Clearly, the alliance between the Conservatives and the peasants was a sham because it was impossible to reach an agreement or achieve peace between the exploiters and the exploited. This became increasingly apparent every time a conflict arose between the peasants and the forgers of Guatemala's destiny. the landowners.[4]

---

4. See, for example, outcome of land dispute in San Juan Sacatepéquez in May of 1847: Indian chiefs were severely punished while the interests of the _ladino_ landowners were protected by Conservative authorities. A.G.C.A., B1, folder No. 28538, dossier No. 18.

The contempt that the Conservatives and the renegade Carrera held for the Indian peasantry was evident by their tolerance of the practice of forced labour in the countryside, which not only meant farm work, but the construction of public works, roads in particular. There is an abundance of records which detail the violent ways in which the representatives of the Conservative government forced the peasants to provide personal services and the complaints and demands for justice that went unheeded.[5] However, it must not be forgotten that there were some people, although few in number, prepared to recognize certain Indian rights, based on earlier Indian legislation. For example, in an agrarian dispute which arose in 1870, a Government official was determined to prove that the laws prevailing in the country provided that in issues concerning land tenure, communities should have priority over private parties. These concessions were generally made when the private parties represented a sector of the ruling class interested in undermining the economic and social bases of the traditional oligarchy.

The dispute over the character of agrarian property

Guatemalan agriculture was evolving independently of the whims and desires of most Conservatives and die-hard traditionalists. The feuds between the large peasant communities with their vast stretches of fallow land, and those who advocated development in the form of agricultural export production, went beyond the control of Conservative authorities and the possibility of any solution. After Independence, many *ladinos* had settled on communal property, and, as noted by a *Corregidor* in 1866, since they were already accustomed to making use of this land, *"they were not inclined to accuse them",*[6] undoubtedly for fear of giving rise to lawsuits which they risked losing. When, in light of the unbridled and continual invasion of communal property by private parties, another *Corregidor* wrote that *"it is unjust that one should prosper at someone else's expense"* and asked for

---

5. Ibid., folder No. 28576. This folder contains interesting documentation on the subject.
6. Ibid., folder No. 28604, from J. Domingo Segura to the minister of the Interior. September, 28, 1866.

authorization to stop the invaders. Central authorities hastened to consult invalid statutes in the _Leyes de Indias_, while they
asked the Corregidor who had made the accusation for sugges-
tions and recommendations. On the 19 february 1866, the _Fis-
cal Protector de Indios_ pointed out that

> _"It is imperative to recognise the need for a decree_
> _which will cover any eventuality whose obstacles could_
> _be neither anticipated nor halted. In order for this_
> _decree to serve a purpose, the Fiscal deems it necessary_
> _for the Corregidor to prepare a draft decree based on the_
> _order of prohibition which figures in any contract_
> _governing the sale, the leasing or the subleasing of_
> _property, which, according to law, is the task of the_
> _Corregidor alone, and which establishes the laws_
> _governing such contracts with all other prescriptions the_
> _Corregidor should consider appropriate. The Fiscal_
> _believes that this is the only way to avoid the problems_
> _which necessarily come about as a result of the_
> _prosperity, the development and the wealth of a people."_[7]

_"These acquisitions have all been made thanks to the support
of the local authorities",_ stated another _Corregidor_ to the Minister of the Interior, making reference to the fact that some private parties had received more communal property than others
during the plundering process, because of the central government's tendecy of tolerating abuse of authority and favouritism.

> _"Some of them have their land marked out with a cord_
> _measuring twenty five yards, others with cords of twenty_
> _eight and even thirty two yards, and it seems to me that_
> _the only way to avoid such friction is to establish a_
> _uniform measure, twenty five being the fairest. It should_
> _be made known that everyone should carry out their_
> _measures geometrically in order to avoid problems. In_
> _almost all the land grants, I have witnessed an absolute_

---

7. Ibid., folder No. 28607, from the _Fiscal Protector de Indios_ to the Minister
of the Interior, February 19, 1886.

*lack of legal formulae to sanction the land acquired in a
satisfactory fashion. But since the Municipality insists
that these grants be respected and because these lands
are under cultivation, there is nothing to be done about
it. The grantees are under the obligation of cultivating
only coffee. It is forbidden to cultivate sugar cane, but
they can plant twenty five* cuerdas *of banana. However,
when they take possession of the land granted to them,
they forget everything and plant whatever they want.
Finally, they transfer the land titles to other persons
without notifying the authorities and without paying the*
laudemio *and* alcabala *taxes. This important aspect has
to be settled, not only for the convenience of the National
Treasury, the indian landowners, the new owners of the
right to cultivate, the municipal funds, but also for
everyone's tranquility, and for the praise worthy objective
of thus silencing the direct owners of the plots of land."[8]*

In the middle of 1867 the *Fiscal Protector de Indios* advised
the Minister of the Interior to prohibit foreigners from taking
possession of communal property. Private parties already in possession of communal property could transfer this property to
their children, or make other transfers or conveyances deemed
"legal". Only the municipalities had the right to lease their property and this had to be done without pressure or coercion and
at public auction. A private person was also entitled to lease
the communal property he owned, but only with permission of
the municipality.

*"As such, the municipality may interfere if it considers
the leasing or the transfer of property to another
individual inappropriate. And if an Indian should
cultivate a plot of land which has not been leased to
him, and desires to sell it in order to purchase more
plots and sell them, then the sale may only be made at*

8. Ibid., folder No. 28607, Gabriel Cárdenas to the Minister of the Interior, January 25, 1866.

> *an auction and will be recognized as perfectly justified.*
> *Any sale conducted in any other way other than the*
> *prescribed, shall be considered null and void, as duly*
> *provided far in Statute 27, heading 1, Book 4 of the*
> Recopilación de Indias."[9]

Communal property leased in perpetuity was often prepared for coffee growing. This factor underlines the socio-economic impact of coffee growing on Guatemalan agriculture and the fallacy propagated by the agrarian bourgeoisie which suggests that land suited for coffee growing was never occupied by Indian peasants. Conservative authorities stipulated that after conveying communal property to a private party, the latter had to plant coffee on that plot of land no later than one year after occupying it. If the party failed to do so, the land would be taken away from him and he would *"lose the right of usufruct of that property, which then could be transferred to another person."*[10]

It was common for private parties settled on communal property not to pay the annual tax which they had promised to pay upon taking possesion of it. Pretexts for not making these payments were infinite: either it was a bad harvest or animals or locusts had destroyed the seedbeds. The truth is that the lessees considered themselves the owners of the property belonging to the municipalities and were confident that sooner of later the Government would recognize them as the rightful owners. This is exactly what occurred when the *"Liberals"* came to power. However, before this happened, the Conservatives stipulated that the payment of this tax was a prerequisite for using and enjoying the fruits of the land taken from the communities. Any person who did not meet the required payment over the course of the next three years was obliged to pay twice the amount owed, otherwise the municipalities had the right to put the property in the hands of the debtor up for public auction, *"in order to recuperate that which was outstanding and to ensure payment of the respective tax in the future".*[11]

---

9. Ibid., folder No. 28612, *Fiscal Protector de los Indios* to the Minister of the Interior, July 11, 1867.
10. Ibid.
11. Ibid.

The move towards commercial agriculture

In practice, most of the measures taken by the Conservatives for the so-called purpose of safeguarding the interests of the Indian communities were not applicable. It was almost impossible to control the use they made of the land leased to them since most of it was quite a distance from the public eye. The *Fiscal Protector de Indios* considered the idea of forcing small- and medium-sized farmers to cultivate the land they held in usufruct, while the rightful owners could freely determine the way in which this land was to be used. According to this same *Fiscal,* either the Government did not stipulate what they were to cultivate, or it did not specify which land was to be used for growing coffee,

> *"since the peasants are as much the owners of their* ejidos *as the landowner is of the property he has purchased, it would be unjust to force the Indians to cultivate a specific plot of land, without making the landowners do the same. There are many landowners who do not even know the number of* caballerías *their* haciendas *have. Consequently, this land risks remaining uncultivated for many years to come, at the expense of agriculture in general".*[12]

It was common practice for a large sector of the ruling class to leave its *latifundios* uncultivated. However, by the end of the 1860s, the remunerative role of the land had grown as interest in coffee growing increased. Within the communities there was a marked interest in using the land for gainful purposes and this took place behind the backs of the municipal authorities. For example, many foreigners interested in settling down and growing coffee would often make offers to purchase land from individual community members who were in need of cash since community authorities had refused to lease land to hem. This permitted a single individual to purchase lots from several peasants and set up a coffee *finca* on communal property.[13]

---

12. Ibid.
13. Ibid., folder No. 28644, Juan Paniagua to the Minister of the Interior, November 20, 1874.

The buying and selling of communal property became customary among the Indians themselves, some of whom had to sell their property title out of dire necessity, hoping to be able to recuperate their land at a later date. The debts contracted by the Indians were often of a religous order. Frequently, *"after having paid their cofradías (religious association) and rented religous icons"*, the Indian peasants were forced to dispose of their land, only to buy it back shortly thereafter at a higher price. Some peasants were obliged to buy small plots of land to grow items which would help them meet their expenses. In those cases it is likely that the parties' mutual need to carry out such a transaction made speculative interest of secondary importance.

> *"They come to our* ranchos*", explained the peasants of San Juan Ostuncalco on one occasion, referring to the men selling land, "and since we are country and working people with* cofradías *to maintain, Indians and* ladinos *come here to sell us plots of land. We make endless sacrifies to be able to buy them and often end up without enough to feed ourselves or our families or to plant sufficient grain to cover our parrochial commitments, let alone those to the* cofradía *etc."[14]*

Occasionally, community members became exploiters of their own class, due to these land transactions and the cultivation of commercial products, such as coffee. This seems to have been the case with Luciano Ramás, a member of the Samayac community, in the department of Suchitepéquez, who went so far as to fight with foreign *finqueros* over men from whom they had exacted forced labour on their coffee plantations. In 1865, Ramás requested that Conservative authorities make him exempt from paying land tax on property he had leased from his community.

> *"When José Loarca was* Corregidor *of this Department, I was obliged to pay taxes on the few tracts of land I*

---

14. Ibid., folder No. 28602, Peasants of San Juan Ostuncalco to the President of the Republic, March 14, 1865.

> had in my village", recounted Ramás to the Corregidor
> of Suchitepéquez, revealing his absolute lack of interest
> in improving the lot of his own community, "but I
> believe my Indian blood should relieve me of such an
> obligation."[15]

A surveyor explained that Ramás owned *"five thousand odd
cuerdas planted with such things as coffee, etc."*, and that, in addition, he owned one hundred and twenty head of cattle and *"many
other financial assets which warrant his being called a capitalist".*[16] The Indian authorities of Samayac, on the other hand,
asserted that

> *"it is difficult to justify this man's having appropriated
> close to one third of the* ejidos *of this town, setting up
> pasture lands and establishing small plantations of
> coffee* (cafetales), *taking over more land every day and
> selling property which is part and parcel of the* ejidos,
> *as he has just done with 1,000* cuerdas *of fodder grass,
> putting hundreds of head of cattle out to pasture, to the
> detriment of the other farmers..."*[17]

---

15. Ibid., Luciano Ramás to the *Corregidor* of Suchitepéquez, May 3, 1865.
16. Ibid., From the *Corregidor* of Suchitepéquez to the Minister of the Interior,
August 5, 1865.
17. Ibid., From the Municipality of Samayac to the *Corregidor* of Suchitepéquez, October 10, 1865.

CHAPTER VI

COFFEE AND LABOUR

The land tenure issue and the problems which resulted from attempts to redistribute communal agrarian property to persons interested in coffee growing were closely linked to the problem of procuring an adequate flow of migrant labour to level the land, sow seeds in seedbeds and transplant seedlings into nurseries, attend to coffee plants until the first harvest, pick and process coffee, etc. The problem in itself was nothing new. We have already seen how Spanish colonists, as early as the first half of the sixteenth-century, distributed land, together with the men required to work it, as they saw fit. Their offspring, *criollos* and *mestizos*, did not hesitate to follow suit once they came to power. The year 1830 witnessed the legalization of forced labour and by the time the Conservatives came to power the recruitment of teams of labourers called *cuadrillas* had become a common practice in the peasant communities when seasonal help was required on the *haciendas* of the privileged class. When coffee growing first began, State authorities ordered the departmental *Corregidores*, by means of *mandamientos*, to see that the

Indian villages provided the coffee growers with enough men to work on the newly established plantations.[1]

In his Memorandum of July 23, 1859, the *Corregidor* of Verapaz informed the Minister of the Interior that

> *"agriculture is developing in the villages of this Department at such a pace that many pairs of hands are required to get the work done".*[2]

On this same occasion, the *Corregidor* recounted how the agricultural entrepreneurs and newcomers to the Department had come to him for assistance in the procurement of workers, who were only found in the Indian communities, according to already established methods of securing forced labour.

The main problem facing the entrepreneurs who pressured Conservative authorities into furnishing the necessary manpower, was that the communal peasants refused, for a variety of reasons, to work for foreigners. In economic terms, it could be said that the peasants were not willing to leave their own crops unattended in order to work for the *finqueros* for a miserly sum of one real per day, that is, the same wages the landowners used to pay during the colonial period. Under these circumstances, it became customary to bribe rural authorities to force unwilling Indian peasants to work on the coffee plantations.

Capitalist agriculture and forced labour

One of the chief characteristics of commercial coffee production in Guatemala is that almost since its introduction it has been a lucrative activity predominantly controlled by foreigners. While Guatemalan coffee growers and *finqueros* followed in the foreigners' footsteps, combining the use of modern technology in coffee production with rational methods of organization and administration on the plantations, the foreigners knew how to incorporate the system of forced labour, prevalent in the count-

---

1. A.G.C.A., B1, M.G.J., folder No. 28585, Pablo Sierra to the *Corregidor* of Verapaz, May 4, 1861.
2. Ibid., folder No. 28577, Juan E. Valdéz to the Minister of the Interior, July 23, 1859.

ry since the period of Spanish colonialism, into commercial agriculture. In other words, foreign capital knew how to take full advantage of traditional production relations of a precapitalist bent, which already existed in Guatemala and which yielded higher returns from their capitalist ventures.

The first foreign _finqueros_ in Alta Verapaz, a Frenchman by the name of Jules Rossignon and an Englishman by the name of Charles Meany, did not request peasants for their plantations. Instead, they demanded that local authorities employ an archaic methods of recruitment through the issue of edicts known as _mandamientos_, and paid wretched wages so that they might increase the returns on their investment. From the beginning, the _finquero_ diplayed absolute contempt for the physical work performed by the peasant, to whom he was most patronizing. He believed he was superior to State authorities, whom he only considered useful when they served his own interests unconditionally. In 1861, Charles Meany noted that the development of coffee growing in Alta Verapaz was running up against _"serious obstacles"_, because the authorities in the region had _"failed to cooperate"_ with the _finqueros_ and their requests for workers. In a memo addressed to the President of the Republic, Meany urged him to ensure that the _finqueros_ always had the necessary number of workers, in addition to other facilities required for the production, transport and export of coffee in the country.[3]

The Deputy _Corregidor_ of Cobán wrote of Meany's demands in a report to the _Corregidor_ of Verapaz dated May 4, 1861:

> _"Records of visits made by the_ corregimiento _from 1856 to the present, describe in minute detail the practice of supplying private parties with young men and the compliant nature with which they have sown their fields. The chief occupation of this Department seems to be that of giving daily orders to neighbouring villages requesting Indians for the_ fincas, _without charging the_

---

3. Ibid., folder No. 28584, Juan E. Valdéz to the Minister of the Interior, June 1, 1861. In this report mention is made of the Charles Meany to whom we referred earlier.

99

owners a cent. In addition, the Indians have to be delivered to the work site, a common occurrence with Messrs. Meany. And the inhabitants here seem to have been spared the problems which have plagued other Departments since they always manage to get the number of labourers they require for a modest wage of one real, and they are docile, obedient and entirely trustworthy... There are so many of them and yet there's never been a single case of a missing farm tool.[4]

According to that same *Corregidor,* in Alta Verapaz, by the middle of 1861, there were only two *fincas "where the coffee was starting to bear fruit"* and where seedbeds were being prepared in order to establish *"between 8 and 10 fincas before the year is out, which will take from 4 to 5 years to yield fruit".*

"The demands made by the entrepreneurs in the planting season create a lot of problems", wrote the Corregidor *to the Minister of the Interior, "because being farmers themselves, the Indians are busy sowing grain and the authorities cannot force them to do someone else's work and leave their own unattended."*[5]

The *Corregidor* of Verapaz stated that the foreigners were starting plantations in Cobán *"for wages as low as one real a day",* which hardly permits the workers to eat. Accordingly, he ordered the Deputy *Corregidor* not to force the Indians

"to work for less than one and a half reales a day and to increase wages when labour is scarce, as it tends to be done in Alta Verapaz. This will produce an excess of men willing to work as a result of this incentive".[6]

---

4. Ibid., Pablo Sierra to the *Corregidor* of Verapaz, May 4, 1861.
5. Ibid., Juan E. Valdéz to the Minister of the Interior, June 1, 1861.
6. Ibid.

The concentration of labour in the countryside

On the Southern Plain, during the first years of commercial coffee production, cattle ranches and sugar plantations were sown with _"the bonanza bean"_, _the name the finqueros_ used for coffee, and their owners took advantage of the existing labour force and turned those workers into tenant farmers. Those entrepreneurs who acquired land by purchasing it directly from high-ranking officials in the Conservative Government (the case of Herrera, who purchased land in Santa Lucia Cotzumalguapa from Carrera, is only one example) or leasing it from the peasant communities, sought to establish their _fincas_ in regions with a relatively large peasant population, so as to gradually incorporate that population into the plantations as their need for labour increased.

The _finqueros_, following the example set by the earlier _hacendados_ who settled landless men on their own property, managed, with assistance from the local authorities, to attract poor peasants by offering them a daily wage which was slightly above the going rate in Alta Verapaz. To complement that daily wage they granted the peasants a plot of land on which to plant corn, beans, and other staples and live with their families under one roof. During the Conservative dictatorship, group labour was not widespread in Guatemala. As pointed out earlier, peasants were considered to be free men as long as they were not indebted to any landowner. Local authorities had instructions from their superiors to supply the _hacendados_ with day labourers, as a contribution to the economic development of the country. In fact, and paradoxically so, the Conservative Government tended to promote the idea of wage labour in production relations. However, the scarcity of hard cash in the country and the custom whereby a plot of land on the property of a _hacendado_ was viewed as partial payment for the personal services rendered, impeded the development of the concept of wages in worker-employer relations.

Instructions to _Corregidores_ to foster the creation of small villages within or near the coffee plantations, were often accompanied by recommendations that the labourers not be subjected to overly rigorous working conditions. If a worker was maltreated on a plantation, he was free to change his place of employment, providing he gave due notice to the local authorities. In 1862, almost the entire population of one *hacienda* in Escuintla, asked the *Corregidor* if they could be transferred to another *hacienda* where it was believed they could enjoy improved working and living conditions. Arguing in favour of their transfer, the workers informed the *Corregidor* that the *hacienda* where they were living only had a *"small coffee plantation, not the large plantation everyone thought, which meant that the inhabitants of the* hacienda *were sufficient in number, if not excessive, to double crop".*[7] In his report to the Minister of the Interior, the *Corregidor* of Escuintla, making reference to the workers, stated that

> *"their modest wage of one and a half* reales, *and all the construction work on the* fincas *and other buildings, which they are forced to do during holidays, is the reason why they want to move to that sugar mill where they can earn two* reales, *the work is less irregular, the tasks reduced and the land more suitable for growing corn. It is also less crowded because there are fewer cattle than in the village, where the livestock business is thriving. For the reasons stated above, I responded to their request".*[8]

As already pointed out, in addition to land speculators and agricultural entrepreneurs, landless men and poor Indian peasants from small communities of the *Altiplano*, without enough land for their growing population, were also able to lease land on the plains in the southern part of the country. Because these poor farmers were often rejected by the Indian communities when seeking assistance from the local authorities, they became a potential labour force since the latter looked for ways and means to set them up in the vicinity of emerging coffee plantations, upon the instructions of their superiors. The Indian aut-

---

7. Ibid., folder No. 28590, Luis Martíinez to the Minister of the Interior, July 1, 1862.
8. Ibid.

horities of these small communities opposed the idea that some of their community members should move to other parts in search of land, because they were afraid of seeing their villages decimated and of being unable to confront future invasions by more powerful neighbours or by outsiders. The _Corregidores_ and their subordinates, however, were authorized to keep these authorities from forcing community members to return to their villages. In a Memorandum dated May 19, 1864, the _Fiscal Protector de Indios_ wrote that

> "speeches delivered by the priest of Tejutla and the Municipality of Tajumulco demonstrate that because of a lack of land to grow staples on, some Indians from these villages have had to go to the Southern Plain, (but) this departure is only seasonal".

For political and economic reasons, the _Fiscal_ suggested to the Minister of the Interior that he advise the _Corregidor_ of San Marcos to

> "see to it that the Municipalities in the villages of his District don't stop the Indian families from settling in those places they so desire and that they stop their being brutally removed from there by the Mayors. For it is said that this is what has been occurring. To subsist, these Indians seek out those very places where labour is scarce and fincas are being established. Furthermore, these spots are near the border and it is worth protecting their villages by granting them such freedom..."[9]

Forced recruitment of labour

By issuing edicts which provided the _finqueros_ with teams of labourers, the Conservative Government literally perpetuated the violence and different outrages unleashed against the peasantry. The _Corregidores_ themselves, most of whom were lan-

9. Ibid., folder No. 28597, From the _Fiscal Protector de Indios_ to the Minister of the Interior, May 19, 1864.

downers, knew how to take full advantage of the orders they received from the Central Power to benefit themselves as well as their friends and protégés. The realtive autonomy they enjoyed to take measures which they thought fitting for the development of coffee growing in their districts, permitted them to act as they pleased and according to their own interests. In 1864, the *Corregidor* of Suchitepéquez appointed a *"country judge"* in his district, who was specifically delegated the task of *"providing the* haciendas *with young and able men"* from the region, enlisting all the inhabitants of the *rancherias* dispersed in the mountains and *"seeing to it that all these men found work"*.[10] That same year, another *Corregidor* forceably recruited teams of peasants whom he sent to work on his own private plantation. This practice, colonial in origin, became even more prevalent when liberal *finqueros* ruled the country.

> *"As stipulated by the* Corregimiento *of Sacatepéquez, groups of twenty or more men from our village are taken periodically to work on the Southern Plain, a three day journey from Sumpango, on the plantation of the* Corregidor*"*, complained the community members of Sumpango to President Carrera on July 17, 1864, adding that *"the Secretary who calls himself Commander D. Carmen Pellecer is in charge of seeing that this is carried out, which always means violence and extreme harm for our village. Not only do they remove men from their homes without making exception for heads of family, but they transport them to infernal climates, escorted by troops and then whip them should they fail to follow orders. They are kept there until another group from the same village arrives and if one should manage to escape, he is treated as a criminal and incarcerated, following orders from the Secretary".*[11]

---

10. Ibid., folder No. 28595, Joaquín Faye to the Minister of the Interior, January 14, 1864.
11. Ibid., folder No. 28596, from the Municipality and Leaders of Sumpango, Sacatepéquez to the President of the Republic, July 17, 1864.

The peasants were well aware of the brutal treatment imposed upon them as well as the illegality of the demands exacted
by the authorities of Sacatepéquez. For that reason they requested that the Secretary of the _Corregimiento_ be dismissed and
the _Corregidor_ prohibited from issuing orders to send Indians
to work on the Plain.

> _"All this Sir", they wrote categorically to Carrera, "is
> contrary to the leyes de Indias..."_[11a]

In addition to the _Corregidores_, lesser authorities also managed to capitalize on the _mandamiento_ system, either by using
indigenous labour on their own _haciendas_ or by providing the
finqueros with workers, for a commission. All State authorities, steeped in Spanish racism, shared the belief that the lot of
the Indian peasants was to work for the sector of non-Indian landowners, whether the latter were white or of mixed blood. On
May 13, 1863, the Corregidor of Chamaltenango wrote:

> _"The Indian neighbours of the village of Tecpán
> Guatemala, in an effort to manage their own affairs by
> devoting themselves to their work and other necessary
> tasks, according to their own personal circumstances,
> lead an independent lifestyle. That is, they bother no
> one, nor do they contract debts or obligations of any
> kind, as they do in other villages. And while this
> lifestyle may be in keeping with human nature, it has
> nonetheless produced a terrible ill, because, as a result,
> the ladinos no longer have Indians to work on their
> farms. To deal with this labour shortage, these ladinos
> contrived a plan last year in which they asked the
> Governor for mandamientos of Indians to work in their
> cornfields and their wheatfields, justifying their request
> by invoking a law which they claim was passed by the
> Government in their favour. Under this assumption,
> Pablo Olea, as Official Receiver of the Municipality,
> asked the Governor for men to clear the cornfield on his_

11a. Ibid.

> *property, and what is worse, he dared to regulate their*
> *wages by paying two reales a bale, which can take a*
> *poor fellow close to a day, sometimes two, even three,*
> *depending on his age, his stamina and the quality of the*
> *soil. This is always unjust because they don't pay a fair*
> *wage as stipulated by law."[12]*

Not only did the peasants refuse to work for *ladino* landow-ners, but when this work had to be done far from their commu-nities, they were even more reluctant. The objection and resis-tence on the part of the Indians with regard to rendering personal services could be attributed to the fact that they did not want to abandon their own crops in order to care for those of strangers, particularly because, after years of exploitation, they knew that they would be abused and subjected to paltry wages from those who solicited their services. This attitude only served to reinforce the racist vision (emanating from the ruling class) of the Indian as lazy, naturally opposed to the idea of work and only capable of being incorporated into commercial agri-culture by means of forced labour. This prejudice which dates back to the period of Spanish colonial domination was used once more by the *finqueros* in order to control the labour force com-posed of community members, particularly after 1871, when the greater part of their land which was suited to coffee growing was wrested from them.

Sometimes the Indians, despite their unwillingness to work outside their communities, were obliged by circumstance to do so. In Alta Verapaz for example, the peasants found themselves forced to turn to work on the coffee plantations belonging to fore-igners after a bad storm had damaged their own corn harvest. The *Corregidor* of Verapaz could hardly contain himself when he passed on this information to the Minister of the Interior on May 31, 1862:

> *"In the villages of Alta Verapaz, where they produce*
> *basic grains in abundance", wrote the* Corregidor,
> *"excessive water from the past winter ruined the harvest*

---

12. Ibid., folder No. 28589, from the   Corregidor   of Chimaltenango to the Minister of the Interior, May 13, 1863.

_and while there was hope that the so-called summer
milpas would suffice to meet their needs, the total
shortage of water in the summer ruined them and
caused a frightening shortage, so much so that it has
been necessary to supply the lowlands with grain. This
has made corn scarce and dear. However, since Alta
Verapaz has never experienced any shortage, except
under extraordinary circumstances, the Indians are
forced to look for other things to plant such as tubers
like potato and others, rice, etc. Essentially, this shortage
has precipated a situation where the Indian has been
obliged to look for work to meet his basic needs.."[13]_

From 1860 to 1867 coffee exports in Guatemala underwent
a huge price rise. In 1860, the country exported 15,350 _pesos_
worth of coffee. Seven years later this sum reached 415,878 _pesos_
and kept increasing.[14] On the basis of this price increase, foreign and Guatemalan _finqueros_ were able to exert more pressure on Conservative authorities, especially where the procurement of labour for their plantations was concerned. On August
22, 1867, a group of _"coffee entrepreneurs"_ from Sololá informed
Conservative President, Vicente Cerna of the following:

_"We have encountered difficulties in getting the number
of people we require to do our work because this land is
very far removed from any populated area and to
maintain the large fincas which we are establishing
requires at least four hundred families. We have joined
forces for the purpose of building, in the midst of our
plantations, a village which is large enough to provide a
constant pool of labour. To achieve this goal which is so
very important to us, we have proposed that we share
the expenses of providing such a village not only with
land to cultivate but also with a church and a school to
educate its people morally and intellectually, and a_

13. Abid., folder No. 28588, Juan E. Valdéz to the Minister of the Interior, May
31, 1862.
14. Ignacio Solís, op. cit., vol. III B, pg. 911.

107

*hospital to meet their medical needs. Believing our plan
to be not only in our own interest but in those of the
Indians themselves who are not always so fortunate as
to have the luxury of steady and fairly remunerated
employment throughout the year, we ask Your Excellency
to be so kind as to provide us with the means required
to carry out such a project, by ordering local authorities
to furnish us with the assistance we require to resettle
some small population which lives under the most
precarious conditions without land to plant their own
crops. We also request that the Government, once this
village is established, be so kind as to excuse these
people not only from their military but also municipal
commitments as well, since we have no other people to
do all the work which is constantly required on this type
of* finca. *Our efforts to create such a village would be
futile if we could not always count on the services of
such people which are absolutely indispensable. Lastly,
we ask the Supreme Government to please be so good as
to appoint one of the residents of this* finca
commissioner of the Corregidor *of the Department, to
keep the peace in this village."*[15]

If we take a close look at this petition, it is easy to detect certain characteristics which typified the Guatemalan agrarian bourgeoisie from the beginning. The *finqueros* of the last century, like those of the present day, saw themselves as the privileged members of Guatemalan society. Their class consciousness surfaces in the first paragraph. When they speak of the difficulties encountered in finding the manpower they required to farm land confiscated from the peasants, they emphasize that *"people"* are required *"to do our work"* and to *"maintain the large fincas which we are establishing".* Semantic distortion and manipulation have always been the finquero's forte. In effect,

15. A.G.C.A., B1, M.G.J., folder No. 28612, from the "coffee entrepreneurs" to the President of the Republic, August 22, 1867.

their honourable intentions produced a semi-slavelike population whom they promised to provide with land so that they would
not die of hunger with the wretched wages they were prepared
to pay. The Church they had promised to build was meant to
teach them to be submissive and respect the powerful, or in the
words of the _finqueros_, "to sustain their sense of morality". Talk
of a hospital and a school was nothing more than an empty pro-
mise. Even today, it is rare to find Guatemalan _fincas_ where peasant families are given medical attention or primary education for their children. According to the _finqueros_, it was not the
peasants who were doing them a service by farming their plantations, but the _finqueros_ who were rendering them a service
by giving them land. Finally, dissatisfied with their unsuccess-
ful attempts to dispose of the Indian authorities, the _finqueros_
asked for authorization from the Conservative State to actas
constables and bailiffs. The _finqueros_ denied the peasants the
right to refuse work in a foreign environment, which was con-
sistently inhospitable. It is interesting to observe that as early
as 1867, when the _finqueros_ had still not wrested political power,
their growing enrichment caused them to view the State and
the President of the Republic as simple tools to satisfy their
needs and safeguard their interests.

The pro-development sector of the ruling class believed that
the stability and success of the plantation economy in the country depended on the degree of support given to foreign coffee growers and _finqueros_. Under these circumstances, it is not surprising that it pressured Conservative authorities into viewing the
proposal of the agricultural entrepreneurs as a _"useful project
for the progress of agriculture"_, and instructed the _Corregidores_
of the western departments to ensure that the Indian authorities of the communities _"did not do anything to impede the transfer of indigenous families"_.[16]

Because of the concessions granted to agricultural entrepreneurs, the communities were forced to give up a fair share of
their land which was suitable for coffee growing, for them to
enjoy as life tenants, and accept the move of many community
members to developing plantation regions. This accounted for

16. Ibid., Circular from the Minister to the _Corregidores_, Sept. 17, 1867.

109

the increased population of tenant farmers on *fincas* in Sololá, Quetzaltenango (Costa Cuca), San Marcos, Suchitepéquez, Escuintla and Chimaltenango. During the Spanish colonial period, as we've already seen, *hacendados* sought to tie a sector of the peasant population to their land, particularly *mestizos* without land to farm, giving them plots of land in exchange for their services. This practice gave rise to the *latifundia-minifundia* system in Guatemala which resembled colonial feudal domination. Three hundred years later history would repeat itself, except this time with the *finqueros* on top and within the framework of a plantation economy.

By the end of the 1860's, coffee growing, and consequently the coffee producer, were well established in Guatemala. Despite the concessions which the Conservative dictatorship found itself obliged to make for the growers, the latter were not particularly amenable. In 1868, for example, the *Corregidor* of Sololá told the Minister of the Interior that

> *"there have been several complaints made by landowners of coffee plantations and* fincas, *concerning fraud and breach of contract by the labourers who commit themselves to more than one employer at a time and receive advances from them, without having any intention whatsoever of performing the required work, because most of the time they are either drunk or truant".*[17]

The need for labour legislation

The need for regulating labour relations which favoured the agricultural entrepreneurs, and more specifically, institutionalizing forced labour, was placed high on the agenda of the *finqueros* and later became the gravest problem confronting the Conservatives in their rapport with the coffee growers at the end of their rule. In response to this situation, a *Corregidor* suggested that the Central Government, invoking the law of October 2, 1839, as its basis, order all the municipalities to keep a

---

17. Ibid., folder No. 28621, from the *Corregidor* of Sololá to the Minister of the Interior, November 16, 1868.

record of all the names of all the peasants under their jurisdiction, capable of working on the _fincas_, so as to be able to meet demands made by the entrepreneurs both quickly and in an orderly fashion. The _Corregidores_ suggested that each worker have a page reserved for his name and the _"length of his engagement"._ At the same time, the municipalities were also to send the _Corregidor_ a list of those persons whose names figured in the records _"so that the Corregimiento could issue orders to accommodate the entrepreneurs and avoid confusion"._ The _finqueros_ had to pay one _real_ to the community fund for every man they received; and the community, in turn, had to give the municipal secretary one fourth of what was collected _"as compensation for the additional paper work"._ Obviously, this was an easy way of luring a second rank authority, through bribery, to keep an eye on the delivery of community members. The _Corregidor_ suggested to the Indian Mayors that they undertake, in conformity with the circular issued by the Supreme Government on August 13, 1847 and the edicts issued thereafter, to persecute any person who tried to evade honourable work, and capture and turn in those individuals caught fleeing the _haciendas_ with pay in hand, for the fraud committed. In this case the fugitive was obliged to pay the costs incurred from his arrest.

If the Mayor failed to carry out these orders, both he and the fugitive were subject to physical punishment and imprisonment. On the _fincas_, the entrepreneurs were expected to treat the workers _"with utmost respect and pay them their wages on time, without forcing them to stay or dismissing them"._ The Government was to fine those _finqueros_ who did not abide by these rules. To avoid deception, the latter were not supposed to accept workers

> _"without demanding beforehand that they settle all their debts with their former employers and that they furnish proof thereof to the respective Mayor"._[18]

Actually, this was simply an attempt to legitimize the outrages committed by the landowners against the rural workers,

18. Ibid., folder No. 28622, _Corregidor_ of Amatitlán to the Minister of the Interior, April 7, 1870; folder No. 28623, Miguel Zelaya to the Minister, December 12, 1870.

111

which by 1870 were occurring throughout the Republic. This is evidenced by a complaint filed before the Court of First Instance in Izabal by some workers from a coffee and sugar plantation belonging to a foreigner in the jurisdiction of Santo Tomás. In a formal document drawn up by the Court in October of 1870, it stated that the workers had complained that on the plantation, in addition to the maltreatment they received, the finquero would often fine them for those days they did not work and force them to work on holidays. The work day lasted until 8:00 p.m. On the *finca* there was a store and when a worker purchased an item, the price of the article was entered in an account book which also included the names of all the workers. The owner of the plantation made use of any and every opportunity to juggle with the figures recorded. The fines imposed on the workers by the *finquero,* together with the fraud which went on in the store, meant that the workers were permanently indebted to the landowner. The men who appeared before the Judge stated that they were prepared to pay their debts but that the *finquero* had refused their offers, labelling them as *"fugitives"*. Before passing sentence the Judge wanted to know if the men who had registered the complaint had, at the time they were hired by the *finquero,*

> *"entered into some sort of contract whereby they had promised to pay, with work, the sums they owed, or had promised to work for a specified period of time, being prohibited however to default on these commitments. They answered unanimously that there had been no such arrangement and that they were led to believe that they could leave the job when they so desired by paying their debts with cash."[19]*

Even though the charges against the *finquero* warranted an investigation which would have brought about the acceptance of the workers demands, the Judge, perhaps due to pressure from the *landowners,* ordered that they return to the *finca.* The grounds on which the Judge based his decision included the fact

---

19. Ibid., folder No. 28626, Petition filed by the workers against Mr. Camilo Esmenjeaud, October 10, 1870. Drawn up by the Judge of the Court of First Instance.

that a) the season was particularly dry when the incident occurred and the sugar cane had still not reached full growth _"which is when it yields the most"_; b) the landowner lost ripe coffee for lack of manpower and because of the difficulty he encountered trying to find workers; c) in general, work on the _finca_ was behind schedule, particularly the planting and clearing of sugar cane, and _"it was impossible to make good use of the upper part of the sugar cane because it had flowered and no longer served for planting, and the land had already been tilled and was overgrown once more;_ d) _"sugar was scarce throughout the Department at the time"_, and e) when the workers who came before the Judge abandoned the _finca_, the others left behind _"were unsure whether they would stay or leave, wanting to see what became of their co-workers, thus many days were lost and they didn't fell much like working"_.[20]

Conservative legislation recognized the peasants as free citizens with the right to accept or reject work on the _fincas_, as the _Fiscal Protector de Indios_ had reminded the Minister of the Interior on February 24, 1869. He considered that the _Corregidores_ were not _"authorized to force the workers to perform wage labour"_. However, at the same time, the _Fiscal_ recognized how convenient it was to provide the _finqueros_ with the men they required for work on the coffee plantations, and to keep a close watch over the number of inhabitants in the country, particulary the community members.[21] This ambiguous attitude made it possible for innumerable outrages to be committed against the peasantry, and supported the continuation of the _finquero's_ violent activities in the countryside, namely the invasion of communal property and the forced conscription of Indian labour. In 1869, a German diplomat wrote that _"by this time, discontent prevailed throughout the country"_.[22]

Obstacles in the development of agrarian capitalism

According to Franz Sarg, one of the first Germans to arrive

20. Ibid.
21. Ibid., folder No. 28621, from the _Fiscal Protector de Indios_ to the Minister of the Interior, February 24, 1869.
22. DZA Potsdam, A.A., No. 52610, from F. Augener to the A.A., January 1, 1869.

in Alta Verapaz during the latter half of the nineteenth century and precursor of coffee growing in this region, in 1868,

> *"continual and growing demands made on the Indian
> population by agriculture (should read by the* finqueros*),
> to work on the* Fincas; *by the exporters to transport
> coffee; by the Government to construct roads, created a
> situation where, in time, the people no longer had any
> desire to work. This manifested itself in the continual
> problems facing the (agrarian) enterprises".*[23]

The re-election of Vicente Cerna as President of Guatemala in
1869 magnified the political, economic and social problems in
the country. By 1867, the armed struggle against the Conservative Government had already broken out and turned into a
guerilla war, with Occidente and Noroccidente, the very region
where coffee growing was developing at a healthy pace, as its
battleground. This was no coincidence. The most important guerilla leader, Serapio Cruz, had the support of the pro-
development sector of the ruling class which was interested, above all, in elminating all the pitfalls which hampered the complete development of a plantation economy. Medium-scale coffee
growers from San Marcos and Quezaltenango, such as J. Rufino Barrios, closed ranks around Cruz's movement, conscious of
the existing limitations in the Conservative power structure and
the obstacle which this dictatorship represented for the development of their interests. The columns of Serapio Cruz were
composed of hundreds of poor peasants who hoped to gain access
to the land owned by the Church and by other large-scale landowners of colonial descent, especially from Oriente. The peasants felt extreme sympathy for Cruz's movement and both protected it and identified with it. Sarg explained that the Indians
were *"very uneasy and exasperated"* by the Conservative regime's unpopular policy.[24] However, to a large extent, Cruz's
demagoguery confused the peasantry. On one occasion, for

---

23. Franz Sarg, op. cit., pg. 21.
24. Ibid., pg. 22.

example, while asking the peasants to join the guerilla movement "en masse" against the Conservative dictatorship, Cruz told the tenant farmers on a coffee plantation in Verapaz that their struggle was for the entrepreneurs who needed more land and more men to work it.[25]

The theocratic State, controlled by the Conservatives and used by them as an instrument of power and domination for more than thirty years, became an ineffective and obsolete tool for the _"progressive"_ sector of the ruling class, given its colonial and feudal origins. The interests of this sector called for the monopolization of the country's principal means of production: the land and the men; the hegemony of political decision-making; the hierarchical reorganization of society, based on an economic and political liberalism capable of promoting and advancing reforms in the cultural and ideological superstructure; and the permanent establishment of a State and institutions where the government bureaucracy and the elite responsible for repression against the people shared the same interests as the sector composed of _finqueros_ and commercial and agricultural entrepreneurs, which considered itself the trailblazer of progress in Guatemala. By 1871, the _finqueros_ had already gained sufficient economic power to venture to contend for the political supremacy of the discredited Conservative clique, which had ruled since 1839. The emerging bourgeois sector of the ruling class in Guatemala, not unlike others in Latin America during the latter half of the nineteenth century, was very keen on extirpating the power of the Catholic Church, which was held to be the bastion of feudalism in the country. They also wanted to do away with a series of State taxes and monopolies detrimental to its interests. But, above all, the growing agrarian bourgeoisie believed it was necessary to establish new judicial, political and economic institutions which truly responded to societal changes. This would occur after appropriating communal property through legal means, subjecting the Indian peasantry, fraudulent labourers and fugitives to permanent exploitation, and by controlling all capital.

---

25. Ibid.

CHAPTER VII

THE LANDLORDS IN POWER

A number of historians have considered the coming to power of the Liberals on June 30, 1871, as a direct result of the alliance between the merchants of the Capital city and the coffee growers of Los Altos of Guatemala, who had been led respectively by the old native demagogue Miguel García Granados[1] and the military adventurer J. Rufino Barrios.

However, in light of new documentation, we have realized that this interpretation needs to be thoroughly reviewed, in order to fully understand the role played by commercial capital in Guatemala's economy and politics during the second half of the nineteenth century, as well as the intimate relation which existed between commercial and agricultural capital. Only a more profound interpretation makes it possible to understand the fact that the most important financiers of the armed forces which removed the conservative dictatorship, were prominent politicians and merchants, and — at the same time — the country's biggest coffee growers and exporters.[2] Commercial capital nee-

1. His real name was Miguel García Zavala, born in Spain. The García family to whom this historic personage belonged, exists to this day, having changed the name to "García-Granados" in order to appear aristocratic. Taking into consideration that Miguel Garcia Z. is better known as M. García Granados, we shall use this name from now on.
2. DZA Potsdam, A.A., No. 52610, Augener to Bismarck, February 3, 1870 and June 9, 1871.

ded the development of agricultural capital in order to achieve its full expansion, and this was not possible without the control of the political power which permitted the liberal bourgeoisie to eliminate all the obstacles in the way of commercial coffee cultivation, and the consolidation of their class domination.

During the period of Spanish domination of our country, the richest merchants who had settled in Santiago de Guatemala, devoted themselves to large-scale cultivation of the indigo plant which since 1580 had been the country's principal export.[3] The colonial merchant-landlord is not, however, to be seen as a modern type of trader-farmer who has been transformed into a capitalist entrepreneur, but rather as a wealthy man trying to take over the means of production, quickening the slow conversion process of a fundamentally rural economy to a market economy.[4] Towards the end of the eighteenth century, the principal indigo exporters of Guatemala were also big farm-owners who produced the dye. But in the general context of indigo producers, they were but very few. The majority of the producers were reapers, who were dependent on the Capital's merchants who used to give out licences, and supplied them with money and goods in order to "acquire, maintain and exploit the workers", who were being employed in agricultural production.

> *"Briefly", affirms a researcher of business capital activity in the Kingdom of Guatemala, "during the eighteenth century in Central America, the agricultural, sheep-breeding, mineral production, etc., was dominated by the business capital: wealth belongs to those who can make the extra product circulate, and not to those who extract it".[5]*

Independence opened the doors to foreign colonization and capital allowing English, German and other entrepreneurs —

3. Murdo J. MacLeod *"Spanish Central America. A Socioeconomic History, 1520-1720"*, (University of California Press, Berkeley-Los Angeles-London, 1973.), p. 220.
4. See what Jacques Le Goff says regarding the medieval merchant: *"Mercaderes y Banqueros de la Edad Media"*. Editorial Universitaria de Buenos Aires, 5a. Edición, 1970, pp. 44-46.
5. Víctor Hugo Acuña Ortega: *"Capital Comercial y comercio exterior en América Central durante el siglo XVIII. Una contribución."* In: *"Estudios Sociales Centroamericanos"*, (San José de Costa Rica, May-August/1980, Year IX. nr. 26), p. 87.

who had gradually succeeded in controlling and dominating import-export commerce — to come to the country. This new group of tradesmen differed from the penny pinching merchants of the colonial period, and were reknown for their industrious and diligent spirit, showing interest in agricultural production for export. They took the country out of its economic stagnation and isolation, caused by the lack of communication with the world, and made improvements and capital investments in agriculture. Important cochineal growers and later, coffee and sugar growers too, and great monopolists of commercial agricultural products for export, came out of the ranks of this new group of tradesmen once they got land and men to work it. One of them in particular, Carl Friedrich Rudolf Klee, the greatest grower and exporter of cochineal in the middle of the nineteenth century, can be considered as the father of Guatemala's present day agricultural-exporting bourgeoisie.

Before 1871, a strong contradiction arose between the Guatemalan merchants of colonial origin, who tried to preserve their commercial supremacy from the foreign trader's energetic and dynamic force, and this new element in the economic scenario, which was constantly being strengthened by new waves of representatives of foreign capital, who were willing to invest in agriculture and then export most of their profits to their homelands. In turn, these profits would be invested in the development of commerce and industry.

However, the major contradiction existing inside the ruling class was that its conservative sector was interested in maintaining the colonial power structure. This assured them a parasitic life as landlords, usurers and bureaucrats, enjoying permanent incomes from the exploitation of rural workers, from financial and mercantile speculation, from the "alcabalas" (a sort of tax), and from the State monopolies. Meanwhile a "progressive" sector of the bourgeois liberals — spearheaded by foreigners — wanted to change Guatemala into one great plantation, widening capitalist coffee cultivation, as a means of obtaining greater profits. Many men who occupied important positions during the liberal dictatorship were, by 1870, already distinguished coffee growers, anxious to gain direct power as rulers of the country and to destroy the political and economic

119

foundation of the Church which was the principal ideologic bastion of the traditional conservative oligarchy.

The needs of the landlords

In order to assure the absolute domination of the landlords in the country and eliminate all obstacles that prevented free development of commercial coffee cultivation, Miguel García Granados, who a few weeks earlier had appointed himself as the liberal government's provisional President, asked the plantation owners to express *"their most urgent needs, and the way in which they could be satisfied," in writing.*[6]

What the plantation economy undoubtedly needed most of all was to eliminate the traditional economic foundation of the Guatemalan peasantry — communal ownership of the land and communal work — and incorporate it "en-masse" into forced labour on the coffee and sugar cane farms and thus into a market economy. During the second half of the nineteenth century cultivation featured the production of fruits meant almost exclusively for the world market, and efficient economic measures, a rational organization and modern technology were applied. Its activity was based on the employment of a numerous non-skilled and semi-skilled working force, badly remunerated, exploited as much as possible, but who were capable of producing great profits for their owners. It is a well known fact that the exploitation of rural workers has been the basis of wealth for the Guatemalan rural bourgeoisie as well as for the thousands of foreigners who have plundered our country. The activity of these agrarian entrepreneurs was concentrated initially in those places which had favourable conditions for the development of large-scale coffee cultivation. When there were no rural workers to be found in those areas, thousands of native peasants were moved there as *"cuadrilleros"* (working-teams). Once these peasants had been expropriated and pulled away from their land, they were given the heavy task of removing forests, building the

---

6. A.G.C.A., M.G.J., folder nr. 28629, dossier nr. 23, Gustav Bernouilli and other landlords of Suchitepéquez to the departmental Political Chief, August 16, 1871.

infrastructure for coffee production and carrying out its cultivation. However, in order to attain this, it was necessary to annul the conservative laws concerning agriculture and to reorganize the country's economic and political systems. Thus responding to the request which was made by García Granados, the landlords enumerated what they considered as mistakes and ambiguities of the old conservative government in relation to the encouragement of Guatemala's agricultural development, and gave priority to the problems the liberal bourgeoisie's government would have to solve in order to definitely establish and consolidate the landlords' power:

a) The institutionalization of the forced labour and the _"peonaje"_ system.

b) the definitive expropriation of communal land and encouragement of the bourgeois ownership of the land.

c) the annulment of the taxes existing in Guatemala from the period of Spanish domination, particularly the tithe, and

d) the implementation of an infrastructure more suitable to the needs of the development of a modern plantation system.

> _"We consider that what is most urgently needed" —_
> _wrote the farmer Gustav Bernouilli to the Political Chief_
> _of Suchitepéquez on August 22, 1871, referring to the_
> _plantation owners' supposed needs — "is a strict and_
> _definite agreement on the system of day-labourers or_
> _rural-workers. Such a contract should clearly and_
> _explicitly define the relationship to be established_
> _between those who provide and pay for work and those_
> _who do it, and should at the same time decide the_
> _punishments which transgressors ought to receive._
> _In a country whose future lies only in agriculture, these_
> _measures have the most important consequences; one of_
> _the reasons for the dissatisfaction with the last_
> _government was the fact that it did not take into_
> _consideration the repeated claims of the growers', who_
> _already were desperate about the losses in their work_
> _caused by the fact that they did not get any support from_
> _the authorities. We will begin — even if it is not really_
> _necessary — by describing the past and present State of_

affairs in this Department. A landlord — no matter how many men he needs for his work — can not get them if he does not give them a 'habilitación' (a certain amount of money in advance), which varies regularly between ten and fifty pesos. Once this money is spent — on paying back a former master or on other debts, or in buying clothes or liquor — the day-labourer begins work.

But one can be sure that he will never be able to pay his debts, because as soon as he only has a little left, he asks for more, something that the master can not refuse if he wants to keep the day-labourer. It is easy to understand that these 'habilitaciones' *represent lifeless capital of considerable value, which amounts to several thousand pesos on the big farms. But even this loss of interests can be supported, if one had at least the guarantee of not losing the very capital. We are not talking about a worker's death, in which case the master obviously loses the money he has payed in advance, but of the impunity enjoyed by those day-labourers who are fugitives or by those who unfairly ask advances to different masters. There have been attempts to avoid some of these difficulties by using statements of account, but this solution is completely insufficient, because there are thousands of ways getting around them, above all due to the fact that there has never been a punishment against transgressors. This is the case with the idle and drunk worker; it is true that the latter is obliged to pay a fine of 1 or 2 pesos, but who really pays it, if not the master? The situation is so critical that — in order to get a certain number of workers — a landlord is obliged to give* 'habilitación' *to almost twice as many workers than he needs. The greater part of the exposed matter is valid not only for the day-labourers who work in the fields but also for the other classes of servants, workers, domestic servants, craftsmen; and the fact is that this system is as ruinous for one side's pocket as for the other's morality. Without any doubt the* _simplest remedy, for all these troubles, would be the abolition of these 'habilitaciones', but nothing is gained by demanding things which are impossible to achieve or to carry out, at least for the time being. After some generations, our successors, may be willing to do that, when the working-class develops a different attitude toward work, when they no longer vegetate in a State of brutalization so unavoidable, when they have other ambitions besides that of getting drunk. In a country, where the facility of surviving is as big as on these coasts it will take a very long time to perform the afore mentioned change, through education and adequate rules. There are well-known examples, where many landlords have tried to put a stop to the custom of giving 'habilitaciones', in paying a higher daily wage in compensation, but the experiments have been in vain, because they have been compelled to go back to the old system for lack of day-labourers. Those who know the character of these workers will not be astonished that this happens._

We are not thinking, therefore, of putting a stop to the custom of giving 'habilitaciones', but we would like guarantees to be given to the masters, and punishments for the day-labourers who deserve them. For this purpose, it will primary be necessary to find a way to control the people, in order to know the provenance and the place of origin. Consequently we will suggest the basis of a regulation that we think will fulfill the more legitimate and urgent needs, and that, at the same time, presents very little difficulty in the execution.

We will give orders to all masters in each Municipality who will, on a fixed date, then present to us a list of all their subordinates: day-labourers, servants, artsans, workers; together with an indication of their native village and an observation if they have the 'habilitación' or if they work voluntarily. The land-owners will have to enclose a complete list of the workers who live on their *land. With the help of these documents, the municipal authorities will be able to draw up a register of all the citizens, and each of them will receive a note-book with his name, his provenance, and a note indicating if he owes something to the master or not. This note-book will serve as a passport for it's bearer, and without presenting it, it will not be possible for a citizen to move freely. Nevertheless, if this were to happen, both the master and the day-labourer would be punished severely, the former fined, the latter with public work. No subordinate, whatever qualification he might have, will be able to leave his master without the consent of the latter, if he has received the 'habilitación', even if he returns the amount due, because the money has been given an account of the work and not as a loan; nevertheless, inspections will be done in case of maltreatment or other legal and well justified complaints against the master.*

The day-labourer who owes something to his master and does not work during the week-days, will be punished with public work, unless he is ill, or has got permission, explicitly given by his master. The same thing will happen to those who are found drunk. These punishments will be unchangeable, and the judges will have to notify them in the day-labourer's note-book, as well as the other punishments that could be imposed for other transgressions. Lastly, it is understood that any falsification in the above mentioned note-books will be treated very severely. We will add that the same regulation is recomended for the sort of women who seek work either as servants, or in the fields, etc. In what has been said, we think we have put forward the basis for an efficient and simple arrangement of easy execution. With it — at least — the day-labourers will be prevented from using a great part of their tricks to cheat their masters, for instance, asking for 'habilitación' to different ones, running away from a farm where they owe money in order to work on another one, or using many different names in different places. Nevertheless, the best laws will not have a good effect, if they are not executed accurately, and — therefore — we count, in the first place, on firm support from the authorities, and severity in punishing the offenders, a requisite we have been claiming in the past in vain. It will be recommended to the municipalities — principally to the native ones — a strict observance of the orders, and the obligation of consigning, without subterfuges, the individuals of their respective jurisdictions, when they are claimed by their masters. As for the rest, we will leave at the Supreme Government's disposal the extension of a regulation such as this one, whose Foundations we have just pointed out. It will determine the kind of individuals who will be included in the regulation and the parts of the Republic in which it will be in force. As far as we are concerned, the greater the extention of the regulation, the better it will be, and by becoming a general one, it will serve not only for the purposes which interests us here, but also will be useful from other points of view, such as, in helping the judges in many cases to identify persons, to know their past, etc., etc. We are not forgetting that to carry out our project requires time and work, as for every new thing, but with help from the authorities, this will not be so important. As to the large towns, an accountant will be needed to write out the necessary registers and file the note-books. By setting a higher price for the note-books, whose real value is insignificant, or by requiring from the masters a minimum tax for each servant, the salary for the accountant would be collected without any expenses on the part of the Supreme Government or the Municipalities. We believe that the masters willingly will give a little contribution in order to avoid the losses which are more considerable than those which hitherto have been exposed. We believe, moreover, that it will not be difficult to find in each department one or more

125

*persons who, if necessary, will render their voluntary
services for the execution of a work so important for the
public benefit.*

*Some measures indispensable for the transition from
one system to another are still to be proposed. Inevitably,
many individuals who have two or more masters will
turn out, since they have demanded and received
'habilitación' from many parts. In order to simplify the
investigation of these cases, many copies of the register
will be made, in order to send them to the neighbouring
populations, where they can then be compared. The
landlords will have the right to ask, by means of their
respective municipalities, for the registers of the villages
from where they chiefly recruit their day-labourers.
As far as the servants who owe some money to many
masters are concerned, a rule will be brought in, that
the actual master will pay the debt of the others, if there
is no other private agreement between the different
masters. It is understood that in different parts of the
Republic, different customs as regards the day-labourers
of the fields are in force. In this way, for example in the
Verapaz, the greatest number of landlords work with
teams of natives who are appointed by the authorities
and relieved every fifteen days. This custom can not be
convenient except in a country where there is an
excessive number of workers and little work.
Nevertheless, we would like to recall that the same
decrees regarding the teams of native day-labourers exist
for the rest of the Republic as well, but that under the
past administration, the mayors (at least that of
Suchitepéquez) have got strict orders of not granting
them, a State of affairs which must be admired, in that
a Government lays down laws and then forbids their
execution. We would like the afore mentioned decrees to
stay in force and be effective for the whole country,
because these are the circumstances under which a
landlord is obliged to suddenly employ, and for a short
number of days of weeks, more day-labourers than he*

can give 'habilitación' to. The abuses that could occur regarding this matter, would be easily avoided, by leaving the concession in the hands of the political chiefs, who would not grant it if they do not consider it urgent. Concluding with this subject we could proceed with another which is equally serious for the development of the country and particularly for this Coast: we could discuss land distribution, a delicate and important matter, whose solution is dependent upon urgently needed, prudent and sweeping legislation. We could complain about the unfair and hateful tithe tax, but we know how other more skilled pens treat the mentioned subjects. The only point which we cannot leave unmentioned is the disastrous State of the communication system in this Department. This is a question of life or death for agriculture, but we do not want to dwell on this point, because we cannot say anything that the authorities do not already know as well as we do. We confine ourselves only to ascertain the ruinous State in which the past administration had left this Department, one of the most productive of the Republic, such a complete ruinous State that not even the taxes which had been collected here, had been invested in the roads of the Department.

With the opening of the port of Champerico, the actual Government has proved that it is not thinking of limiting care to the Capital and its inmediate interests, but also of taking care of the remote districts as well; therefore we have alluring hopes of seeing improvements and progress in reality, and not only in the columns of the Official Gazette."[7]

---

7. Ibid., Gustav Bernouilli to the Political Chief of Suchitepéquez, on August 22, 1871. The Political Chief replaced the *corregidores* of the Conservative period

The militarization of the workers

The measures which were adopted by the liberal authorities to resolve the agricultural problem responded not only to the economical interests of the landlords, but also served the purpose of preserving social peace, and the extension of the liberal State's political power. This was noticed particularly in the subordination of all the rural population scattered in distant regions from the Capital, to a central Authority. As we have previously said, many hid in the mountains, and in communities that were cut off from the rest of the country, avoided all social and economical contacts, often even with their neighbouring communities and populations. The librals did not look favourably upon this rural mass which, as a matter of fact, refused to accept their authority. Under these circumstances, since their coming to power, they undertook to submit the peasantry to the yoke of the agricultural entrepreneurs, by means of mechanisms which allowed the close mutual collaboration between the State which was based on the coffee-cultivation and the landlords. To function as the political authority of the Central Government was one of the principal tasks which was committed to the landlords' charge. They were invested not only with civil and political authority, but also with military authority. The result of this was a great similarity between the systems of forced work and political control which hade been adopted by the landlords led by J. Rufino Barrios, and those in force in the Kingdom of Guatemala during the second half of the eighteenth century.

In this way, for example, during the period of Spanish domination many of the rural workers were obligated to take part in so called *"militias"* of the colonialists. In 1784, in the *"Regulation for the Distribution of Workers to the Indigo-plant growers"* it was stipulated that

---

as representatives for the central Power in the inland Departments. Their authority and administrative functions are similar to those of the ancient *corregidores*. They were appointed directly by the Chief of State, before whom they were responsible. Actually, they came to be miserable dictators of the district, many times not less cruel and rapacious than the Governor occasionally in charge.

> _"as to the punishment of the militiamen in cases they
> occur, the Judge and Deputies are to inform the colonel,
> if he is in town, and if not, the captain or highest
> ranking officer, who will then sentence and punish
> accordingly with jail, the whip or whatever they
> consider suitable and which is not improper for the
> category of these militiamen, being cautious that there is
> not to be any indulgence as to this point. The military
> judges will not allow any complaints or let the
> militiamen become idle and miss work due to lack of
> punishment, because this can not serve as an excuse for
> vice and laziness to which this people are so inclined,
> not even its institution will dispense them from being
> compelled to earn their living by honest means, usefully
> taking upon themselves the task which belong to their
> class. If someone or some of them in order to avoid
> working were to escape or move from one group to
> another, as easily happens because many of them are
> lazy and without roots, the landlords will ask the Judge
> and Deputy of their territory their capture and return
> them to the area where they are registered. And the
> landlords of the places where the militiamen have been
> found, will sentence them and return them to the
> villages, proceeding all of them at this point with the
> necessary caution in order to avoid the countless crimes
> and disorders that are caused every day by this criminal
> freedom. This will take place without a competent
> jurisdiction but by means of a mutual agreement
> regarding the capture, extermination and punishment of
> these wanderers..."[8]_

The greatest part of the peasant population was concentrated in the western part of Guatemala, where J. Rufino Barrios

8. Regulation on the Distribution of Workers to Indigo-plant Growers, 1784,
A.G.C.A., A1.53(3), folder Nr. 623, dossier Nr. 5771. Cited by Manuel Rubio Sán-
chez in his work _"Historia del Añil o Xiquilite en Centro América"._ (2 volumes,
San Salvador: 1976, vol. II, Appendix 4), pp. 365-373.

made his headquarters. This group had shown a strong tendency towards self-imposed isolation and mutiny during the period of Spanish domination, because it was here that the forced work systems introduced by the Spaniards had become most deeply rooted. In the second half of the nineteenth century the owners of the region — many being *"mestizos"*, descendants of the first iberian colonizer — decided, with Barrios' support, to militarize the workers, in the same way as their ancestors had done. This measure, which was made official by the Liberals, allowed a sector of Conservatives who had been displaced from Power to approach the Government thereby widening the political base for the new regime.

"Urban militias" were created from amongst the most important farmers, doctors, lawyers, *"and those who were leading members of trade enterprises"*, all of them were appointed as *"troop captains"* of the *"Civil Guard."* The active militia were made up of the city's and the country's poor people, who weren't *"tenant farmers or temporary workers"* in the plantations. The so called *"reserve militia"* were organized *"by servants and tenant farmers from plantations, sugar factories and other agricultural enterprises"* and with workers from the *"salt mines and the fishing industry"*, *"and with those who work regularly and receive a monthly wage, in whatever useful occupation"*.

The old landlords, as we have already seen, had the custom of physically punishing their workers, placing them in the yoke and in prison when they were reluctant to work, escaped from the farms or committed acts of insubordination. According to the proclamation issued by J. Rufino Barrios as *"General Comander of Occidente"* on August 9, 1871, the reserve militia was to be formed by recruits aged between fifteen and fifty years. On the farms, the owners or their representatives had to *"read through the list"* every Sunday, they had to *"inform the Headquarter of their jurisdiction of the state of the militia under their command, in which they exposed the increases and decreases which had occurred during the week."* The workers would form peasant teams, as there had to be on each farm a *"team under the authority and the command of the master, to whom the enlisted men would bestow all respect and consideration as a Chief"*. *"All lack*

130

of subordination would be severely punished, in the same way in which misbehavior towards superiors is corrected in the active militia". "The lack of subordination" would be judged militarily, thus were all the landlords of the country informed. The Political Chief of Suchitepéquez indicated that the landlords _"have understood the good that is done to them and approved the measures as suitable to the circumstances", as "agriculture was given an effective means to avoid insolence and fraud on the part of the farm workers."_ It has been called the 'reserve corps' because it will be able to serve militarily when really necessary.

Without any doubt, what was most satisfactory for landlords like Gustav Bernouilli, was the new article of the previously mentioned proclamation:

> _"Decreases in the teams will only take place in the case of a soldier's death, retirement granted by the master, or escape. In this last case, the fugitive will be considered a deserter and be officially persecuted inside and outside the Department. Therefore, the masters, according to the punishment which is convenient, will not omit any increase or decrease in their weekly report, and will not grant any retirement without the solicitor producing the previous permit of his chiefs."_[9]

Actually, unofficially, the peasantry and all the farm workers were subjected to these regulations until 1944, that is to say, a period of 73 years during which the first dictatorship of the landlords came to power. An attempt to solve the problem regarding the lack of institutional regulation of the forced labour system on the farms in 1877, when the so called _"Regulations of day-labourers"_ were decreed; nevertheless by the end of the century, the liberal State was still obligated, apparently without great success, to appeal to civil-military taxes, in order to compel the rural independent population to work in the farms. This appears in a confidential report which was sent by the German

---

9. A.G.C.A., B1, M.G.J., folder Nr. 28629, dossier Nr. 31, from the Political Chief of Suchitepéquez to the M.G., September 1, 1871.

Consul, as well as wealthy landowner Richard Sapper, to the German Chancellery, in July 1899:

> *"The new military law, which has recently been decreed, seems to be done in order to favour agriculture and the establishment of plantations, because it states that while each indian (in Alta Verapaz 95 % of the population) has to pay $ 10.00 every year to be released from active military service. The native workers who live and work in the plantations are free from paying this tax, on the condition that they could prove, with a certificate issued by the owner, that they are working regularly. The owners only have to pay an annual sum of $ 1.00 on the workers charge, in order to pay the stamp duties. We hoped then that the indians who did not carry on any work relationship with any plantation near their residence, would endeavour to establish this relationship, thereby saving the annual $ 10.00 destined to the Army. But this beautiful law, as many others, has remained until the present as written word. Instead of being useful for the landlords, as they had hoped, it has turned out to be harmful for them, because the workers of the plantations have payed the $ 1.00 in stamp duties, but the indians who live off the land did not pay their $ 10.00; thus the workers of the plantations have become very discontented, complaining that they had to endure the expense of the stamp duty."[10]*

A regulation regarding day-labourers had been discussed *"very actively"* by the committee of agriculture in the Economic Society headed by Mariano Ospina, a rich coffee grower of Colombian origin, even before the landlords came to power.[11] According

---

10. DZA, Potsdam, A.A., No. 53916, Sapper to A.A., on July 10, 1899.
11. San Marco wanted to put into practice measures which regulated the system of work-contracts on the coffee farms under his jurisdiction, observing that *"as different punishments are imposed on them, both on the landlords, and day-labourers who receive money to work on them, the Attorney General thinks that*

to the Attorney General who was in charge of the protection of the Indians, in a note written to the Minister of Government on February 8, 1871, the legislation regarding day-labourers was still _"in its cradle"_, and did not allow the _"establishment of fixed rules for the development and progress of agriculture"._

> _"Therefore, it seems indispensable to await the handiwork of time to collect general and uniform pieces of information, and dictate regulations as every branch of the industry requires" as "such arrangements run the risk of being unfair and not suitable to the aim they are adressed to, being able as well to become harmful to the improvement which they try to favour."_[12]

The Attorney General considered that the most profitable for the development of agriculture would be for the local authorities and the central Power to _"controll the farmers in order for them to give a better treatment to the day-labourers"_, as they did not seem necessary to persecute or abuse the workers who did not want to be employed by the landlords, because

> _"the entrepreneur who pays a better wage, and behaves reasonably, has always had great ease in recruiting the number of day-labourers which he needs..."_[13]

The Supreme Court of Justice of the conservative government was also interested in forbidding the system of _'habilitaciones'_ or advances in money which the landlords gave the workers in order to contract debts and submit them to servitude for life. This was a typical system of forced work during the Spanish colo-

---

the publication of that document is not opportune; because we are at present examining the project of the Regulation about Land-works, which has been drawn up by the Economic Society, and it seems to us convenient to await its result." A.G.C.A., B1, M.G.J., folder Nr. 28633, dossier nr. 63, from the Attorney General to M.G., on January 9, 1871.
12. Ibid., folder Nr. 28625, From the Attorney General to M.G., on February 8, 1871.
13. Ibid.

nial period, with the intention of avoiding that *"the landlords apply the ways of coercion by themselves".*[14]

In 1880 this court tried the swiss landlord Georg Bramma,

> *"for having whipped three natives and kept them in the yoke all night, making them work by day on his farm 'San Agustin' (...) because nobody is authorized to take justice into his own hands, nor to inflict corporal punishment, and even less to use whipping which was abolished in the beginning of this century..."*[15]

The conflict which arose during this period as a result of the dispute about political power between the conservatives and the liberals did not allow for the adoption of an agricultural legislation which would be completely favourable to the interests of the landlords, and which officially would not take into account the rights of the peasantry and of the farm workers who were forced into servitude by the agrarian entrepreneurs. Not before the Liberals resorted to the institutional use of coercive and forceful measures, could the landlords regularly obtain the work force which was needed to develop the coffee economy of the country.

Having turned the workers into *"militiamen"*, does not always seem to have been completely beneficial for the landlords, especially during the dictatorship of J. Rufino Barrios, who was inclined to military adventures and aggression towards the neighbouring countries. Even in 1878 an english traveller observed that in spite of the *"disadvantages"* of not existing a good means of communication in Guatemala and the *"possibility"* that at any time a war could be declared and the workers incorporated into the military service, many foreigners were settling down in the country in order to devote themselves to the cultivation of coffee.[16]

---

14. Ibid., folder Nr. 28624, from the Supreme Court of Justice to M.G., on January 14, 1870.
15. Ibid.
16. H.W. Bates (Editor): *"Central America, the West Indias and South America"*, Standford's Compendium of Geography and Travel. Based on Hellwald's *"Die Erde und ihre Völker"*, (London, 1878), p. 102.

After the failure of the reckless attempt of the *"Central American Bismarck"* to conquer El Salvador, in March 1885, a german diplomat in Guatemala noted that the mobilization of the militia in all the departments of Guatemala, its concentration in the Capital, and later its dispatch to the front line, in spite of its short duration, meant a big set back for the normal development of agriculture and a blow to the plantation economy, as these militia constituted *"the nucleus of the productive and consumer population in the country"*.[17]

The conditions of productive work

The newly created liberal bureaucracy decided to find out about the situation which existed in the country, before officially pronouncing itself on matters of agricultural legislation. In that way, in the memorandum which was sent to the Political Chiefs of the departments on September 19, 1871, the liberal Minister of Government requested information about the population under the authority of the Municipalities, Preventive Judges and Political Commissioners. They also wanted to know the salaries received by the Political Commissioners and about the convenience of disolving some Municipalities and transfer the local power into the hands of the Preventive Judges and the Political Commissioner. The minister was interested in knowing the exact number of the native and the mestizo population, the state of the *"communal funds"* of the peasant communities, the way in which these funds were collected and their destination. They particularly wanted to know about the customs existing in the countryside *"concerning wages"*, the obligations that the farm workers had, and ways in which working conditions could be *"softened"* on the farms and, at the same time, *"guarantee the rights of the owners."*[18] According to the Political Chief of Chimaltenango, in the center of Guatemala, in all the villages of the department there were municipalities, and two of them, San Martín and Parramos, had Political Commissioners. The abo-

17. DZA Potsdam, A.A., Nr. 52612, Sarg to Bismarck, March 31, 1885.
18. A.G.C.A., B1, M.G.J., folder Nr. 28629, Memorandum of the ministry of Government and Justice to the Political Chiefs of the Departments, September 19, 1871.

lition of the municipality in some villages was not considered convenient by the Political Chief, because *"it is an institution so ancient, that it would be difficult and dangerous to attack it"* besides, *"under a liberal regime",* the municipalities were *"the corporations which are more familiarized with the local customs"* and the only ones which *"were able to enlighten and put into practice superior orders".* These orders consisted, in most cases, of compelling the municipalities to *"provide people for farming in the important farms of the Santa Lucia Coast, whose owners complain and lament constantly about the great losses they suffer due to the frauds of the above mentioned natives, without ever finding neither help nor protection from the authorities".*[19]

> *"It usually is a custom to pay the day-labourers one real and food daily, or one and a half reales without any food; and if the payment is according to the work they have done, which regularly consists of forty yards, two reales are paid; but in reference to these who are engaged monthly, both abuses by the masters and innumerable frauds by the servants were committed; the month-labourers are engaged with a great difference in salaries: they earn from 12 reales to 6 pesos monthly, not because their masters keep them busy; they all do the same, they even work on holidays and even by night if the master consider it urgent, but those who do not know about the treatment of the month-workers will be surprised by the fact that the master who pays twelve reales has 100 or more workers, and, proportionally, others pay more but have less of them. The reason for this is that the master who has many workers does not keep them busy daily, but only during certain periods, and leaves them free for the rest of the time, when they are lazy, drunk, and cheating other growers from whom they get money in advance, and, when the time to repay comes, they remain with the other master. This life means pleasure for them and therefore they prefer the*

_____

19. Ibid., from the Political Chief of Chimaltenango to M.G., September 26, 1871.

_twelve reales payment to the 6 pesos, because the master
who pays this makes them work daily and they get no
chance to become lazy and drunk. The master, in turn,
commit great abuses as well: they do not keep account of
the months for their workers according to the calendar,
but they consider a four week month, and fix eight days
of work a week. Instead of demanding what can be done
in one day, they demand great tasks which require two
or three days work and in this case the workers are paid
for one; if in the contract it is the obligation of
maintaining them is stipulated, the ration received is so
limited that they do not get enough to live, and this fact
compels them to ask for money daily, without any hope
of ever becoming free with that miserable wage. The
indians are naturally lazy because of their vices; because
they have got no hope of improving their conditions: it
seems that they are satisfied with servility, and without
modesty or shame or incentive they let life go on, taking
care neither of the future, which is based on cheating,
nor of their children's future, which they know will be
the same._

_The question about how to regulate work and soften the
future of the day-labourers has been debated very much
and with reason has worried the soul, because it is a
vital question for the nation, whose prosperity is based
on agriculture._

_But I think that the longer and more complicated the
regulations dictated on this particular subject are, the
more confusion and trouble they will produce, this being
a fact that will remove them from their objective.
Referring to this, I thought about a proclamation which
had to be published in this department, but as it is
essential to absolutely forbid the placing of "meseros"
(monthly payed workers) to work in the fields, because
these contracts are of the kind which actually hinder
having any rules in the branch. As this headquarter's
does not have the faculty to order such a prohibition, I_

137

take the opportunity of presenting the project for the consideration of the Supreme Government. It is to be noticed that there is not any restriction or limitation concerning the sums which are given to the day-workers, not even concerning the time under which they are to be engaged, because this is not only antieconomical, but also against the freedom of contracts, no matter what the restriction. It would be prejudical if something like this were to be fulfilled, but being against the interests of the growers and dayworkers, they would always elude it, and it would become useless. To improve the condition of the indians, there are difficulties which are almost impossible to overcome as they are satisfied with their present situation, as it has been indicated. This conformity makes them so passive to everything that nothing can persuade them, not even violence, to free themselves from it; and in the violence which drinking brings out in them, social civilization means nothing.

Therefore, they refuse education, the only thing that with time could remove them from their present state. They also refuse it because they consider it more useful to earn a 'cuartillo' (approximately 3 cents) which their little son gives them for grass or firewood he has collected, and which is later spent at the liquor store, than the time their son spends in school, learning, if he learns anything at all, and what use would it be later on in life anyway. They do not want their children to go to school, because they do not like the idea of their children mixing with the mestizo children. Their actual customs present big problems because in their service to the 'cofradías' (religious organization) they become ruined because if they had not learned to drink liquor before they do so here. Even though they are convinced that the 'cofradías' are their principal ruin, there is no power which could remove them, as it is only here that they find stimulation and where they place all their *pride. Their participation in 'cofradías' fills them with pride, elevates them to positions of consideration and respect among their class. The members of the 'cofradías' are recognized as 'PRINCIPALES' (community leaders), a quality which opens the door for them to obtain the posts as Mayors and Governors.*

Their ambition being reduced to such a tight circle and without any other moral scale than that of the 'cofradías', schools of drunkness, they are not able to live without it, or to avoid being subjected to its consequences. In spite of the brutalization of this unfortunate class, it cannot be denied that they have a soul which always impels them to rise, I do not think the remedy is so difficult, nor that the time in which their actual situation could be changed is so far away; and even if this point does not concern the others of the present report, I believe it to be the government's intentions, and I take the liberty of pointing out the remedy that, certainly, could be adopted. It consists in declaring that all natives who know how to read and write and know the Christian doctrine have to be considered mestizos and be released from any type of services, and contributions to the parish as well as the municipalities to which this class have been submitted.

This would be a real incentive; because as mestizos, the radius of their aspiration is widened and they are released from many taxes which hang over them. This idea has its origin in the fact that it has been observed that when an indian knows how to write, he tries to abandon his customs, to adopt the customs of the mestizos and search the company of these, and gradually separates from those of his class. If schools for only indians were to be established in the villages, in order to remove them the unpleasantness of attending the same schools with the mestizos, and establishing obligatory assistance for those between seven and fifteen

139

> *years of age, the present generation would perhaps*
> *completely change its character."[20]*

The Political Chief of San Marcos, in Occidente, was informed that in the Municipality of San Lorenzo, place of birth of J. Rufino Barrios, the day-labourers got one and a half reales for their daily work on the coffee farms. The landlords claimed that, upon receiving money in advance, the workers *"either work badly or do not repay what they are given".* Nevertheless, on the farms along the Coast where they were payed two reales daily, the workers used to accomplish their tasks, *"and so it is there that they gather the most and escape the least."[21]* In the neighbouring areas of San Antonio Sacatepéquez the workers received one and a half reales as well, as part of an old custom, in exchange for a task carried out on two *'cuerdas'* of 25 yards in cold climate and one in the coasts, where,

> *"they have the propensity to get employment and receive*
> *sums of money in advance for work they will do, which*
> *later is very difficult for them to accomplish, and it*
> *turns out that they are accused of deserting the farms*
> *and of fraud... because they not only owe to one part but*
> *to different persons."[22]*

In El Rodeo, San Marcos, a local Political Commissioner said,

> *"the custom is to pay one real daily to the servant who*
> *is fed in the house of his master and if not, is one and a*
> *half reales, no matter whether the work is for*
> *completing a task or on a daily basis. These payments*
> *are always made in advance in order for them to make*
> *partial repayments of debts, and nobody works and*
> *receives his payment day by day. Many of these escape*

---

20. Ibid.
21. Ibid., from the Municipality of San Lorenzo to the Political Chief of San Marcos, on November 7, 1871.
22. Ibid., from the Municipality of San Antonio Sacatepéquez to the Political Chief of San Marcos, October 9, 1871.

*from service, because as a great quantity of work-craft is
needed, they get engaged without any guarantee, and
thus arise the great losses suffered by the masters. The
obligation of the servants in many places here, are the
tasks to which they are alocated during one or half an
hour by their master and by the local authorities as
well, every sunday, or on as many holidays or festive
days as there may be (...) Often the discussions the
master and the servants occurred because of falsification
of the accounts, that is to say, the lack of formality in the
account-books; because in many cases, there are just
"pretend accounts", as they are formulated in a simple
note or cash-deduction, perhaps written down completely
wrong, if written at all, or it happens that the
registration of accounts are torn up or concealed. This
raises suspicions, and because of the contradictory
character of the subject, some doubts appear. This is not
the case when using corresponding books, that are kept
right, and which would be respected by the labour laws
which are under formulation and considered necessary.
Such a necessity has led the other nations to meditate
and promulgate the "labour laws". I, Sir, have had
occasion to become acquainted with the laws from the
State of Chiapas, which have been sanctioned by the
supreme authorities of the Republic of Mexico, and my
attention was greatly attracted to the concerned books,
for their consequences..."[23]*

The Preventive Judge of San Antonio Coatepeque, *"in whose
jurisdiction numerous coffee-farms are situated,"*[24] stated that in
this region

*"the day-labourers earn one and a half reales daily, for
clearing twenty-five square yards of land, and get*

---

23. Ibid., folder Nr. 28630, dossier nr. 101, from the Political Commissioner of
El Rodeo to the Political Chief of San Marcos, November 3, 1871.
24. Ibid., dossier Nr. 106, from the Mayor of Quezaltenango to M.G., January
2, 1871.

'habilitaciones' in advance, because otherwise they do not work, even if half a day's wages are given to them". According to him, "the way of softening the situation is to punish the day-labourers for the absenses on duty which are so frequent, as there are many who do not perform the task, and others who perform two or three tasks while doing the same work, and therefore earn three reales daily. It would be a positive step to instate a labour law, imposing penalties on the authorities which do not obey it, to the masters who do not respect it, and to the servants who do not fulfil their duties because of their laziness, as these are a kind of men who are rather authorized thieves, who request money under pretext of their work..."[25]

In Occidente, generally speaking, wages oscillated in 1871 between one real and a half and two reales, even if this *"custom"* had its origin in the middle of the century, when the coffee cultivation began in the whole region. Everything seems to point to the fact that during the eighteenth century, the wage of the temporary workers on the farms and coffee and sugar plantations was seldom higher than two reales daily, that is to say, $ 25 cents. As a matter of fact, it was common to pay between 5 to 10 cents for a 10-12 hour work-day. The abuses and frauds of the owners against the workers were many; they consisted of submitting the workers to heavy burdens and ill-treatment, as is pointed out by the rural authorities in their reports to their superiors. Marx used to say, with much reason, that daily contractual work constituted *"the most precarious of the wage forms".*[26]

The low wages in the plantations were so advantageous for their owners, that even during periods of low coffee prices on

---

25. Ibid., folder Nr. 28629, from the Preventive Judge of San Antonio Coatepeque to the Political Chief of Quezaltenango, October 23, 1871.
26. Karl Marx: *"El Capital".* Economical Culture Foundation, thirteenth impresion, (Mexico, 1978), Vol. I, chap. XXIII, p. 601. This observation is especially for those who would like to use the term *"embryo of wage",* which does not mean anything.

the local market, there were plenty of entrepreneurs who were willing to establish plantations in the country. In 1886, for example, when the price of the last harvest had not been more than $ 10.00 in gold for a quintal of coffee,[27] the German Vice-Consul in the rich coffee district in the South-West of Guatemala noticed that the new coffee plantations increased annually without interruption.

> _"Although the actual low level of the prices did not produce great profits for the coffee growers," the above mentioned diplomat wrote to his Chancellery, "the price, however, is apparently still good to such a degree that the investment of capital in a plantation is considered as income-yielding."_[28]

---

27. According to the report of the German diplomats who resided in Guatemala in the second half of the nineteenth century, the prices of coffee on the local market, starting in 1871, were the following:
1871: $ 10.00 per quintal of coffee in parchment;
1877: $ 14.00 per quintal of coffee in parchment;
1881: between $ 3.00 and $ 4.00 per quintal of coffee in parchment, considering the prices as very low;
1883: $ 5.00 per quintal of coffee in parchment, considering it _"a low price";_
1884: between $ 7.00 and $ 8.00 per quintal of coffee in parchment. The report says that "the conjuncture of coffee is improving";
1885: between $ 8.00 and $ 10.00 per quintal of coffee in gold. These prices are still considered as "low";
1886: between $ 11.00 and $ 12.50 per quintal of coffee in parchment. The report speaks of "favourable prices of coffee";
1887: between $ 11.00 and $ 17.50 per quintal of coffee in parchment;
1888: between $ 14.00 and $ 20.00 per quintal of coffee in parchment;
1889: $ 23.00 per quintal of coffee in parchment. The report says that "during the last years the price of coffee has been high";
1893: $ 31.00 per quintal of coffee in parchment;
1895: $ 44.00 per quintal of coffee in parchment;
1896: $ 28.00 per quintal of coffee in parchment, $ 35.00 per quintal of coffee in gold;
1897: $ 14.00 per quintal of coffee in parchment;
1900: $ 9.00 per quintal of coffee in parchment, considering it an "extremely low price".
During harvest time a worker picked no less than 25 pounds of coffee in parchment daily, for an average wage of 10 cents dollar. In Costa Rica, the daily wage was not inferior to $ 1.00.
28. DZA Potsdam, A.A., Nr. 52620, Gustav Boy to Werner von Bergen, May 25, 1886.

143

Not only the high price that coffee could obtain on the markets was advantageous, but also the low costs of production as well, costs that allowed the cruel exploitation of the peasants of Guatemala by the native and foreign landlords. Only under these conditions was it possible for the new land aristocracy to rapidly become rich, and the flow and boom of foreign capital could take place, especially German capital. Thus, in 1899, a German noted that the values of real property had *"greatly increased", "particularly the value of the houses and the coffee plantations, as well as that of the lands which are not cultivated but are suitable for coffee cultivation."*[29] The fabulous profits that the coffee entrepreneurs had obtained, starting in 1886, led every member of the ruling class who had respect for himself to try to purchase, at least, one coffee farm, in order to take part in the great banquet of high prices.

> *A foreign observer wrote that "everybody wanted to own a plantation, and the purchase prices which had been requested and paid have been fixed, particularly by the end of 1889, in accordance with the high price the product has been obtaining during the last few years. An infinite number of new plantations have also been established, often without taking into account the fact that in many parts of the country there are very difficult conditions to get workers, even thinking that with such good prices, if necessary, it could be possible to pay higher wages."[30]*

As a result of a favourable price situation, it was nearly only the foreigners who could keep their plantations, as they very soon proved to be the only ones capable of administrating their properties in a rational and economical way, particularly during periods of bad harvests, low prices, or after the periodical *"frosts",* that struck the Alta Verapaz and the Antigua region, which are devoted to coffee cultivation. In this way, valuable and famous

---

29. Ibid., Nr. 53911, Franz Sarg to Bismarck, May 6, 1889.
30. Ibid., Nr. 53911, Franz Sarg to A.A., September 5, 1890.

properties soon became the property of foreign joint-stocks companies, particularly German.

> _"It may be said that for the owners of coffee plantations
> 1889 was a brilliant year", a German diplomatist wrote
> to his Chanceller in September 1890, "as besides having
> obtained great dividens for their investments, the value
> of their plantations increased. Many farms changed
> owners. Some of the most important ones in the country
> became the property of German societies; as, for example,
> the farm_ El Porvenir, _situated in the department of San
> Marcos, belonging to the heirs of ex-president Barrios,
> which was bought for 2.000.000 marks by the
> Guatemala Plantagen Gesellschaft, from Hamburg; and
> the plantations Las Viñas, in the department of Santa
> Rosa, and_ Los Diamantes, _in the department of
> Escuintla, which were bought for 4.000.000 marks by
> the consortium Hanseatische Plantagen-Gesellschaft,
> with headquarters in Hamburg as well. It has been
> proved that these capital investments are highly
> profitable, thereby increasing German participation in
> the total coffee production of the country with 5 %."_[31]

Towards the end of the nineteenth century, the Germans had invested more than 200.000.000 marks in the purchase of about 300.000 hectares of the best lands in the country, suitable for coffee cultivation, thus more and more reducing the number and economic importance of the native Guatemalan entrepreneurs.[32]

> _"Anyway", the Political Chief of Quezaltenango informed
> the Minister of Government in October 1871, "in Tierra
> Fría agricultural work is regularly accomplished_

---

31. Ibid., Nr. 53911, Franz Sarg to A.A., September 5, 1890.
32. Ibid., Schaeffer to the Fürsten zu Hohenlohe-Schillingsfürst, May 1, 1901.

because of the abundance of labour and the facility to obtain it: but where we are really suffering, is on our Coast; we lack labourers in the very places where the most valuable products for export are produced, and where we may say with valid reason that our future is based. The few workers who are available always want some sum in advance; otherwise they do not get engaged; they get demoralized and corrupted to such a point that they cheat the poor owners, causing them considerable losses. Among us exists the system of 'habilitaciones', which consists of giving a certain sum in advance when the high period for certain work comes, such as the trimming of coffee plants. What usually happens is that none of them respect the obligation they have contracted, and go to other distant coasts, where it can be difficult to find them. The owner loses his money and the labour he thought he had secured. If the workers are persecuted and legal actions are taken against them before the Mayors of the villages, these do not show any interest in compelling them to fulfil their obligation, and if they take any measures it is most likely as a compromise which rather covers up these deceivers. This of course discourages the undertaking of work in a greater scale, the grower suffers losses because he cannot reap the whole harvest, and as he needs two amounts of capital, one for the workers who escape and another for those who stay on the farm, he has to make double commitments, and lastly, ruins himself. That is where we have the principal difficulty. Which would be the best remedy to solve these problems? We are of the following opinion: abolish the ruinous system of 'habilitaciones'; enforce a 'mandamiento' law (a forcible recruitment of workers) so that the Mayors of the villages could provide those workers who are needed, the interested party giving a small sum for the transportation to the farms and another one to the municipal funds; increase the daily wage to two reales and make sure that each department

_exploit the labour it has at its disposal for its own
benefit. We have numerous villages in the Department
which are capable of carrying out all the necessities of
our present agriculture with their labour force and even
more; but the native is naturally lazy. As he has few
needs, he can easily satisfy himself. As he is inclined to
get drunk easily, he spends the little sum he earns on it,
and when he asks for 6 or 8 pesos in advance for work,
he does not spend them on anything else, but alcohol,
and it is painful to be obligated to repay it within a
three or four month period that which he enjoys, as he
says, during a three or four day period. He goes
unwillingly to work, when this is the case, and then
runs away; because the custom is to receive as many
'habilitaciones' as he can from the agents of the
different farms, without contracting any compromise,
except sometimes with the last one who gives him a
'habilitacíon'._[33]

The Political Chief of Quezaltenango thought that it would be
good for the villages that were in a _"miserable"_ state, if its inhabitants were compelled to work on the coffee farms along the
Coast, _"where, with the incentive of getting a regular week wage,
they would be stimulated and acquire a sense of greed and thus
would not misconduct their work."_

_"Wouldn't it be more advantageous for the grower to
always count on workers, even if more expensive but
safer? We believe so, because he loses much more on the
workers that escape. It is convenient for the landlords to
pay them honestly and treat them with consideration,
because otherwise they will not be able to count on
getting anyone to work. We have noticed that workers
from the farthest farms are brought to the villages of
this Department, farms that belong to the jurisdictions
of Sololá and Chimaltenango, and those of Panam and_

33. A.G.C.A., B1, M.G.J., folder Nr. 28629, dossier nr. 41, Political Chief of Quezaltenango to the Government Minister, October 12, 1871.

> *others. Is it really fair that, when there are as many
> workers in those villages as there are in these, the
> owners must go and look for the workers they need and
> take them from those villages, thus harming those from
> here? We believe this is not fair, because it means
> harming a region in order to make another better. It is
> more natural, more economical, that every Department
> contribute with its own workers towards its own
> improvement in agriculture. Now, if we add to what has
> been exposed so far, a severe protection of the owners by
> the authorities, and request that mestizos be released
> from the military service, we believe that the condition of
> the fourth article of the Circular will be fulfilled, that is
> to say, to guarantee the rights of the masters and to
> soften the conditions of the labourers."[34]*

The cultivation of coffee in Oriente

In the eastern part of Guatemala the owners faced similar problems as those of the rest of the country. Here, coffee cultivation had begun a little later than in the regions of the South, Center, Occidente and Verapaz, and in the nineteenth century, its production never became as important as in these regions. Chiquimula, as we have already pointed out, was an important region which produced cochineal, and this attracted and gave work to small and medium independent growers and tenant farmers. Generally, agricultural exploitation of this Department belonged to the most conservative element of the country. Vicente Cerna, Rafael Carrera's successor, was a rich farmer and Mayor of Chiquimula before becoming a President. Many of the farmers of the region inherited their properties from their ancestors who had obtained them as *"royal gifts"* during the Spanish colonial period, and they had enlarged them through *"agreements"* or had acquired them as a result of the coming to power of the Conservatives, by purchase or embezzlement. At any rate, major cattle farms with dozens of *'caballerías'* were common. The

---

34. Ibid.

farms, besides having pasture lands, used to give shelter to land-less peasants who cultivated corn and other food-stuffs on small land plots, in exchange for a part of the products which were cultivated or personal services to the landlords.[35] Nevertheless, in 1864 coffee cultivation had already begun in the Department, as the Mayor of the place, Vicente Cerna, points out:

> *"In this important place, and in other places as well, besides going on with the cultivation of the fig-tree, though not in the same extension as over the last few years, other seedings have been started, such as the indigo-plant, coffee and particularly cotton, which had a regular harvest and whose products are being sent to Europe..."[36]*

The interest for coffee cultivation led hundreds of poor peasants to clear land in the mountains and high regions of the department of Chiquimula, and reguest them as their own property as they were uncultivated lands.[37]

By 1870, a comission of the Consulate of Commerce acknow-ledge that in that region existed an *"increasing coffee producti-on"*.[38] With the victory of the Liberals, the authorities tried to

---

35. In 1853, the municipal Mayor of Chiquimula, referred to the fact that the farmer Manuel Cordón had appeared before him, asking that the indians of Chiquimula be obliged to pay him *"the rent of the land"*, corresponding to a two year period which they owed him as a result of *"having made corn fields"* on his land. Cordón assured that *"the above mentioned indians, are not only aga-inst the repayment of that debt, but they also influence the other peasants on his lands, whose number amounts to forty-one, to do the same"*. The payment which was demanded by the farmer was 48 corn fanegas (a weight measure) for two years. Rafael Carrera rejected the petition of the peasants concerning them as owners of the land they cultivated, and urged Cordón *"not to prevent the indi-ans from taking advantage of the land for growing and farming, and not to inflict another tax on the indians than charging a moderate and equitable rent"* See: A.G.C.A., B1, M.G.J., folder Nr. 28560, dossier nr. 5. Still in 1872, the Political Chief of Chiquimula referred to the fact that part of his jurisdiction "has rema-ined for a long time under feudal conditions". See: Ibid., folder Nr. 28635. Poli-tical Chief of Chiquimula to M.G., June 17, 1872.
36. Ibid., folder Nr. 28595, from the Mayor of Chiquimula to the Minister of Government, August 8, 1864.
37. Ibid., folder Nr. 28617, from the Mayor of Chiquimula to M.G., July 10, 1864.
38. Ibid., folder Nr. 28623, Report of the Comission to the Consulate of Com-merce, July 17, 1870.

improve the planting of coffee on the lands of the native communities of Jocotán, *"as it was the best fruit produced in these
lands"*[39]; Quezaltepeque[40]; and San Juan La Hermita.[41] The
wages the owners payed the day-labourers was 1 1/2 reales daily, though they used to talk about *"the lack of labour".* The indigenous authorities refused to collaborate with the mestizo-
owners regarding sending men to work on their plantations,
because of the exploitation and ill-treatment to which those men
were submitted. As a result, the Political Chief of Chiquimula
decided that the wage should not be lower than 2 reales *"for each
team of ten men which was send to work".*[42] The Political Chief
nominated an *"agricultural Judge"* in Quezaltepeque, who was
to procure the teams that would be requested,

> *"being careful of sending persons who do not have any
> legal problem which could make them want to escape,
> and also controlling that the native class be treated
> conscientiously by the owners with regard both to
> financial matters as to personal treatment."*[43]

In Jutiapa there were too many cattle farms, and sugar cane
was cultivated on a great scale.[44] In 1859, *"all the peasants who
enjoyed some type of comodity"* were ordered to cultivate coffee.[45]

---

39. Ibid., folder Nr. 28634, from the Political Chief of Chiquimula to M.G., May
31, 1872.
40. Ibid., April 28, 1872.
41. Ibid., Act of the Municipality of San Juan de la Hermita, March 25, 1872.
42. Ibid., Act drawn by the Political Chief of Chiquimula in the Municipality
of Jilotepeque, April 7, 1872.
43. Ibid., Act of the Municipality of Quezaltepeque, April 28, 1872. In the act
it is expressed that an *"Agricultural Judge"* be nominated, who is to engage
himself in *"handing out the tasks to be assigned to the day-labourers, when this
be needed consequently between master and worker, taking care of the extension
of the kind of work and of the remuneration it deserves; at the same time, he will
make sure that the wage be payed punctually to the worker and that if he has
been engaged, will be paid enough and given good food, and get two reales daily
while his commision lasts".*
44. Ibid., folder Nr. 28578, from the Mayor of Jutiapa to M.G., February 1, 1859.
Statistics about agricultural production of Jutiapa, which was elaborated by
the departmental Mayor in April 1853, referred to the existence of 16 farms
and 112 *"herd"* of cattle, amounting to a total of 16.798 heads of bovine cattle,
277 oxes, 490 mules, 2038 mares and 829 horses; 116 sugar-mills, 317 cane seedings, 2 small coffee plantations, a nopal plantation, 9879 corn seedings and
568 kidney-bean seedings. See: folder Nr. 28559, dossier Nr. 54.

In 1870, the local representative of the government (known as Jefes Politicos after 1871) pointed out that coffee was being cultivated _"with determination"_ in the region,[46] and two years later, it was made known that in Oriente too, the workers _"refused to pay with work for that which they had received on condition of work"_[47] The Political Chief of Jutiapa informed the Government Minister on July 17, 1872, that

> _"In order to avoid the frauds often caused by the day-labourers, who ask for_ 'habilitaciones' _from the farmers of this Department or escape to the Departments of Santa Ana and Ahuachapán, Republic of El Salvador, to do the same thing, I adressed the Governors of the above mentioned Departments, and wrote to them that if they considered it convenient, they would request from their Government faculties to stipulate an agreement which would permit in an economic way and through the local authorities, to expel the law breaking day workers from the Department... they were positive to it; as a result of this, I hope that the Minister will be kind enough to give me the authority which he considers convenient to accomplish such an agreement, which will contribute profitably towards the agricultural development of this Department. The authority will be used for a purely economic agreement. It must be noticed that those who suffer more are the growers in this Department, as those of Santa Ana and Ahuachapán have very severe regulations, which they put into practice against the law breaking daylabourers, in order to protect the growers..."_[48]

---

45. Ibid., folder Nr. 28557, from the Mayor of Jutiapa to M.G., March 7, 1859.
46. Ibid., folder Nr. 28622, from the Mayor of Jutiapa to M.G., April 6, 1870.
47. Ibid., folder Nr. 28633, file Nr. 302, from the Political Chief of Santa Rosa to M.G., April 19, 1872.
48. Ibid., folder Nr. 28633, dossier nr. 287, from the Political Chief of Jutiapa to M.G., July 17, 1872.

The contradiction of the habilitaciones system

During the period of Spanish domination in America, the *"distribution"* of indians to the farmers was a terrible practice that caused the death of thousands of natives who could not stand the brutal conditions of forced labour and the abuses and humiliations to which they were submitted by the colonialists. In that epoch, however, many members of the religious Orders raised their voices in protest to defend the indian, who was considered by them to be human beings with rights and who should not be oppressed by the system and by the circumstances of having been *"conquered"*.[49] The same colonial authorities used to apply, from time to time, measures of protection for the indian, against the racistic european colonizer's greed for the land of the communities and the men who inhabitated them. In this way the formation of an american nobility which would be capable of fighting the King of Spain over absolute sovereignty of the land and the inhabitants of America was avoided. The peasants always tried to shun the work which they were obligated to do through the distribution system and when the Spanish Crown decreed the freedom to elect work in the fourteenth century, *"it was proved once again, that the indians did not want to work for a wage, in the required number and for long periods of time"*.[50] Faced with this situation, the colonial authorities compelled the peasants to appear in the squares of the villages where the Spanish owners were supposed to engage them in order to work for short periods, with the base of a wage which was satisfactory to both of them. As a matter of fact, the distribution of indians for forced work in the farms continued during the whole period of Spanish domination in America, although due to the immediate needs of a labour force on the part of some of the land owners led to the generalization of the practice of granting the

---

49. See Juan Friede's interesting works: *"Bartolomé de las Casas: precursor del anticolonialismo"*. Editor Siglo Veintiuno, s.a., 2nd. edition, (México, 1976); and Lewis Hanke: *"Estudios sobre Bartolomé de las Casas y sobre la lucha por la justicia en la Conquista española de América"*. (Universidad Central de Caracas, 1968).

50. Richard Konetzhe: *"América Latina. La época colonial."*, Historia Universal, Siglo XXI Editor, s.a., (Madrid, 1971), p. 191.

workers money in advance, food, or tools, in order to secure labour when competing with other farmers who were also engaging workers. In that way, the _"habilitaciones"_ appeared. The peasants never showed any real wish for doing personal services, for which they were paid, to the arrogant and tyrannical europeans and their descendents, who lived off the forced work of the former. The farmers, in turn, as the ancient colonialists had once done, considered the indigenous workers as vagabonds and lazy by nature, with a great inclination to vice and deliquency. They believed that the only way to obligate the indigenous workers to join the labour force on the coffee and sugar plantations was through forced labour. Many Political Chiefs shared this opinion. One of them, for instance, affirmed in 1872 that the indigenous workers

> _"must be accustomed to submission, for which the use of some rigour is indispensable, because that is the miserable condition of this race. It is a consequence of the savageness in which they have been mantained."_[51]

Gustav Boy, a farmer and German Vice-Consul in Retalhuleu, speaking in the name of the plantation owners of Costa Cuca, affirmed that the very development of coffee cultivation had led to a great scarcity of workers. He nonetheless attributed this scarcity to the fact that _"the indian race is indolent and lazy by nature"_.[52] The scarcity of workers did not make the plantation owners pay higher wages and improve working conditions, instead made splendid advances in cornering and monopolizing the labour force in the countryside. Under these circumstances it is not strange that the workers, being conscious of the exploitation they were submitted to in the coffee farms, would be inclined to cheat the owners, who were considered to be _"satisfied with being able to solve their momentary difficulties and to obtain profit in spite of having procured greater expenses"_.[53]

According to one farmer, the system of _'habilitaciones'_ increa-

---

51. A.G.C.A., B1, M.G.J., folder Nr. 28631. dossier nr. 188, from the Political Chief of Chimaltenango to M.G., June 21, 1872.
52. DZA Potsdam, A.A., Nr. 57917, Gustav Boy to A.A., December 15, 1886.
53. Ibid., September 14, 1889.

singly alienated the peasant population, because it encouraged them to commit frauds.

> *"By paing the worker a high sum of money in advance",
> the farmer pointed out, "he is bound to the plantation
> for a short time, but when the owner, who has
> distributed money enough between the workers, is no
> longer willing to continue giving money in advance, he
> runs the risk of causing the indian to leave the
> plantations, secretly leaving behind another debt. Thus
> he goes to another department and does the same there.
> Here some other farmer gives him another splendid
> 'habilitacíon', with hopes of recuperating his investment,
> until he finds himself in the same position as the farmer
> before him, or worse still because the law does not
> protect him in any way so that at least the advance
> would be returned when it is discovered that the worker
> already had a previous debt with another master."*[54]

It was a fact that the system for obtaining workers through the *'habilitaciones'* system led, sooner or later, to forced permanence on the farms and to slavery. And this did not occur without the knowledge of the authorities who encouraged it, nor of the free peasants subjected to extortions and all sorts of pressure on the part of the owners and rural authorities. This was stressed by the Political Chief of Chimaltenango in 1872:

> *"In this district an almost feudal system has established
> itself among the workers as a consequence of the
> 'habilitaciones' system. Four or five of the more well-off
> persons have monopolized the labourers giving a certain
> amount of money to each, which they never will be able
> to make up because pay them, besides their keep, from
> 12 to 24 reales a month maximum. This salary, not
> being sufficient for a man, is even less for one with a*

---

54. Ibid.

> _family to support. Thus in order to fulfil his needs, he has to increase his debt until he becomes enslaved because it is inherited by the children when their parents pass away."[55]_

Whenever conflicts arose between owners and workers, the Liberal authorities protected the interests of the plantation owners. This led the peasants to feel that the only purpose of the _'habilitaciones'_ system was to enrich the plantation owners. As an example, the case of six towndwellers of Chichicastenango, can be edited, who in August of 1871 sent a memorandum to the provisional president (of the Republic) in which they expressed the following:

> _"Several days ago, the owner of the Hacienda 'El Corralito' of the region of Sololá, came to our town. Because our needs are so many, we had to compromise to work on the above mentioned Farm in order to give agriculture a push, and thereby enrich the Nation, but unfortunately, we have not been treated with the required mildness, and instead of the consideration we deserve as we are the strongest arm for agriculture, we were mistreated when we came to the above mentioned farm. Not only were we not given the necessary 'habilitacíon' but we were paid according to a tariff. There is an unfair fine of five pesos as well which was imposed on us and charged on our account... Because we enjoy the privilige of the law as we are natives and we had to do the most important work in order to survive and not observe the_ 'gracia de permiso' _from the master, therefore, we humbly beg and supplicate to continue with the information on the matter and prevent the above mentioned farmer from treating us in accordance with our class and our ignorance, as what we ask for is just."[56]_

---

55. A.G.C.A., B1, M.G.J., folder Nr. 28631, dossier nr. 188, June 21, 1872.
56. Ibid., folder Nr. 28630, dossier nr. 14, Manuel Calbo and companions to the Provisional President of Guatemala, August 7, 1871.

The landlord refused the charges of the towndwellers and stated:

> *"First they complain about how they are ill-treated and*
> *that because of their needs, they have to compromise*
> *themselves in receiving money; secondly, that they are*
> *not given the* 'habilitacíon' *they need; thirdly, that they*
> *do not get paid accordingly to the fee, and fourthly, that*
> *improper fines are imposed on them for not completing*
> *tasks." According to the landlord, the workers "achieved*
> *the ability of not paying until a certain time what they*
> *received from the* 'habilitador' *(he who gives*
> 'habilitacíon') *in account for the work they completed. I*
> *have this to say to the first accusation, that on my farm*
> *every servant is as well treated as his behaviour*
> *requires, and they have been treated better, because as*
> *they are new servants and as I would like to get more*
> *people from that village, it is clearly in my interest to*
> *keep them satisfied. That they compromised themselves*
> *because of their needs, I do not consider as a reason to*
> *complain. Everybody has to compromise in order to*
> *satisfy needs, remaining thus inevitably obligated to*
> *comply with the requirements.*
> *The second accusation can be nothing more than an*
> *excuse to annul their compromise, as only with their*
> *current accounts of 'habilitacíon', and work can it be*
> *understood not only that they receive, but that they*
> *receive more than their due, something which everyone*
> *recognizes. On my farm no worker is denied money,*
> *much less when they are new.*
> *In reply to the third accusation, I answer that I pay on*
> *my farm exactly what the servants earn, according to the*
> *custom established in all those places; but if they*
> *demand a wage for the six tasks a week they are*
> *supposed to do, and have not done, they would have to*
> *get paid daily and not weekly. It is perfectly*
> *understandable that such a demand is unacceptable and*
> *against any right.*

> *On the fourth and last case, I have never imposed any*
> *fee to any servant and if they consider it a fee when I*
> *add to their accounts the expenses I incur when I pursue*
> *them upon escape, then I do not think that it is the*
> *correct term, nor do I think this legal. Nevertheless, the*
> *persons who presented this can not affirm it, as the*
> *considerations which I expressed above protected them*
> *from charging them with any expense, as I ought to*
> *have done, carrying legality and justice to a pure and*
> *impartial end. They made a mistake as well when they*
> *said that the landlord himself had appeared in Santo*
> *Tomás in order to pay them in advance, as it was my*
> *employee, who lives in that village."*[57]

The landlord considered the attitude of the rural-workers as
"unreasonable", in his opinion, they looked only for a way to
"annul" their debts; he pressed the Political Chief of the region
to order *"his"* workers to *"pay by their work"* as soon as possible
the balance due him *"as well as all the others who owe me* (referring to the landlord) *in that village".*[58] *"All the others",* about
twenty members of the village, supported their companions who
presented a new complaint and adressed it to Miguel García Granados. They said that the circumstances by which they had been
bought by the native *'habilitador',* a neighbour, were unfavourable, and that the conditions of work they met in the coffee farm
were hard and oppresive.

According to the peasants new testimony, the *'habilitador'* had
verbally promised to pay them four reales daily for the working
day.

> *"We agreed",* said the peasants, *"and for that we*
> *received a sum of money and went and stayed at that*
> *hacienda working during four months. We worked*
> *double because they did not keep the promise of paying*
> *us four reales a day as they put us to work by task. That*
> *is to say, we cleaned and weeded the coffee-trees by*

57. Ibid., Emilio López to the Political Chief of Sololá, August 29, 1871.
58. Ibid.

> 'cuerdas' *(surface measure in the Antillas) of twenty*
> 'brazadas' *(armful) each* 'cuerda'. *This took three days to*
> *complete and we got paid only two reales. In order to eat*
> *we had to buy maize and he charged us for a hundred*
> *cobs a week and two reales, that he gave us for chilli*
> *(red pepper) and salt, so that we earned only four reales*
> *a week just to loose a peso, this because we bought the*
> *cobs and we had to put the* 'machetes' *for the work*
> *ourselves. Is this fair, Mr. President? The sicknesses and*
> *privations that we suffered each moment on that coast*
> *and the treatment we received has caused us to return to*
> *our homes; but now they require us to go back to the*
> *same farm. In virtue of being poor and as we do not*
> *know how to actually return the money we owe, we*
> *would like to be allowed to repay over a two year period*
> *and ask to become soldiers for Our President, as there*
> *are fifteen of us who offer our services as soldiers*
> *because this is the only way to free us from that lord,*
> *who persecutes us and says that he who does not want*
> *to work on the Corralito has to pay 5 pesos of his wage*
> *free; otherwise, he will be punished..."*[59]

This case is also an example of how the landlords and rural public officials of the Liberal government viewed negatively the complaints of the rural workers which came before the Central Power. They did not like their authority to be underestimated by the rural workers, as it frequently happened be during the conservative period. At the same time, this demonstrated a change which occurred among the ruling class, where there already existed a strong tendency to force the rural workers to serve the interests of the powerful class, binding them to the plantations for their debts. During the Conservative era, the representatives of the government often received instructions to support the rural workers who wanted to leave the plantations where they were mistreated and badly payed. However, the Liberals sho-

---

59. Ibid., Twenty neighbours of Santo Tomás Chichicaltenango to the Provisional President of the Republic, September 7, 1871.

wed very quickly what the so-called freedom of work and cont-
ractability meant for them. The Liberals believed that the landlord and what he represented — the development of agriculture
and the country's progress — deserved undeniable protection,
particularly in those regions where the peasants had tradicio-
nally conserved a rebelious and independent spirit.

> _"It clearly appears that the persons presented have in
> mind only to gain time to see if they can keep the
> 'habilitaciones", said the Political Chief of Sololá. "I
> have also noticed that not all resist, but three or four,
> particularly Manuel Calvo. Thus with the objective that
> they would not go on bothering the Supreme
> Government, I condemned the above mentioned Calvo
> for his illegal complaint to fifteen days, and the other
> three to eight days. All the others agreed voluntarily to
> go to the farm 'El Corralito' and pay their debts, from
> the first of the month onwards, and they have been given
> a serious warning about the fact that they are to work
> hard. As the citizen Mariano Rodas was present as well,
> it turned out that during the confrontation he had with
> the complainers, there was not one who had been
> charged the five pesos fine which they referred to, and it
> is not true that they have been offered four reales daily;
> and if it is true, it must be that the complainers
> themselves asked for that sum, without anybody
> compelling them to do it. As there is not any motive to
> proceed against Rodas, I am just warning him; first,
> that he has not to give 'habilitaciones' when the
> workers are drunk; second, that he has to give the
> 'habilitaciones' before the respective Mayors; third, that
> he does not have to beg them to accept money because
> otherwise they will make the excuse that they had been
> forced..."[60]_

According to the Political Chief of Chimaltenango, no more
attention was to be paid to _"the continous demands of the indi-_

---

60. Ibid., The Political Judge of Sololá to the M.G., September 15, 1871.

ans", who slowed down the development of the country's economy in opposing themselves to the wishes of the Liberal government and of the landlords, that is of *"developing and broadening agriculture"*. During the Conservative era, the above mentioned Political Chief was asked,

> *"which request, made by the peasants in the presence of a hundred or two hundred individuals was not taken into account?"*. With this he was trying to demonstrate it was time *"to force this unfortunate class to give up bad habits, and to lead them toward progress."*[61]

The plot to bind the peasants with the system of *'habilitaciones'* counted on the sometimes open, sometimes concealed support of the Liberal authorities. The peasants very frequently received a promissory note instead of actual money, with which they could buy over priced articles in the landlords' shops. A swiss observer noticed in 1880 that *"the art"* of administrating a plantation consisted in not giving the workers too much money in *'habilitaciones'*, as well as in knowing how to cheat them when the time came to settle the accounts of salaries and amount of time worked. The landlords had to try to keep indebted the most laborious workers. The amount of money paid out in advance to a worker had to be measured by his degree of intelligence and his physical craft, as well as by his attitude towards alcohol and the work on the plantation. Comparing the average wage given to a worker as *'habilitacion'*, with that which had to be payed for a black slave in other regions of the planet, the foreigner considered that it was cheaper to enslave a man from Guatemala through debt.[62]

Merchants and coffee cultivation

> *"Business here has always had something to do with*

61. Ibid., folder Nr. 28633, the Political Chief of Chimaltenango to M.G., July 16, 1872.
62. Otto Strow: *"Guatemala, Reisen und Schilderungen aus den Jahren 1878 — 1883"*. (Leipzig, 1886), pp. 88-89.

agriculture", wrote the German landlord and diplomat who lived in Alta Verapaz: "the Department can only accept foreign merchandise, as long as its agriculture prospers. Unfortunately, the latter is in a situation of stagnation. The expenses of a plantation rise constantly. It is all the more difficult to recruit workers, creating enormous capital demands. Each day protection against workers deceit, escape and similar fraudulence becomes more illusory. Even if the Government takes some good measures in order to avoid these anomalies, the Institutions charged with their execution do exactly the contrary of what the landlords expect them to do. The question of the workers is the key to the efficiency of production in this Department, and, with it, the capacity to purchase imported merchandise."[63]

The intimate relationship between the development of commercial agriculture, import trade, and social and political organization of Guatemala in the second half of the nineteenth century was a typical feature of the plantation economy which already ruled in the country and which little by little was being completely controlled by foreign capital that had predominant interests in the development of coffee cultivation. The latter had to be based on the existence of low salaried workers, in order to ensure the strengthening of the landlords. That was equivalent to preventing the development of the national economy in order to favour a reduced number of landowners and entrepreneurs.

José María Barrundia, one of the Liberals who was very close to J. Rufino Barrios, considered that it was not convenient to totally submit the peasantry to the service of landlords, because this only promoted the well-being of the plantation owners, while it hindered the improvement of the standard of living of the working people. Barrundia understood that real national development was impossible in Guatemala, when an enterpri-

---

63. DZA Potsdam, A.A., No. 52619, Türkheim to A.A., May 5, 1886.

sing elite grabbed systematically the product of the work of the country's peasantry.

> *"It is true that the growth of agriculture has to be protected", said Barrundia in a note adressed to the Minister of the Government, in February 1872, just after he became an important coffee grower thanks to speculation, "but according to me, this must correspond both to the labouring class as well as to the proprietary class. The custom of assigning a wage to the daylabourers of three or four pesos monthly, pretending daily tasks, not making out their accounts correctly, and ill-treating them, is quite an irritating question existing for many years, and for which there is no well established contract reasonably formulated respecting the day-labouring class, whose situation requires the attention of the Supreme Government."*[64]

What Barrundia wrote reflected the thought of the traders in the Capital City, who found themselves dissatisfied. They were not able to increase their transactions, because the rural workers were not payed adequately, this in turn hindered their purchase ability and limited the development of an internal market for products of foreign manufacture. Already in 1865, the import traders noted that the native peasants consumed *"very few, if any, foreign products".* The traders had noticed that in Guatemala there existed an extremely unfavorable relationship between commerce, generally speaking, and the number of inhabitants. This situation was unfavorable to their interests as commerce in the country was

> *"on the average, of two milion six hundred thousand pesos annually, and the number of its inhabitants that of one milion two hundred thousand. Each person 'le toca' the minimum amount of two pesos and sixteen cents."*[65]

---

64. A.G.C.A., B1, M.G.J., folder Nr. 28634, José María Barrundia to M.G., February 29, 1872.
65. Ignacio Solís: cit. work, Vol. III, p. 879.

In 1868, the most important foreign trader in Guatemala referred to the fact that, thanks to the constantly increasing amount of coffee seedlings, the country had a brilliant future. The
coffee harvest had already reached the quantity of 100.000 quintals and in a couple of years this number would to be triplica-
ted. What aroused the greatest enthusiasm in the foreigners
was the _"excellent quality"_ of the product, which was _"particularly appreciated in Germany"._[66] A year later, however, the same
person stated that all the traders' shops were full of european
merchandise, as they had bought very much more than the population could afford to buy.[67] According to a representative of the
landlords:

> _"If the native does not presently consume more than the
> immediate products of his work, it is because they turn
> out cheaper, and for this reason, as the native is strongly
> attached to his habits, he goes on living with little
> change, just as he has lived before the Conquest, that is
> to say, he does not count on anybody else than himself
> for what he needs. Supposing that he spends less in
> wearing european cloths, that he acquires needs for
> other articles of foreign origin then, when the
> predominating element of progress and the division of
> labour have penetrated that society, we will see the
> native race devoted to agricultural production which we
> will contemplate, while nourishing an abundant
> external commerce."_[68]

Werner Von Bergen, one of the most important foreign diplomats to have lived in Guatemala in the second half of the nineteenth century, considered in 1878 that the Central American
countries, in spite of their unbelievable riches and natural resources, were as far as commercial development goes, still in a _"res
nullius"_ situation. _"Not only their external commerce, but the state
of communications and internal commerce as well are presently
of the most primitive nature"._[69]

---

66. DZA Potsdam, A.A., Nr. 52602, Augener to Bismarck, January 15, 1868.
67. Ibid., Nr 52610, Augener to Bismarck, January 3, 1869.
68. Ignacio Solís: cit. work, Vol. III B, p. 880.
69. DZA Potsdam, A.A., Nr. 52602, W. v. Bergen to Bülow, November 2, 1878.

José María Barrundia thought that a decision about payment of wages which could function as the principal system that regulated the relationship between the landlords and the workers, would become *"the fundamental basis of the development of agriculture and commerce"*, considering the role of the liberal state as that to preserve the order and tranquility in the country.[70]

The ruling class in Guatemala had divided opinions as regards the role of commerce in the development of Guatemala's national economy, and its relationship with commercial agriculture. While sector fought so that the traders of Guatemala would play a dominant part in the external commerce of the country, and tried to prevent their falling into the hands of foreigners, another group which was mostly bound to the new land aristocracy, led by J. Rufino Barrios, was more interested in strenghtening the supremacy of the landlords and of foreign capital in the social, economic and political structures of Guatemala.[71]

The search for political supremacy between both factions culminated with the retirement of the *"liberal-conservative"* Miguel García Granados, in 1873, from the presidency the definite establishment of the dictatorship of the landlords led by J. Rufino Barrios. The foreign traders who already in 1885 constituted the 83,50 % of all the active import traders in Guatemala were strengthened as a result of the quarrels between the Liberal sectors.[72] The major part of these traders had strong interests in coffee cultivation, which was the main feature of the plantation economy in our country. All the commercial transactions fell under the influence of the price of coffee on the international

---

70. A.G.C.A., B1, M.G.J., folder Nr. 28634, José María Barrundia to M.G., February 29, 1872.

71. In my research on the Trade Treaty of 1887 between the German Empire and Guatemala, I have tried to cast some light on the support J. R. Barrios gave to German capital in our country, in order to favour the landlords who exported coffee and to the detriment of the position of the traders of Guatemala in the national economy. See: *"El Imperialismo Alemán in Guatemala. El Tratado de Comercio de 1887."*, Published by the Institute of Social and Economic Investigations (IIES), University of San Carlos of Guatemala, (Guatemala, 1977).

72. In the import-trade that was carried on in Guatemala in 1885 participated various nationalities: spaniards (35 %), germans (30,11 %), americans of U.S.A. (9,14 %), french (4,76 %), swiss (1,87 %), italians (1,14 %), belgians (0,79 %) and South-americans (0,49 %). DZA Potsdam, A.A., Nr. 52612, Franz Sarg to Bismarck, April 29, 1885.

market. If the production obtained good prices, all deals seemed to flourish; otherwise they weakened.[73]

The foreign traders used to invest in agriculture a good share of the profits obtained in commerce, thus strengthening that sector of the agricultural bourgeoisie which was interested in the development of the plantation economy.

> "The commercial situation in Alta Verapaz during 1885 was variable enough", wrote a german landlord, who devoted himself to the import-export trade as well as in representing the interests of Germany in the North of Guatemala, "however, at the end of the year a satisfactory result could be seen; there was enough coffee, the country's principal export article, as its price had also been increased in comparison with the previous year. The currency circulation that this produced in every sector of the population naturally influenced commerce in the whole region, two thirds of which were to be found in the hands of the Germans."[74]

The ruralization of the foreign traders was not liked even by many prominent members of the Liberal burocracy, who were bound by family relations, to the traders of Guatemala who had been placed in second and third position by the activity of foreign capital in the commercial and productive spheres. As an other German trader-diplomat and landlord communicated to his Chancelor:

> "We foreigners are envied and hated because we succeed in our work."[75]

The speculative activity in coffee cultivation by the foreign traders, particularly the Germans, consolidated its supremacy in the plantation economy of the country and held back, for more than seventy years, the free development of the national bourgeoisie in Guatemala. This contributed to the settlement in Gua-

---

73. Ibid., Nr. 53916, Türkheim to Bismarck, January 21, 1889.
74. Ibid., Nr. 52619, Türkheim to the A.A., April 13, 1886.
75. Ibid., Nr. 52610, Doeding to Bismarck, April 24, 1876.

temala of a foreign bourgeoisie, completely foreign to the idyosincrasies of the people of Guatemala, alien to their needs, and unable to understand their aspirations to be masters of their destiny and achieve a higher standard of living. For these foreigners and their subordinates, who dominated Guatemala during the past century, the profits which were obtained through agricultural production for export were sufficient to enrich themselves, to maintain a State based on coffee cultivation and to maintain a State burocracy in unconditional service, and even to nourish the commerce of imported merchandise. The landlords knew that the high prices of coffee would contribute to an increased purchase power on the part of a priviledged sector of society, and that little by little other sectors of the population would increase their possibilities of consuming articles manufactured abroad.[76]

In 1888, a rich German landlord and trader who had lived in Guatemala since 1860 wrote that

> *"the high prices of coffee have greatly influenced the market; the scarcity of cotton clothes have been substituted well enough by the increase in the import of wool and silk clothes. The taste of the inhabitants of Guatemala was guided according to their possibilities, for the purchase of jewels and precious stones; they order clothes made in Paris, consume expensive wines and the finest alcoholic drinks. From this comes the great increase in the import of these articles, for which the trader finds a market principally in the class of the plantation owners."[77]*

For many traders, the entry of the peasant population into the process of commercialization of imported articles depended not only on the increase of wages the workers obtained in the plantations, but also on the capacity of those workers to obtain funds as small producers of maize, beans and even coffee. Türkheim wrote to his Chancellery in 1889 that

---

76. Ibid., Nr. 52620, Boy to Bergen, April 27, 1889.
77. Ibid., Nr. 53910, Sarg to Bismarck, April 28, 1888.

*"A moment of great importance in Alta Verapaz was
when the enormous native population began to take a
bigger part in commercial life. All this great population
had cultivated, until a short time ago, was simply maize
for its own use. Since last year, however, these natives
have started selling coffee at the market. This has
occurred after having had a long standing hostile
attitude towards coffee cultivation. Their principal
cultivation is still maize, but also the value on the
market of this product has increased. This increase in
price is principally due to the various bad harvests that
this Department has had."[78]*

The phenomenon of the *"ruralized"* trader was personified in
the second half of the nineteenth century by the major part of
the German Consuls. In most cases they were great import traders, important landlords and coffee exporters. This seems to
point out that among them the interest of making the greatest
possible profit from coffee cultivation, prevailed, even when the
expansion of the internal market for imported merchandises was
postponed. This also seems to indicate, however, that the economic situation of favourable coffee prices which began towards
the middle of the 1880's, turned many peasants into small coffee growers and good customers for the importer.

*"The commercial year was generally speaking very
satisfactory", wrote one of the above mentioned German
Consuls once, referring to 1892, "as well being has risen
as a consequence of a splendid coffee harvest. For this
reason the commerce of merchandise may be considered
good as well. This is principally found in the hands of
the Germans, who take care of imports from Germany
more than from any other country. The buyers consists
principally of indians."[79]*

The trader-landlords preferred that the system of forced labour continued in Guatemala as a generalized salary system in

---

78. Ibid., Nr. 53916, Türkheim to Bismarck, January 21, 1889.
79. Ibid., Willy E. Dieseldorff to Caprivi, August 20, 1893.

the countryside would mean higher salaries and this would prevent obtaining super profits like those obtained up to the present time. The traders who became landlords were very soon convinced that it was much more profitable to secure a steady labour force on the plantation, binding it to the farm either by debts or by providing a parcel of land, than to pay high wages to the workers which would be spent in purchasing imported products. Contract and work conditions which developed in Guatemala of coffee cultivation did not exclude the wage system, as we have seen, but this system did not become a general one, that is, the tipically capitalist relations of production did not become the predominant ones in the country. The system which developed was more or less of extraeconomic coaction precapitalistic in nature. In order to increase their profits, the import traders devoted themselves energetically to smuggling, bribing custom authorities on all levels, falsifying bills and altering the prices of the goods which had been bought in the industrialized countries.[80]

The dispute over the labour force

A large monetary circulation in the country and the system of free engagement of workers for the plantations were also obstructed by the competition and labour-theft which appeared among the farmers from the moment when coffee cultivation began to produce great profits for the agrarian entrepreneurs (trader-farmers, exporters, interest holders and private investors). In 1873 it was denounced that the farmers of Chimaltenango

> *"greatly damage the agriculture in this village, as they pay the workers half a 'real' and a fourth of a 'real' daily", and taking advantage of the fact that they take turns acting as Mayor "they send formen and policemen to the plantations in order to take the workers by force, when the other growers have payed them two reales";*

---

80. About the unlawful practices of the import traders, see: J.C. Cambranes: *Desarrollo Económico..*', pp. 150-153.

_besides, "when someone asks the Governor for some
workers for a particular service, and the referred
gentlemen know about it, they strongly scold the
indigenous authorities for having provided workers to
the 'ladinos', and warn them not to do it in the future.
This can be testified by Manuel Forris and Juan
Mijangos, who did not get a single worker, because the
Mayor had forbidden it by threatening with prison sentence."[81]_

In San Pedro Yepocapa, also in the department of Chimaltenango, the neighbours complained about the indigenous governor, who was payed by the entrepreneur Manuel María Herrera, forced them to work on the farm of his employer.[82] The
Political Chief of Escuintla referred similarly, in 1873, to the
fact that in that department, besides coffee, a great variety of
fruit, sugar cane, cocoa, brown sugar, rice, maize, mixt (pump-
kin seeds), building wood, salt, cana fistula (a medicinal plant),
cotton, vanilla, dye-sticks, tamarind, sarsaparilla, moscabado
(type of spice) and rubber are grown. Furs and many different
sorts of precious wood are exported as well. Many inhabitants
devote themselves to hunting and fishing, therefore _"there is a
lack of workers for the enterprises"_ and the entrepreneurs are
thus forced to _"employ all diligency to get workers, giving them
sums in advance in order to assure themselves of their labour for
some time"._

_"But these (workers), who are not faithful in fulfilling
their contracts are skillful cheaters and get engaged in
other parts. The new masters who were looking for
labour, engage somebody else's workers. This is the
reason for the permanent desertion of day-labourers, the
conflicts and disagreements on the part of the
entrepreneurs, and the paralization of the work."[83]_

---

81. A.G.C.A., B1, M.G.J., folder Nr. 28639, from Juan Gálvez to the President
of the Republic, May 23, 1873.
82. Ibid., from the Political Chief of Chimaltenango to the M.G., April 14, 1873.
83. Ibid., from the Political Chief of Escuintla to the M.G., August 13, 1873.

Trying to avoid the hoarding of workers, a rural authority received instructions to convene all the farmers of his region and
ask them to declare the number of day-labourers they had at
their service, the sum of money the workers had got in advance,
the kind of work which was destinated for them *"and the conditions of employment and the possibility of prolonging the engagement, at the convenience of the masters and workers".* Next, it was
decided

> *"that all persons wishing to employ a worker should do
> so before the first Mayor, registering them in accordance
> to the required terms. He who does not present himself
> in the time indicated for the inscriptions, will not have
> the right to demand the workers the fulfillment of their
> contracts. Every master was to pay one 'real' as tax for
> every worker, and the Secretary was to take a third part
> of this money for his work, the rest going to the funds. A
> worker who owes a master was not to be able to get any
> other sum in advance from another master, while he still
> had not paid. The persons who engage workers without
> the above mentioned requisites, will have no right to
> legally demand work or repayment. If the worker was to
> resist fulfilling his contract when the master asked him
> to do so, the worker was to be punished as fraudulent".*[84]

In a note which was adressed to the Minister of Government,
at the end of 1874, the Political Chief of Sacatepéquez informed
him:

> *"The agricultural enterprises have vividly resented the
> cheating rooted in the working class, to which the
> owners had contributed to a degree. It has been stated as
> a principal that as regards agriculture, the producers
> must be left completely free; but this theory fails in*

---

84. Ibid., from the Political Chief of Chimaltenango to the M.G., September 7,
1873.

*practice because instead of the good faith that the
contractors were to observe, they used a mass of
subterfuges in order to eliminate their compromises, and
therefore the resulting confusion, the disorder, and the
slow development of agriculture. As the number of
entrepreneurs increased, a harmful competition for the
acquisition of labour has developed among them. Every
one of them complained about the fact that he had to
fight against various obstacles in order to reach his
goal. During the last administration, the mayor Juan
Ignacio Irigoyen established the inscription of workers,
through which the owners came to the villages to
distribute money, paying half a 'real' of the inscription
and the right of having a worker for a six month period.
The aspects of this system, which then seemed to be the
most suitable, began to work in an adverse way. The
owners of great commodities, against whom lower scale
owners could not compete, came to the villages to
subscribe for all the day-labourers, without leaving
anyone for the others. In order to always keep them in
their service, the owners burdened the workers with
'habilitaciones'. Also, in order the worker was
transformed into a perpetual slave, became bothersome
and tired, and the wish of get rid of that situation
encouraged him to cheat. The prisons were full of rebel
workers who went to work unwillingly. The secretaries,
due to their interest in receiving part of the registration
fee tried to inscribe workers who were already registered.
The other owners, trying to neutralize the influence of
the most powerful, flattered the workers and offered
them money in order to lead them away from their
previous employers; this was done in order to weaken
the system of hoarding workers by a few powerful
landowners. That was the origin of two destructive
extremes: the tricks of the owners and the cheating of
the day-labourers. The correction of those abuses could
not be other than a suitable regulation in order to
immediately facilitate the intervention of the authorities.
This was the situation I found when I took charge of*

171

> *this Department. The wish to solve the problems and the knowledge acquired on this branch led me to fix my attention on the problems I have spoken of My intention was to form a brief law, which was based on the observation of agricultural contracts, giving guarantees to the owners and to the day-labourers, and persecuting fraud with an inmediate punishment."*[85]

According to the Political Chief, his intention was:

> *"to use the people available, making them available to all the owners; not to disturb the people; to conciliate interests; eliminate the slavery indirectly established; to assure the greatest liberty between owners and workers, who will be satisfied with having worked, having the possibility of being free from work within one week or to renew his contract at his own will. The owner is thus satisfied as he obtains the work of one worker and has the possibility of replacing that worker. Against the abuses which could be committed, there is the action of the authorities according to determined rules. As I mistrusted my opinion, I exposed it to the cencorship of the growers, whose interests it concerned, and after having discussed it suficiently, they approved my proposition with some small aditions, which are named in the respective act."*[86]

Projects for labour legislation

The farmers considered agriculture as the branch which would be the base of their wealth and welfare, and the foundation of the progress of Guatemala. The duty of the Liberal authorities was to impel the development of the agricultural economy, by giving the entrepreneurs *"the necessary action for their mainte-*

---

85. Ibid., folder Nr. 28644, from the Political Chief of Sacatepéquez to the M.G., November 16, 1874.
86. Ibid.

nance" particularly in the period of the agricultural work, and arranging

> _"in an adaptable and economical way the teams of workers who were frequently required by the farm owners."_[87]

Nevertheless, in some occassions, some minor functionaries wished to

> _"root out the abuses which have been introduced from time inmemorial between masters and day-labourers, where fraud and the slow march of the enterprises was born, due to lack of workers and the 'habilitaciones."_[88]

The labour law which was elaborated by the Political Chief of Sacatepéquez and the farmers of the region, stated that the Mayors of the peasant communities had to send the Political Leadership lists of all the peasant men between fourteen and fifty years of age who lived in the villages. This was to be done in order to form a team with all the workers who were at the disposal of the farmers. At headquarters, a register of the registrations would be made, where the number of peasants obligated to work on the farms would be kept, including the time they were to work and the _'habilitacion'_ each received. Each farmer would not receive more than fifty workers as part of the team and the communities thus were forced to provide the required amount of workers. Each team would be renewed weekly, and the farmers would pay half a _'real'_ for each worker's registration. This money would be assigned to the people's municipal fund. The Governors or indigenous Mayors were to send to headquarters the lists of peasant men from the villages who were to work at a particular farm, including the name of the farm and the amount of time to be worked. In that way, the Political Chief could see if _"the obligations of the people"_ were being literally fulfilled. The farmers were authorized to pay money in advance to

87. Ibid., folder Nr. 28644, from the Political Chief of Sacatepéquez to the M.G., November 10, 1874.
88. Ibid.

173

the *"habilitados"* (the workers who got the money), who were considered as *"their"* day-labourers, and had to indicate in advance *"the period of work and the amount of time they needed to pay the registration".* The community authorities, moreover, had to send to the farms the number of peasants who were required by the owners, thus avoiding that the former made agreements with different farmers. These demands, nevertheless, could be avoided if the peasants were busy with their communal or private fields. The claims of the owner could also be refused if the peasants were working on the settlement, on roads or on other public works, or *"if they did not pay the nine 'reales' for not working personally, and wanted to compromise with some master".* Any farmer would then have the "right" to a worker, who had not previously been registered. When the work was finished, the employer was obliged to inform the leadership if he wanted to register the workers again, *"in order to avoid this the worker could take money from different employeers".* The worker who refused to fulfill his agreement after being registered, and the worker who had got *'habilitaciones'* from different farmers, would be punished by the political leadership *"with a penalty of fifteen or thirty days of public work, changeable for two of four pesos, according to the importance of the crime".* The transgressors, called *"luneros",* for whom the master could pay the fine imposed, had to repay it by working two weeks, as well as the value of the registration. The farmers who gave *'habilitaciones',* knowing the worker was engaged for work on some other farm, had to pay a fine of five pesos and also lost the sum which he had given in advance. Nevertheless, the farmers who were in this kind of dispute could make a deal between themselves regarding the use of the peasant labour, though they were obligated to inform about the negotiations to the Political Chief. The farmers who had workers who were bound to their properties by debts, had to make a list of them and send it to the Political headquarters, *"specifying the village to which they belong, the sum of money (which they owe), the time and the manner of repayment of the debt".* Otherwise, they would lose the *'habilitaciones'* already granted and the money indebted, becoming this money a part of the fund at headquarters. The farmer had no right to fine their workers nor to allow their administrators and fore-men to do so. If _"the worker had not done anything serious, the farmer would lose the 'habilitacion' and registration; besides having to pay a fine no lower than or higher than fifty"._ The far-mer who retained the payments of their workers would also be fined twenty pesos, he would also have to pay the day-labourers the days lost. Similarly, the indigenous authorities of the com-munities who did not send the required work teams would be fined twenty or twenty five pesos. Instead of a Secretary, there was to be a specific employee who would handle the registrati-on books, receiving a monthly wage of twenty five pesos, _"which was to be paid from the same registration fund, and the remai-ning part, will be destined for the municipal fund of the Depart-ment"._ This fund would provide the possibility of creating seed beds for tobacco and coffee, _"and other articles which are proper to impulse agriculture and favour those, who due to lack of reso-urces deserve the consideration of the authorities"._ Eight percent of this fund will be given to the authorities of the communities, _"for the work which this law imposes on them"._[89] The farmers considered that they had the right to fine their workers, tho-ugh not to _"actually"_ ill-treat them, as, according to them, many workers did not go _"to work some days of the week"._[90]

The central Government had already accumulated sufficient regulation projects, and considered that _"the same subject could not and ought not to be the matter of different laws",_ and for this reason decided not to recognize what had been elaborated in Sacatepéquez.[91]

The greater part of the projects for the regulation of workers which were sent by the farmers were based on the law of 1784, and on some arrangements of the Conservative Government which were aimed at regulating in the country labour contracts given by the landowners (articles 22, 23 and 24 of the agrarian law of October 2, 1839, and the memorandum of August 13, 1847, which was mentioned earlier here). In all cases, particular refe-

---

89. Ibid.
90. Act of the Secretary of the Political Chief of the Department of Sacatepéqu-ez, Enrique Carranza, November 16, 1874.
91. Ibid., folder Nr. 28646, from the Fiscal Protector of Indians to the M.G., November 18, 1874.

rence was made to the "crimes" which the workers used to commit. The fact that the peasants were actually the victims of greed and robbery of part of the owners was mentioned only in passing. It was also usually the wish of the owners to make lists of the peasants, as if they were objects of private ownership for an inventory list. Thus, for example, the farmers of Chimaltenango asked once that

> *"the Mayors and Governors of each village keep books where a register was to be kept with all the men in the respective neighbourhoods who were able to work";* stating *"the occupation or skill which every one is engaged in, expressing which occupations these are, and if they are full time or seasonal; if they have debts and in that case for whom, to specify who the lazy ones were in order to hand them over to a teacher who was to teach them the skills needed, if they are young, or to look for work for them or engage them in public works as a way of correction, if they were older than fifteen years old."*[92]

The specific tasks that the workers had to do on the coffee plantations, the working-hours, the kind of food the farmers were to provide the workers, were not mentioned anywhere. Neither was there any mention of an acceptable wage for the peasants who were always well disposed toward productive work in their own communities, but who refused to do forced work on the farms. It is evident that this attitude shared by the great majority of the peasants and the cronic lack of workers which resultes was caused by the farmers themselves as they mistreated and humiliated the workers, submitting them to their own interests. However, this did not encourage the owners to increase wages or stop their arrogant behavior and absolute disdain for the man who fed and enriched them with his work. The only thing they had in mind was the gain of profits no matter how, through the practice of forced work teams and the hidden enslavement of the worker, who was not spared violence, terror, pri-

---

92. Ibid., folder Nr. 28629, file Nr. 35, from the Political Chief of Chimaltenango to the M.G., August 31, 1871.

son or hard labour in public works, which in many cases meant being sentenced to death. Among the Cuban slaves of that period, a _"black rural labourer"_ did not earn less than 30 pesos monthly (which were equivalent to 240 reales in Guatemala) for his work on the sugar plantations.[93]

When we state _"the landlords in power"_, we want to point out clearly that the Liberals were the very same landowners who had finally succeded in institutionalizing the tyranical system through which they subjugated their workers on their farms. We have already seen that the very J. Rufino Barrios was a small coffee grower before 1871. Since then, as a result of and thanks to his powerful position, it did not take long for him to become the greatest and most important coffee grower in the country, transforming the whole of Guatemala into a farm, when he laid the foundations for the Coffee-State which we still know in our days.[94]

The sources of labour

In 1874 the Political Chief of Quezaltenango said the following refering to Costa Cuca:

_"The General President, Mr. José Rufino Barrios,
ordains the settlement of villages which are needed in
this region, both in order to favour agricultural interests_

---

93. Juan Peréz de la Riva: _"La Contradicción fundamental de la Sociedad Colonial Cubana: trabajo esclavo contra trabajo libre"._ In _"Economia y Desarrollo"_, nr. 2, April-June 1970. (La Habana), p. 146.

94. Corruption and speculation amongst the Governors of Guatemala began from the first years of the country's independence; nevertheless, since the dictatorship of J. Rufino Barrios, the unlawful enrichment of the high state burocracy, the Chief of the State at the head of it, has been a constant factor. It has been affirmed that J. Rufino Barrios took no less than 5.000.000 dollars every year from public funds (DZA Potsdam, A.A., Nr. 12441, p. 81, _"Weser-Zeitung"_ from June 30, 1885). The German Representative said that the Government of Manuel Lisandro Barillas, the successor of J. Rufino Barrios, was so corrupted, that the State Ministers called one another thieves. _"Groups of women often march in front of the President, shouting to him that he steals more than his predecessor"_, said the diplomat. DZA Potsdam, A.A., Nr. 1555, W. v. Bergen to Caprivi, March 2, 1891.

177

*and to offer convenient expanses of land to those who
want to work."[95]*

Costa Cuca was 3000 feet above sea level, with very fertile land
which was very suitable for coffee cultivation; this had attracted agricultural capital, which had already established *"the
many farms which were in existence"*, according to an official surveyor. *"The good road towards the Pacific Ocean"*, and the proxi-
mity of important urban centers like Retalhuleu, San Martín,
San Felipe and Coatepeque, residence of the greater part of the
coffee growers who had their plantations in other regions, gradually gave a *"modern"* and *"civilized"* aspect to the country.
The only thing missing was to lay the foundation for more and
more villages, with thousands of men and women who could be
incorporated into capitalist production of coffee. As we have already seen, the first coffee growers in the South-West did not have
great difficulties in obtaining labour. Many of them simply changed what was cultivated on their old properties, after noting the
success that coffee production had in Costa Rica and the support it got from the Conservative Government. They could use
the permanent labour which already existed on their farms. Those first entrepreneurs like Guardiola in Suchitepequez, who
were able to penetrate and establish themselves in communal
lands, employed the peasant men of the nearest villages. Moreover, many landless were incorporated on these first coffee farms
as workers. They arrived at these rich regions after having been
refused plots of land to cultivate by the indigenous communities, because they were too poor and were not able to pay annual
tax which was required in order to begin any commercial cultivation. They did not have the support of the rural authorities,
which was reserved for the powerful landlords. The arrival of
all these men and their families increased the population of the
whole region which was going to be *"coffeecultivated"*, thereby
satisfying the voracious entrepreneurs. Nevertheless, as more
and more farms appeared like *"mushrooms sprouting up thro-*

---

95. A.G.C.A., B1, M.G.J., folder Nr. 28652, file nr. 70, from the Political Chief
of Quezaltenango to the M.G., August 25, 1874.

ugh the earth", there were not enough workers to satisfy the need.[96]

This constituted an obstacle for coffee cultivation. An attempt to solve this problem was through the practice of recruiting work teams which would sooner or later provide a new generation of permanent workers for the coffee plantations. But as the richest farmers and some rural authorities monopolized the labour force, and the resistance of the peasants into enslavement through debts, meant that the Liberal and Conservative authorities resorted to the settlement of a greater number of villages, where all those poor peasants who were still dispersed in _'rancherias'_ (settlements) distant from the main road or belonging to the communities of the highlands had no suitable land for cultivation in their places of origin. However, this resettlement project was based, as during the period of Spanish domination, on purely economic and political considerations. It was not as the Liberals used to say, that it was _"to protect those who wanted to work".[97]_

> _"Populations which are concentrated complying with human nature, attract rich tradesmen, facilitate governmental operations, assure justice, guarantee tranquility, and prompt all branches of industry and instruction. Men often live like beasts and not as intelligent creatures as long as they are dispersed among these great mountains. They are ignorant and superstitious, opposing progress and civilization. As a consequence, they are poor and unhappy among all the richness their land offers them.[98]_

One year before the official proclamation of the _"Legislation for day-labourers",_ the central Government ordered in a memorandum dated November 3, 1876, that the Political Chiefs guard the newly settled populations and peasant communities and pro-

---

96. Otto Stoll: cit. work, p. 80.
97. A.G.C.A., B1, M.G.J., folder Nr. 28652, dossier nr. 70, from the Political Chief of Quezaltenango to the M.G., August 25, 1874.
98. Ibid., Report of the land surveyor Lic. Hernán Escobar to the Political Chief of Quezaltenango, January 5, 1875.

179

vide the farmers with the labour they required.[99] The Political Chief of San Marcos, in reference to this memorandum, wrote in a note sent to the Minister of Government on April 3, 1877, that his Department allowed all kinds of cultivation, because it had temperature ranging between *"the coldest to the warmest regions"*, but that it has preferred coffee and as a result *"beautiful and large farms have been and are being settled"*.

> *"The harvest (of coffee) still in process, from which the last shipments are still being sent to the Port of Champerico, produced more than fifteen thousand quintals in gold in the Rodeo square, and even on the actual farms the price reached fourteen pesos per quintal, and thereby fundamentally proved that just by sale of this product alone, two hundred and ten thousand pesos flowed into the agricultural transactions of the Department. It could have been even more, had not the freights for the transport of the goods to the neighbouring port of Champerico been two pesos per quintal. However, it is expected that prices decrease as the road from The Rodeo to Coatepeque is to be finished this year. This road will facilitate the transport of the above mentioned product, of which large seedings are being started with enthusiasm.*
> *For the time being, I will not mention the other products which are going to assure the future progress of these people, once the cultivation of products such as sugar cane, cocoa, tobacco and others is expanded. More exact information which is needed to make general statistica still has not been gathered. The Minister knows the difficulties which appear in this kind of work, that is in reference to their accuracy, Nevertheless, always supporting and being attentive to agriculture, I particularly recommended the native population a precise fulfillment of the instructions of the*

---

99. Ibid., folder Nr. 28659, from the Political Chief of San Marcos to the M.G., April 3, 1877.

*Memorandum of the First Magistrate of the Nation the
last 3rd November, regarding the provision of workers to
the agricultural enterprises. I explained for them the
advantages that regulation implies, saying that it gives
life and presents a promising future to the Department,
and that the local authorities take care of punishing
economically the crimes and vices of workers, and that
the masters were not to abuse them in any way."[100]*

According to this Political Chief, there were in San Marcos, besides the city of the same name, place of residence of the departmental authorities and the richest owners of the region, two country towns, eighteen small towns *"and a considerable number of villages",* where the farmers obtained *"the workers they needed".*[101] The departments of Huehuetenango, El Quiché and Totonicapán supplied the other departments of the South Coast with men, as well as the farms of Sololá, which, as a well-known fact, had transformed this lastly named department into a *"flourishing and progressive"* one. According to its Political Chief:

*"The spreading of the coffee enterprises in the warm
lands, above all in the district of Patutul, influenced the
activity and circulation even in the most distant villages,
as there were 53 farms on lands already owned, and 81
farms which were already on the census were being
built up. Everywhere coffee machinery is seen, working
very successfully..."[102]*

The Costa Cuca in 1877 had also become a centre of wealth for some of the big coffee growers, already producing seventy thousand quintals of coffee, which, like the production of San Marcos, were to be exported through the port of Champerico, *"whose good position has given the region life and trade".* The Political Chief of Quezaltenango said, *"referring to the day-labourers"* that *"the permanent claims of the growers has been whenever possible satisfied".*[103]

---

100. Ibid.
101. Ibid., from the Political Chief of San Marcos to the M.G., May 14, 1877.
102. Ibid., from the Political Chief of Sololá to the M.G., May 12, 1877.
103. Ibid., from the Political Chief of Quezaltenango to the M.G., May 15, 1877.

The general Consul of the German Empire expressed the following to his Chancellor:

> *"The importance of port Champerico, on the southern coast of Guatemala, is quickly increasing, at this time, the coffee exports which in the past were exported predominantly through the port of San José de Guatemala, are now more and more directed towards Champerico, particularly since the installation of an iron quay. This port has as hinterland the Costa Grande and the Costa Cuca, the country's richest coffee lands at present. In the Costa Cuca, amongst others, is the plantation 'Las Mercedes', which is owned by the German Firm Hockmeyer and Co., and is considered to be the biggest and most beautiful in all Center America as well as South America; it could also be considered one of the most remarquable in the whole world, with its annual harvest of 18.000 quintals coffee."[104]*

---

104. DZA Potsdam, A.A., Nr. 52602, W. v. Bergen to Bülow, December 11, 1878.

CHAPTER VIII

THE MANDAMIENTO-FORCED
LABOUR SYSTEM

Through the *"Reglamento de Jornaleros"* (Wage Labour Regulations) passed on April 3, 1877, and the decree 243 of April 27, 1894, entitled *"Reglamento del Servicio de Trabajadores Agricolas"* (Regulations on Landworkers' service), the *finqueros* institutionalized the practice of forced labour which, in fact, had existed in Guatemala since the Spanish Conquest. However the Liberals tried to show that it was a *"painful but necessary"* measure for the development of agriculture, trade and industry or, as they put it, the progress of the country.

In reality, the *finqueros* faced with a pressing need for labour, succeeded, by means of instrumentalizing agrarian legislation through their *diputados* in legitimizing the forced conscription of workers. In addition to being able to procure teams of peasants from the different communities, the so-called countervagrancy laws permitted the *finqueros* to appropriate landless men and poor peasants not belonging to any particular community, many of whom were brought to their place of work on foot, tied and bound and escorted by militiamen, across hairpin curves, mountains and ravines.

According to Government provisions, any man fit for work was obliged to carry on his person at all times, a document which bore details attesting to his integrity, his productivity level and his solvency with the *finqueros* Any person who failed to do so was treated as a *"vagrant",* subject to a cash fine and immediately sent to a plantation or public works site, where he remained consigned as a debtor to a *finquero* who would pay a minimum fine of 5 pesos and a maximum of 25 pesos.

Wage Labour Regulations served to fuse together what William Z. Foster referred to as the *"three fundamental forms of vassalage":* slavery, group labour and wage labour in the countryside.

A German diplomat, in a note to his Chancery concerning Wage Labour Regulations, wrote that:

> *"According to these regulations, all workers when they show up at the plantation in search of work, must prove, by means of a small document which they are to carry on their person at all times, that they are not indebted, in any way, to a former employer. The entrepreneurs are obliged to make entries in these documents concerning what the worker earns and what he in fact receives, and furnish him with a weekly statement of his accounts. In addition, they are to erect livable dwellings for these workers and if work should be lacking on the plantation they are to provide them with a plot of land, at no charge, which the worker may cultivate, or permit them to work on other plantations. No employer is obliged to advance a sum of money to an employee. His only obligations includes the provision of an adequate food supply, if the worker is under contract, and the construction, at no cost, of a school on the premises, should there be more than ten families living there; that is, a school for the children actually working on the plantation. Children of full age are to receive classes both on Sundays and in the evenings. A school shall operate daily for the little ones, granted that there are no other comparable facilities located in a nearby village.*

The finquero _who fails to meet these requirements shall
be fined anywhere from five to fifty dollars (pesos). The_
finquero _who prohibits those workers who are proven to
be solvent from working on another_ finca _shall be fined
anywhere from twenty to one hundred dollars. No_
finquero _is entitled to punish his employees, and should
they commit some offence, he is to send them to the
competent authorities. By the same token, each and every_
finquero _is expected to treat his workers fairly. If an
epidemic should break out on the plantation, the
workers should not be obliged to remain there, but are
expected to return once the infirmity has passed. Every
worker is to receive a daily or weekly advance, when he
deems it necessary. Workers living on the plantations as
tenant farmers are naturally obliged to work there. The
compulsory term is arrived at by mutual agreement.
This should not exceed four years. Employees should not
accept advances from other entrepreneurs if they have
not settled outstanding debts with former employers. All
workers are obliged to send their children to school. The
authorities should check, insofar as possible, that the_
finqueros _have a sufficient number of workers at their
disposal, and that they pay a tax for every worker and
the corresponding period worked, namely 6 1/4 to 12 1/2
cents for every worker."_[1]

These regulations reflected the increasing difficulties confronting the _finqueros_ when looking for labour to work on their coffee plantations, because of the Indians' unwillingness to work.
Most of the rural workers transported to the plantations came
from the more temperate zones of the country and the climate
and long work days were often fatal for them. In Alta Verapaz,
where it is said to rain thirteen months of the year, the physical
stamina of these workers was truly put to the test. A German

---

1. DZA Potsdam, A.A., No. 12435, W. v. Bergen to Bülow, June 12, 1877.

finquero, in praise of these poor victims, wrote in a letter to a relative in Europe observing that:

> *"In Alta Verapaz the rain never stops. No sooner do we wake up to a bright and glorious day, do we find ourselves beset with that dreadful rain. How these pitiful coffee pickers, dressed in tatters, can stand it all day, is beyond me. There is no doubt in my mind that the Indians can take more than we can."[2]*

Despite the fact that these Regulations stipulated that no worker was to receive an advance, this can really be interpreted as a veritable mockery of the peasantry on the part of Liberal legislators because they were designed specifically so that the *finqueros* could freely hand out cash advances and thereby secure labour from the different villages. The Regulations stipulated that the *finqueros* were to treat the worker fairly and justly, not deceive him where his accounts were concerned, supply him with adequate food and accommodations and schooling for his children, etc., but only those provisions which served the interests of the entrepreneurs were recognized, i.e. legilization of forced labour and debt slavery. Given that the interests of the Government and the *finqueros* were one and the same, these Regulations were nothing more than a legal device used by the ruling class to distribute men as if they were speaking animals, capable of working under the most difficult conditions.

"Today the farmer finds support and many elements of wealth which are the future of nations", claimed a *finquero* from Occidente in 1878, while he attempted to give advances to all the rural labourers in the vicinity of Chimaltenango, where he had vast tracts of land.[3] Another *finquero* from Alta Verapaz stated that plantation owners were finally getting justice with the Government helping them to *"find the necessary labour".*[4]

2. Howard-Tilton Memorial Library, Special Collections Department, Tulane University, New Orleans, United States, Erwin Paul Dieseldorff Archives: Box 4, Folder 7, E.P. Dieseldorff to Arthur Dieseldorff, Cobán, November 22, 1920. (Hereinafter referred to as *"E.P.D. Archives").*
3. A.G.C.A., B1, M.G.J., folder Nr. 28665, from José Nájera to the Minister of the Interior, March 7, 1878, and from Rafael Escobar to the Minister of the Interior, March 2, 1878.
4. DZA Potsdam, A.A., Nr. 53915, Türkheim to W. v. Bergen, January 24, 1878.

Resistance to the mandamiento system

Many Indian authorities responded to the issue of the Wage Labour Regulations by refusing to permit their men to be recruited.[5] In many departments, peasants were reported to have fled from their communities and settled in the virgin bush or moved to neighbouring countries where they hoped to be safe from Liberal law enforcement officers.[6]

For example, the _Political Chief_ of Izabal informed the Minister of the Interior in 1879 that many peasant families from Lanquin and Cahabón, Alta Verapaz, were "roaming" the jungle of Izabal.[7] The _Political Chief_ of Alta Verapaz, in response to inquiries made by the Minister of the Interior on the issue, said he was not certain of _"the number of families actually roaming through the mountains headed toward the north of the lagoon in that department because of hardships imposed by the authorities of that department"._

> _"Cahabón is the only village where the number of families which have emigrated is noteworthy. This is due to the fact that because of the absence of any sort of enterprise in that village, the Indians living there are not accustomed to any kind of work, and because of the need to protect the coffee industry in Senahú, I found that Indians from this village and from Lanquin were being sent in groups, upon request and on a weekly basis, for this purpose. It is true, Your Excellency, that, in support of agriculture and commerce, the general population of these villages are being forced to work, but without these efforts, agriculture and commerce, the source of wealth in this Republic, would suffer and this would produce unemployment which would be detrimental to the interests of the private sector and the public treasury."[8]_

5. A.G.C.A., B1, M.G.J., folder Nr. 28665, from José Nájera to the Minister of the Interior, March 2, 1878.
6. J.C. Cambranes, "Desarrollo económico...", op. cit., p. 105.
7. A.G.C.A., B1, M.G.J., folder Nr. 28669, Luis Molina to the Minister of the Interior, May 14, 1879.
8. Ibid.

187

According to official sources, many villages in the Alta Verapaz region were unable to continue planting in their communities *"for lack of manpower"* which was the result of the *"huge
wave of Indian migration to the Department of Izabal"*.[9] In Chiquimula, it was reported that *"waves of families were moving
to the Republic of El Salvador"*.[10] This migration to El Salvador, as well as to Honduras, *"where it is believed that there is more
work"*, produced *"considerable reductions"* in the population of
the eastern portion of the country.[11]

Even in El Petén, a traditionally sparsely populated department, one could sense the demands made on the peasantry by
the *finqueros*. In 1884, an official of the region observed with
astonishment that *"some fugitives"* from the north were cros-
sing the Chiquibul River which separated Guatemala from the
British protectorate of Belize at Benque Viejo, *"a small town on
the Belize border"*.

> *"Upon analysing the visit made to this department, I
> was surprised by the marked decrease in population.
> But when I started looking into the causes, I found there
> was a great deal of protest for the aforementioned
> reasons. Although it should be pointed out that, in
> effect, most of the people who left were jailbirds,
> foreigners, thieves and unskilled vagabonds..."*[12]

Following Independence, Guatemala declared itself slavefree,
and opened its doors to black slaves desirous of fleeing the
English colony of Belize to settle on its soil. Years later, Belize
became a sanctuary for Guatemalans who sought refuge from
the dictatorship of the *finqueros*

---

9. Ibid., folder Nr. 28683, Report from the secretary of the *Jefatura Política* of
Coban to the Minister of the Interior, March 1, 1880. Also see folder Nr. 28721,
from the Political Chief of Alta Verapaz to the Minister of the Interior, November 26, 1885.

10. Ibid., folder Nr. 28683, Manual Duarte to the Minister of the Interior, December 9, 1881.

11. Ibid., folder Nr. 28715, from the Political Chief of Chiquimula to the Minister of the Interior, February 2, 1885.

12. Ibid., folder Nr. 28706, from the Political Chief of Petén to the Minister of
the Interior, March 28, 1884.

> *"From the day he was born the Indian opposed*
> *anything associated with progress", stated one Political*
> *Chief with respect to entire Indian villages which*
> *preferred the inhospitable but free existence in the*
> *mountains over subordinance to the authority of the*
> finquero, *"and the more the authorities look for ways*
> *and means to integrate them into society, the more*
> *frightened they become, and seeing the person who is*
> *trying to make them useful members of the society as an*
> *evil agent, they disband into groups and go back to the*
> *mountains and agriculture suffers as a result..."[13]*

In Conquistador fashion, the subjugation of the peasant population was carried out in the name of *"civilization"*, while the activities of the profit-oriented finqueros were held to be *"a contribution to the wealth of the nation"*, *"agricultural progress"*, etc. From the nineteenth century to this day, the *finqueros* have arrogantly believed that Guatemala and its working class belong to them and that they have some God-given right to do with it as they see fit.

> *"These people are some of the most reluctant when it*
> *comes to forced labour to benefit agriculture" reported*
> *the Political Chief of Sacatepéquez in 1885 to his*
> *superiors. "I've seen how their work, duly remunerated,*
> *has contributed to the development of agriculture in this*
> *country and I warned them that the* Jefatura *would try*
> *to take this into account insofar as possible, but that at*
> *the moment an order of this kind is issued, it ought to*
> *be fulfilled, and the guilty subjected to punishment."[14]*

One *Political Chief* who mentioned how he had *"to struggle with the Indians who refuse to work on the* fincas *on the Coastal plain,*

---

13. Ibid., Ministry of Development, (hereinafter referred to as M.D.), folder Nr. 14865, from the Political Chief of Izabal to M.F., November 3, 1897.
14. Ibid., M.G.J., folder No. 28714, from the *Political Chief* of Sacatepéquez to the Minister of the Interior, February 10, 1885.

189

as pointed out in other issues raised", admitted in 1885, that the peasant attitude

> *"was due to the scant wages they receive in return for their work, because they're always obliged to do it for a set amount and at ridiculously low rates. And while experts have repeatedly been sent to verify whether each job is being properly remunerated, no one has been able to ascertain this, because on the Coastal Plain the work is very unlike that to which the young men from the Highlands are accustomed, like those of their department who only know how to wield a hoe, not a* machete, *which means that while the tasks are well suited for the people from the warmer regions of the country who are familiar with this tool, they are hardly appropriate for those who must also find the climatic change difficult, which makes them victims of countless infirmities. On these grounds, and as a result of the discourse by the Indians of Santiago Sacatepéquez addressed to the* Primer Magistrado *of the Republic, I have stipulated, as a means of partly neutralizing these problems, that those men who perform forced labour on* fincas *on the Southern Plain, should do so on a daily basis, and earn 3* reales *a day; and that the* finqueros *should pay them additionally for their travelling time, allowing 2 days for 10 flat miles. In my mind, this is imperative, given the general discontent felt by the Indians with regard to this compulsory work system, which is always abusive and inflicted upon them by petty authorities who are incapable of carrying out their orders effectively and reconciling the* finqueros' *interests and the Indians needs."*[15]

In 1893, the *Political Chief* of Chimaltenango, stated that what bothered the peasants most about the *mandamientos* was that

---

15. Ibid., folder Nr. 28716, from the *Political Chief* of Sacatepéquez to the Minister of the Interior, February 10, 1885.

they had to abandon their own chores in the country to attend
to those of the landowners.

> _"Countless problems are arising as a result of the
> system of forced labour", he wrote. "With the exception of
> the larger villages in this department, namely San
> Martín Jilotepeque and Comalapa, all the others are
> obstinate to the degree of disobedience; and since the
> finca owners rely on this method, they request men,
> without respite. However, I'm intent on reconciling these
> problems, but the truth is, the repeated complaints from
> the Indians are disturbing..."_[16]

A short time after this missive was issued, a group of peasants
from Tecpán, upon arrival at a _finca_, demonstrated against the
Comisionado Político and the soldiers escorting them, and refused to continue any further. Only with military reinforcements
was it possible to imprison 15 instigators, after having them
brutally beaten.

> _"Not only are the Indians of Tecpán opposed to the idea
> of forced labour", reported the_ Jefe Político, _"but
> Indians from all the other villages of this department
> have also shown their discontent and I have to deal
> with this every day, since both the Indians and the
> landowners are abusive. The Indians run and hide, or
> register unfounded complaints and flee the_ fincas. _The
> landowners request men, without respite, ordering them
> to perform difficult tasks without paying them just
> wages. They work themselves to the bone just to earn
> two and a half or three_ reales _a day, which is just
> enough for them to scrape by. It is true that the_ fincas _in
> the Costa de Pochuta, Acatenango and Yepocapa
> desperately need men to harvest their crops, but the
> Indians also need time to attend to their own grains..."_[17]

16. Ibid., M.D., folder Nr. 14855, from the _Political Chief_ of Chimaltenango to
the Minister of Development, September 6, 1893.
17. Ibid., October 30, 1893.

Peasants from Quiché, in a note addressed to President José Maria Reyna Barrios, a wealthy *finquero* and relative of the former dictator Rufino Barrios, expressed, in a few words, their rejection of the yoke of forced labour. The petition, simplistic but categorical, shows us, once more, the rebellious spirit of our people who refuse to passively accept such oppressive treatment from the *finqueros:*

> *"The Chiefs and all the residents of San Sebastián Lemoa, humbly express before Your Excellency, that the authorities of our domicile, have told us that the* Jefatura Política *of the Department of Quiché has issued an order for 50 men to go, without fail, to the* finca *"Medio Día", to do forced labour, something they are unwilling to do... and so we ask that Your Excellency order that the sum they want to advance us be returned. Therefore, we humbly ask and beg of you to be so kind as to order the* Jefe Político *of Quiché to return the money to the owner of the* finca *known as "Medio Día", since we have our own chores to attend to and don't want to be subjected to forced labour. It is justice and mercy we are seeking."[18]*

The peasants' need to cultivate their communal and individual property obliged rural authorities for a time to grant *"exemption privileges"* and *"permits"* so that they could plant, clear and harvest during the required seasons. However, these permits were drastically reduced in number and exemptions practically annulled, due to pressures exerted by the landowners. From 1880 onward, local authorities addressed numerous reports to their superiors in the departmental centers or to the Central Government itself, relating how *"the sowing in the communities was never completed for lack of men, because these same people are tied up on different farms",* or that the peasants had been taken *"en masse"* to the *fincas,* without being allowed *"to finish sowing the communal* finca *with corn for general consum-*

---

18. Ibid., folder No. 14850, Eugenio García, and friends to the President of the Republic, November 9, 1893.

tion". Often, it was the women who had to take on tasks once assigned exclusively to men, because the work in the cornfields was left undone.

The lot of the communal peasants grew even more difficult when the government itself demanded forced recruitment of labour to carry out roadworks, railway construction and public works in general. The community members, in these cases, would often receive a card exempting them from work on the _fincas,_ issued by the highest authorities for a period of six months to a year, but, in return for this privilege, they had to join the so-called _"sapper company"_ and bear the weight of the burdensome workload to which they were subjected by official foremen in the different tasks of constructing the infrastructure for the coffee plantation.

The regulations of the mandamiento system

Fulfillment of the provisions of the Forced Labour relations was often problematic for the _Jefes Políticos,_ because they weren't always able to meet the _finqueros'_ demands and attend to the peasants grievances at the same time. It must also be added that the rural authorities had to keep an eye out for the intrigues of the landowners' private _habilitadores,_ who advanced money to the Indians, and the corruption of their subordinates and representatives, particularly the political Commissioners, who were always eager to get involved in shady deals with the most powerful _finqueros. "The Mayors and Political Commissioners, with very few exceptions, have speculated on forced labour",_ confirmed a _Jefe Político_ from Chimaltenango with obvious rage:

> _"The finca owners, in their indefatigable competition for labour, will do anything to get what they are after..."[19]_

The same rural official issued an order for forced labour based on the Regulations of April 3, 1877, in an attempt to eradicate

19. Ibid., folder No. 14855, from the _Political Chief_ of Chimaltenango to the M.D., August 18, 1893.

the abuses committed by both the labour authorities and the ones giving and receiving advances."[20]

To begin with, the advances were for 45 days, instead of 30, as they had been until that point in time. If the workers completed the work for which they had been contracted before the 45 days, the *finqueros* were obliged to *"assist"* a neighbouring landowner having difficulties harvesting his coffee for lack of men, *"by having the wage labourers who had been sent to them by virtue of forced recruitment, move on to the* finca *of an entrepreneur who still required the services of these men".* On the other hand, when the Mayors and Political Commissioners received instructions from the *Jefe Político* to execute an order, they had to *"acknowledge receipt"* of *"delivery"* and record it in the municipal register. Local authorities were to use *"receipt books",* with a list of the names of the peasants advanced money to facilitate *"immediate supervision"* by the *Jefatura,* while the workers were distributed in a more orderly and equitable way. The Political Commissioners had to write weekly reports on the *mandamientos, "the orders issued and the ones which should be ordered, immediately reporting any problems which should arise";* the system was to be "scrupulous and impartial", so as not to overload some workers *"while sparing others".* This required a readily available *"political map of the area and a register of taxpayers".* Local authorities were to be directly responsible for: the rates of the advances granted by the farmer to the peasants, in case the latter ignored the order *"unjustifiably";* the advances effected behind the *Jefes Políticos'* back; expenses incurred by the *finqueros* and losses suffered as a result of the peasants' rejection of forced labour, as well as penalties they were to impose on their *"agents",* should the latter fail to carry out orders and go unpunished.

Only those peasants with physical handicaps who could furnish proof, were exempted by the *Jefe Político* from having to perform forced labour. In addition, and rather ironically, *"those wage labourers indebted to the coffee plantations, and registered as such in this Office..."* [21] were also exempt. That is, workers

---

20. Ibid.
21. Ibid.

already committed to a plantation were, according to the *Jefe* Político, exempt from these duties.

The foregoing were approved provisions by the Central Government. The provision stipulating that the peasants work on the plantations for 45 days instead of 30 *"first appealed to the finqueros",* recounted the *Jefe Político* of Chimaltenango in 1893, since it *"guaranteed their services for a longer period of time".*[22] However, in practice, this was asking the peasants to make an even greater sacrifice. since for the most part, upon abandoning their communities, they had to bring along enough food to supposedly last them the days they were to be in the service of the landowners, and as if reheating their meals for thirty days wasn't enough on top of the abominal working conditions on the *fincas,* the idea of having to cope with 15 additional days made the arrangement absolutely unbearable. Once more the peasants reacted by abandoning their villages, emigrating, and registering their complaints before the President of the Coffee Republic.[23]

> *"Apart from the Indian's systematic rejection of forced labour, even for a limited period of time, as reflected in continual complaints, justified or not, and thousands of excuses and pretexts",* wrote the Jefe Político *to the Minister of Development, "I've found that because they're not given food on the* fincas, *and because the food they do bring along perishes within 15 to 20 days (an acceptable period of time to be away from their homes and their families), I've found myself in a position whereby I've had to regulate the system in the best possible way to ensure that the Indians are paid for the time spent travelling from their home to the* finca, *that the workers are responsible and that those workers with the most time available are selected first, but nothing seems to reduce the complaints which have plagued and continued to plague the President and his Office."*[24]

22. Ibid., from the *Political Chief* of Chimaltenango to the M.D., September 6, 1893.
23. Ibid.
24. Ibid.

Some weeks later, the *Jefe Político* explained to the Minister of Development that:

> *"Because of repeated complaints filed by the Indians of this department, with reference to forced conscription, once again I think it most appropriate to inform you that I'm carrying out your instructions rigorously, and seeing to it that there are three fifteen-day periods; but what the Indians want and something they're very adamant about, is a single and shorter period, because they can't possibly bring along provisions for any extended period of time, particularly during the rainy season when they can't get enough hours in to cancel the advance.."[25]*

The official establishment of this system has helped us to understand the class solidarity which developed between the Chiefs of the communities and the peasants. The Indian Mayors and Governors in particular, tried, in every possible way, to protect the members of their communities. It was not uncommon to see them at the head of the Indian delegation which always came to the Capital to demand recognition of their civil rights. On several occasions, their protests curbed the authorities' tendency to turn them into collaborators and simple local intermediaries of the *finqueros'* dictatorship. In these situations, the fury and powerlessness of the *Jefes Políticos* backfired on these quiet men with an iron will.

The peasant women were also victims of forced labour, suffering in different ways the outrages perpetrated against their class by the *finqueros* and their representatives. Further on I shall examine the importance of women in the development of coffee growing in Guatemala — a noteworthy aspect —, particularly their role in coffee production and processing. For the time being, I shall only mention that they too were subjected to forced conscription, and often outnumbered the men who made up the columns of group labour. On one occasion, a rural authority

---

25. Ibid., from the *Political Chief* of Chimaltenango to the M.D., September 23, 1893.

reported that while reviewing the books of the community, he had discovered that the *finqueros,* in 1882 had requested *"286 women and 15 young men to prune the coffee plants".*[26]

The slave-like conditions to which men and women alike from Alta Verapaz had been subjected gravely affected the sensibilities of one *Jefe Político* with strong Liberal convictions who, unlike most of his colleagues, did a meticulous study of the way in which *finqueros* and rank and file authorities in the region enforced the system. Given that this official represented the interests of the ruling class, it's not uncommon to find in his report, which he submitted to his supervisors, a good dose of prejudices against the Indian peasant, typical of the period, which still exist today. However, his exposé is a curious document of great historical value:

> *"The Department of Alta Verapaz is pure farming country", wrote the same Jefe Político in 1892, "traditionally opposed to progress, despite elements which make it a good candidate for change. Because most of its inhabitants are submissive and abide by all government regulations, it's never difficult to get a new business going which is useful to the public. But because it is dominated today by a small nucleus whose only aspiration is to accumulate wealth for its own selfish gain, it's another story altogether and energy and singleness of purpose are required to put an end to a system which has gradually been feeding on the inhabitants of this region.*
> *Since the authorities of the villages of the Department are largely made up of simple natives, their employees most trivial actions are subject to the wishes of a Secretary who, more than once, has exploited, to his own benefit, the position in which he finds himself, transgressing the law to benefit a tight circle whose chief characteristic has been to exploit the Indian race with pretexts of the contributions the Government is making to agriculture. Superior authorities who*

26. Ibid., M.G.J., folder No. 28704, from the Political Chief of Alta Verapaz to the M.G., February 24, 1883.

*witnessed such conduct with absolute indifference,
perhaps because their interests were tied to those of the
more privileged, permitted this absurd system to take on
all the characteristics of a custom deeply rooted in the
political society which it is my duty to govern; this
explains the constant struggle which I approach with
energy and prudence unable to arrive at any
compromise between the interests of the landowners who
believe in forced labour at all costs and the rights of the
Indians who instinctively shun, in any way they can, the
commitments imposed upon them by the law of*
mandamientos.
*At the same time, it is common knowledge that the land
distribution program in this Department has been
designed to satisfy a hungry few. I don't know how, but
one person can claim fifty, one hundred even five
hundred* caballerías *of land, which were principally
occupied by Indians in their capacity as tenant farmers.
The erroneous interpretation of the very legislation
governing the system of* mandamientos *has led them to
believe that the administrative authorities don't have
anything to do with the citizens and the landowners are
constantly protesting so that they abide by the law.
Which means that, other than the payment of direct
taxes, they refuse to comply with any other obligation
imposed by the authorities for public work utilities, and
this, in turn, has meant that all improvement efforts
initiated before April 2, 1885 are at a standstill. It's
evident that since that date absolutely nothing of any
national concern has been accomplished in this
Department.
On the contrary, only private interests are thriving,
thanks to the exuberant vegetation and then wealth of
our forests. Here they are making fortunes which, apart
from the impatience of the foreigners who want to make
colossal sums overnight to be able to return immediately
to their countries, leave nothing to be desired.
In each town,* finca *and hamlet, whose land belongs to*

a party with individual title, Alcaldes Auxiliares _are appointed, together with ten or twelve individuals called_ Mayores, _whose task it is to exclusively serve the master for a term of one year without compensation from the_ fincas _and without the Municipality of the respective jurisdiction knowing anything of the actions of the residents for whom this has been established._
If the landowners, instead of forcing the Indian to work on Sundays without pay, should adopt the philanthropic idea of giving these unfortunate men religious classes — food for the soul —, as payment for a week's work, we would not have to see the yardstick of justice fall by the wayside — a tragic sight — while the Alcalde, Mayores _and villages turn their backs on the day of the week which educated people, the world over, have set aside as a day of rest._

Entirely subject to the whims of the landowners who govern as feudal lords, impose fines, incarcerate, evaluate and regulate working conditions, act as defendants and jury, the proletariat, exasperated, has no other choice but to seek refuge in the mountains, leave their country, a phenomenon which is occuring with a large number of families who have gone to live in Punta Gorda _in the Colony of Belize and in_ San Luis, _in Mexican territory._

The poor workers cannot move to other fincas, _or seek asylum on municipal property, as they live with the constant threat posed by their bosses who make them virtual slaves by having them carry a little book on their persons at all times, which, because they are illiterate, means nothing to them at all, yet, is a symbol of their commitment to live for four long years obeying the_ master. _The Indian who forgets his status and attempts to go elsewhere, returns to find that his cornfields have been confiscated, his personal belongings and his corn missing, as if he had no property title whatsoever. This process constitutes an absolute transgression of that_

199

which has been established in the Constitution and the laws.

Even the women have not been spared the hardships of the mandamiento system. *Authorities have been known to force their way into the houses of a family man, a husband, a widow, to deliver advances which they have to repay on one* finca *or another pruning coffee plants.*

Tragic situations resulted from this practice. More than once honourable young women have been forced to abandon their virgin white garb to don the threads of the shameless whore; and more than once the wife who was the incarnation of goodness and tranquility in her home has returned, a fountain of sorrow, persecuted by her husband's jealousy. The honourable widow, respected in every cultured society, is looked upon here as a contemptable harlot condemned to live with her offspring under the thumb of frightful foremen who force her to produce riches for the white man while she and her children go hungry. When trying to find the causes of venereal disease there is no need to look any further than the fincas. *It alone can be attributed to the illegal application of forced labour on women.*

The proletariat who works in an Indian community or on property belonging to the Municipality, has been worse off than the tenant farmer. The authorities, obliged to supply the finqueros *with labour, have had to turn to these people, and the Indian who lives on his own plot of land never knows whether he will be able to attend to his own work. No sooner does he work the equivalent of one advance, than along come the* habilitadores *to leave him another, against his will, and force him once more to keep working, with absolute disregard, on the part of the authorities and the* finqueros, *for this poor fellow's own crops which go unharvested.*

Since it is not customary to feed the labourers, as

prescribed in the mandamiento law, _before leaving home they have to stock up on provisions which consist of_ totoposte, tortillas _and_ chile. _After four days, the food starts to decompose, due to the climate etc., but they eat it like that nonetheless for lack of anything else and often get sick and are unable to work. This situation, in addition to their propensity for rickets, makes it impossible for them to get their work done in two or three days. The entrepreneurs, take advantage of their timidity and assign them thirty, thirty-six, even thirty-eight square_ varas _to work. Few_ finqueros _assign the just task of twenty-five_ varas. _This, Your Excellency, is the lot of the Indian race when it comes to_ mandamientos.

In terms of the administration of the Department, you can imagine the difficulties encountered by the authorities when they want to construct even the simplest schoolhouse. As you have seen, the character of the growers is such that they monopolize the labour on their own property and if the authorities should request five, ten or twelve men to work on a national project, they are often turned down categorically and insulted.

As I have said before, the authorities of these villages are often submissive characters who, far from being independent, cater to the whims of many landowners who, unaware of their duties, find pleasure in converting the sacred privilege of authority into a type of stewardship designed to serve their own private interests.

I am determined to make these people aware of their own dignity so that justice may shelter both the rich grower and the poor proletariat alike, by insisting that everyone be given the respect to which they are entitled.

The wealth of a nation should not be calculated in terms of the fortunes of a handful of individuals but by the greatest number of landowners residing there. Since in my mind labour legislation favours the monopoly of

201

*workers to generate capital for a limited circle, I beleive
it is unfair for the wealthy to deposit vast sums of money
in the* Jefaturas Politicas, *when the others are only
capable of paying wages at the time they request labour.*

*On the other hand, since these deposits satisfy the greed
of the Agricultural Commissions, it is easy to see how
this practice has given way to certain vices which are
detrimental to the interests of the proletariats who, in
short, have been victimized since their names have been
entered on debtor lists, suggesting that they have
received given sums of money, which is often not the
case.*

*The coffee grown by the Indians of Cobán on their own
land goes for the same price on the European market as
that grown by the* ladino, *and if the legislator has
established the* mandamiento law *with an eye to
promoting the development of the country multiplying its
wealth by exploiting its jungles and mountains, then
and undoubtedly I have done my duty by protecting the
Indian, as much involved in agriculture as the
foreigner; after all, a difference in colour does not justify
a difference in principles before the law, which judges
all men as equal.*

*The greed of some growers is such that they are not
content with what the law, nature and the elements
provide. There have been numerous crimes committed
which are not tolerated in a cultured society governed by
democratic laws. For example, when an Indian owns a
piece of fertile land which others want, the first thing
the ambitious person does is to invade that property,
under the pretext of having bought it, and once he is
settled, he declares open war on the neighbours, lets his
cattle trample on their sown fields and subjects them to
forced labour, without the authorities being aware of
what is occuring. Then, after having ousted the original
owner, he proceeds to sell the property which was once
the object of his greed.*

For lack of a census of workers which specifies the exact

> *number of men available for work on the* fincas *and a*
> *census of the* fincas *indicating the number of tenant*
> *farmers residing there, it is impossible to proceed in a*
> *normal and just fashion to accommodate those*
> finqueros *requesting labour. Therefore, I think it is*
> *imperative to conduct such a census."*[27]

Rosendo Santa Cruz, *Jefe Político* and author of the foregoing report, belonged to the Liberal movement which advocated a branch of agricultural development in Guatemala which would recognize the labourer's civil rights, unlike those who pretended not to see the blatant social contrasts in the countryside due to the exploitation of the Indian and *mestizo* population by plantation owners.

> *"The labour problem", wrote a German* finquero *from*
> *Alta Verapaz in 1889, "which affects agriculture directly*
> *and trade indirectly, has improved considerably since*
> *May of 1887. Authorities are enforcing existing*
> *countervagrancy laws in a reasonable fashion The*
> *malaise which existed at the beginning of 1887 has*
> *disappeared entierly. However, the time has not yet come*
> *for making free men of the Indians from these parts or*
> *permitting agriculture to develop exclusively on the basis*
> *of privately contracted labour. Conditions still prevail*
> *which permit the Indian to meet all his needs and those*
> *of his family after no more than 60 days of easy work*
> *and it will be necessary to pressure them to work on the*
> *plantations a part of the remaining 300 days of the year.*
> *Widespread satisfaction among the Indians working on*
> *almost all the plantations, suggests that such pressure is*
> *far from excessive. In particular, there have been no*
> *complaints filed against the Germans living here. On*
> *the contrary, the Indians seem to prefer working for*
> *foreign employers rather than local ones. The truth is,*
> *that if it were entirely up to the Indians, they would not*

---

27. Ibid.

> *work at all. This is exactly what Labour Legislation,*
> *which has been seriously criticized, is trying to avoid.*"[28]

Because many *finqueros* often concealed the exact number of their labourers suitable for recruitment for active military service, or public works, the *Jefe Político* of Alta Verapaz ordered all coffee growers to *"take note of the number of persons inhabiting their property, reporting the names of each one to the respective authority. Those who failed to do so were fined accordingly"*.[29] It was a question of drawing up accurate lists which allowed for the more rational and equitable distribution of the labour force among *finqueros* who requested men, so that no Indian was called on a second time before the entire roster was covered. Santa Cruz tried by *"persuasive"* means, to convince the *finqueros* to use mules and vehicles to transport coffee, in an attempt to stop the use of peasants as beasts of burden. He also prohibited local authorities from providing women for forced labour, as he considered it *"immoral"*.

Acknowledging the labourers' demands, he tried to apply rigurously, those provisions of the Wage Labour Regulations which condemned the abuses perpetrated by the *finqueros*:

> *"Given the frequent and well founded complaints filed*
> *by the tenant farmers during this visit, in which they*
> *accuse their bosses of treating them cruelly and*
> *tyrannically, the authorities were advised to inspect the*
> fincas *where they have heard that such abuse is being*
> *practiced, to terminate the said practice in accordance*
> *with labour regulations and to ensure that the Indians*
> *are not treated as slaves. In the hearings in which the*
> hacendados *or* finqueros *judge the workers employed on*
> *the* fincas, *evidence furnished by the Indians will be*
> *accepted, just as it is from the* ladinos, *for, according to*

---

28. DZA Potsdam, A.A., Nr. 53916, Türkheim to Bismarck, June 1, 1889.
29. A.G.C.A., B1, M.G.J., folder Nr. 28825, Orders issued by the Political Chief of Alta Verapaz for the purpose of supporting agriculture as the only element of national wealth in all the villages of the Department, August 20, 1892.

law, they too are citizens, and only sheer aberration has caused the Indians' testimonies to be rejected, leaving the unfortunate man to be judged entirely defenceless."[30]

Because of complaints brought before the *Jefe Político* by the leaders of the Indian communities, which confirmed that the peasants were only being paid two *reales* a day, which was not even enough *"to meet a man's most basic needs",* the latter ordered that the landowners feed the labourers in their employment:

"The landowner who fails to comply with this order has to pay three reales *for every 25 square* varas *— since corn is being sold at such exhorbitant prices — 12, 18 even 25 cents a pound, and the workers have to buy two, sometimes three* reales *worth a day to feed a single mouth, which means that after a hard day's work, not only is a man incapable of saving anything but has a deficit."[31]*

Municipal authorities were forbidden to accept cash deposits from wealthy *finqueros* which permitted them to monopolize the labour force. It was common for the *finqueros* not to register newborn children on the *fincas,* so as to impede official control of the labour force available to them on their very own property. Santa Cruz ordered local authorities to oblige the *finqueros* to *"comply with this law, on the understanding that if they learn that a* finquero *has violated this law, he will automatically be fined between 5 and 25 pesos".* He also ordered them to build a school on each *finca,* in conformity with the Labour Regulations.

"The Jefatura Política*", stated Santa Cruz in the orders passed on to his men, "is informed that many people who have had the occasion to deal with the Authorities*

---

30. Ibid.
31. Ibid.

> *on matters concerning the laws governing the forced*
> *conscription of labour, were rude and disrespectful, even*
> *insolent; for that reason, an attempt is being made to*
> *put an end to such conduct by punishing the offenders*
> *as prescribed by law; should it be necessary, the charge*
> *shall be investigated and brought before a higher autho-*
> *rity.*"[32]

This marked the first time that a rural authority of Santa Cruz's rank had dealt so harshly with the *finqueros*, whom, in the presence of his superiors, he called *"exploiters of the Indian race", "power hungry", "feudal lords", "slave drivers", "monopolists of lands and men",* even *"criminals".* However, the *Jefe Político's* orders did not have much of an affect as far as forced labour was concerned. The same provision which spared females from having to perform forced labour only stipulated that local authorities not provide the *finqueros* with female labour, *"leaving this task to private initiative".* This was equivalent to the right hand not knowing what the left hand was doing. A provision which exempted the peasant who could provide the *finquero* with two beasts of burden from being subject to forced labour was probably invoked by only a few wealthy Indians, but not the masses. Peasant poverty, on the one hand, and the landowners' unwillingness to incur additional expenses on the other, due to the abundance of cheap labour and Indian labourers with strong backs, dampened any hopes of innovating a system for transporting coffee, particularly on the plantations, and from the plantations to the marketplaces. When German *finqueros* from Alta Verapaz found themselves obliged to give up using peasants as a means of transportation because the greater part of the labour market was cornered by the most powerful foreign landowners, they improved routes in the department in order to speed up the delivery of coffee abroad.

> *"The Indians carry their loads in bundles on their*
> *shoulders",* wrote Richard Sapper, wealthy landowner
> *and German Vice-Consul in Alta Verapaz in 1898 to Dr.*

---

32. ibid.

> _von Voights-Rhetz, German Ambassador in Guatemala,_
> _"and they can handle a quintal, even more. In the past,_
> _they were very useful for transporting coffee. However,_
> _with labour being so scarce on the plantations, this_
> _method is used less frequently and on a smaller scale._
> _Beasts of burden and two-wheeled oxcarts have replaced_
> _them."[33]_

Measures adopted by _Jefe Político_ Santa Cruz were not implemented because he was dismissed shortly after having disc-
losed them. This possibly occurred on the part of influential farmers, those whom he fruitlessly tried to show that the Coffee
Republic was governed by democratic laws which treated the
rich and the poor as equals.

By 1890, most of the coffee plantations had difficulties finding
labour. This came about not only because of the numerous _fin-
cas_ that had been established, as one landowner suggested,[34]
but because free peasants evaded forced conscription and hid
in the mountains when the _finqueros_ came looking for them.
The _Jefe Político_ of Alta Verapaz who replaced Santa Cruz advised the Minister of Development to keep the Indians

> _"from violating this law by using a method which seems_
> _unjust but in his opinion is the only way to resolve the_
> _labour problem, namely detaining the wives of the men_
> _that flee for 2 or 3 days to force them to return to work._
> _With the knowledge that their wives will be detained if_
> _they should go into hiding, they certainly will refrain_
> _from doing so and the problem will be solved."[35]_

Some _finqueros_ seriously considered the introduction of foreign labour, particularly Asian _"coolies"._ This had already been
done in Cuba and other regions in America with plantation economies.[36] Apparently the most advanced sector of agri-

---

33. DZA Potsdam, A.A., No. 53916, R. Sapper to Voigts-Rhetz, July 30, 1898.
34. Ibid., No. 53910, F. Sarg to A.A., September 5, 1890.
35. A.G.C.A., B1, M.G.J., folder No. 14859, from the _Political Chief_ of Alta Verapaz to the M.D., September 20, 1894.
36. DZA Potsdam, A.A., No. 53910, F. Sarg to A.A., September 5, 1890.

cultural entrepreneurs considered the free contracting of men on the labour market the most convenient way of solving the problem of scarce labour on the plantations and the ultimate development of coffee growing. On the other hand, the forced labour system had become a rich source of revenue for authorities delegated the task of supplying workers for the *finqueros*, who continually charged more for this service.

> *"The real affliction of the agrarian sector and the reason for its stagnation is the lack of labour", wrote Richard Sapper to Berlin in 1893. "The future is not very bright; workers are needed more desparately with every passing year. The problem is becoming more acute. The Indian population has not decreased but has become increasingly opposed to working. In theory, the pressure once exerted by the Government to force the Indian population to perform farm work has disappeared. In practice. however, labourers can still be procured in exchange for adequate compensation. In fact, a virtual graft system has been created to secure labour which has not only made coffee production more costly but its demoralizing effect on the workers has made the situation more critical every year. This has caused Guatemala's labour problems and the need for radical change in the means of procuring labour to be reconsidered, following attempts to introduce a foreign labour element. The limited success of this effort meant that it would take a long time for such a procedure to gain ground. Some hundred natives from the Gilbert helped in a very small way to remedy labour shortages. Japanese workers have proved, however, to be quite competent and not any more expensive than local labour."*[37]

---

37. Ibid., F. Sarg to the A.A., September 6, 1893.

The mandamiento in road and railway construction

There is no doubt whatsoever that road improvements, port construction projects, promotion of shipping activities along our coasts and modernization of the means of communication as from 1871 has been of utmost importance to the development of plantation economy and capitalism in Guatemala. The principal contradiction, however, of this immense work consisted in its being a function of foreign capital interests, rather dedicated to extracting largest possible profits from the land and exploiting the people put in disposition by the coffee merchants's State, than to arrange for ways to development and progress. The Liberal leaders, with J. Rufino Barrios and his henchmen in the lead, are to blame for this, since they had not taken into consideration the true interests of the Guatemalan peasantry. At the time when the ambitious infrastructural projects were designed and the State's money spent, the plantation owners' convenience weighed more heavily than the interests of the people. Moreover, according to a foreign diplomat with many years of residence in the country, *"the government grants neither building nor supplies' contracts, or any concession, without first being bribed".*[38]

The documentation that we have managed to compile, permits us to establish that already as early as during the Conservative dictatorship, any infrastructural project serving the interests of the peasantry was receiving their full support. There were strong desires to participate in and contribute to the regional progress among the peasant communities. Any road project planned by the *Consulado de Comercio* could count on collaboration from the peasants, provided they did not detect any hidden intentions from anyone wishing to utilize the community members for his own benefit. It was not unusual to see the sons of the people voluntarily putting smaller sums of money from their own funds towards the purchase of building materials at the authorities' disposal upon presenting themselves to the work leader to begin the work. On the other hand, however, projects that

---

38. DZA Potsdam, A.A., No. 1554, Bergen to Caprivi, April 10, 1891.

involved forced labour on the peasants' part, with the aim to make them into workers, were systematically rejected by them. The Guatemalan peasantry has hated the oppressing State and its representatives for centuries, not only because they were robbed of their land and liberty, but also because the working conditions they were subjected to by the foreigners reduced them to talking animals. This did not change when strangers turned up in their communities demanding them to form *"cuadrillas",* work squads, to carry out road work.

In May 1858, *Principales* of Cuyotenango, Suchitepéquez, complained to Rafael Carrera of having been compelled to form a squad consisting of twenty men to work on *"the road to the sea".* Those responsible for recruiting the peasants had — according to the *Principales* — used such violence that the peasants

> *"were forced to leave without provisions, that they were given no salaries and no tools for the work, and among them were also some poor day labourers, whose families were dependent on their income. They were required to bring choppers, pickaxes and machetes that cost more than they can earn during a week, for in these villages tools are more expensive than in the capital".*[39]

The Cuyotenango *Principales* also referred to an estate owner by the name of Valladares who had lead the gang of henchmen, and that all of them, armed with shotguns, had devoted themselves to terrorizing the community members, setting fire to the houses of those opposed to the recruitment of themselves and their companions, some of the peasants having been taken prisoners in the process. As the accusing peasants saw it, Valladares' secret plan was to seize the common land after he had frightened its natural proprietors away, since he could then claim it deserted. The reason for their protest was, if for nothing else, the desire not to keep silent upon the illegal acts committed by the powerful. *"Even if we complain, we will not be heard",* expressed the community members, *"we are poor and Valladares is rich."*[40]

---

39. A.G.C.A., B1, M.G.J., folder No. 28576, from Principales of Cuyotenango to the President of the Republic, May 22, 1858.
40. Ibid.

The Conservative and Liberal dictatorships gave the opposition against forced labour among the peasants such importance that prisons were built in the regions where road projects were in action. By means of repression and punishment, the State hoped to conquer the peasantry's resistance to work that in many cases meant death. The opposition became stronger as road projects were carried out in regions where humidity and excessive heat predominated, working conditions were abominable and the work itself exhausting. Sons of the _pueblo_ Santa Lucia Cotzumalguapa describe how they were risking their lives when compelled to do maintenance work on the _carretera_ to the port of San José. Of the twentyfive men that made up the first work squad, six had died after having worked a short time, and the rest had fallen gravely ill. Those responsible for the project did not pay the workers' wages on time, nor did they give them anything to eat, but compelled them to _"a persistantly hard work in a lethal climate"._[41]

The road work duty often meant that the peasants could not tend to the fields where they grew their food, and this was another big reason why they refused to be recruited.[42]

While the rich contracted out of the work duty through relief payments, equivalent to one _peso_ per working day, the poor were compelled to work not only the three days prescribed by the Road Contribution Law of 1830, but for as long as they were needed for the road project. However long a peasant had been working, three days were always deducted, being considered obligatory, when it came to counting out the wages for the workers. During the men's absence, women and children endeavored to tend to the fields, although domestic responsibilities often prevented the women from filling the empty space left by their spouses. Later they were forced to put up with hunger and misery.

Towards the end of 1858, many communities in Western Guatemala were compelled to work on the construction of a _carretera_ between Quezaltenango on the South coast, and a place called Patio de Bolas. The community members were told that the

---

41. Ibid., folder No. 28628, dossier No. 229, from the M.G. to the Corregidor of Escuintla, December 1, 1861.
42. Ibid., folder No. 28583, from the Corregidor of Escuintla to the M.G., August 30, 1861.

work would not exceed three months, and they were offered a wage of half a *real* a day, which would enable them to buy food. In March 1861 the project had not yet been finished, and the *corregidor* of Quezaltenango informed his superiors that *"various people have begun to set an example of disobedience"*, and recommended that the workers' wages be raised to one *real* a day, so as to quieten the minds of those reluctant to work.[43]

> *"Since three years we have been working on the* camino carretero *going from the town of Quezaltenango to Patio de Bolas", declared sons of the Ostuncalco* pueblo *in a petition directed to President Carrera. "Tired of continuing said work, as a hundred and sixty men are required every other month; they now raise their voices saying: they have known much disaster in their families, for in order to be obedient, and not absent from work during the week when it is their turn, every husband has to leave his wife and children suffering from starvation. To avoid this, they have had to get into debt, pawning their plots of land and the houses they live in, but since they have had a bad harvest, everybody is expecting a great famine, especially among the poorest Indians."[44]*

The community members asked for *"three years of leave to get over our losses."* The government did not take heed to their request, but instead gave orders to the *corregidor* of Quezaltenango that he pay the peasants one *real* and a half a day and that he should not let them be subjected to longer periods of work, with the intention that the peasants take turns with the road, thus giving them enough time to attend to their crops.[45]

In general, the slow progression of the road construction and improvement work did not solely depend on the structure of the land, even though large rocks and huge trees often were almost impossible to remove; powerful storms also frequently destroy-

---

43. Ibid., folder No. 28586, from the Corregidor of Quezaltenango to the M.G., March 14, 1861.
44. Ibid., from the Principales and the Municipalidad of Ostuncalco to the President of Guatemala, March 8, 1861.
45. Ibid., from the M.G. to the Corregidor of Quezaltenango, March 22, 1861.

ed a month's work in one night. A long winter could turn into
the road worker's worst enemy.The foreman of a _cuadrilla_ constructing a road from Tecpán to Totonicapán, reported on one occasion that the heavy rainfalls had made it impossible to move
forward more than a few meters in three months.[46]

The extension of the road projects made many peasants despa-
ir, and it was not unusual that families living in villages close
to the road construction suddenly disappeared from their homes.
As one government official put it: _"they have gone to look for a
living in some other part of the country"._ The pedlars also left
their communities from time to time to pursue their profession
elsewhere, while other community members died during the
course of the road work. In the end, there were very few left to
work with road construction. This, too, delayed the road projects and meant a heavy burden for the peasants, since those who
stayed had to work not only to fulfill their own obligations, but
also those of the people absent. As a consequence, it was not unusual to see twelwe or thirteen year old children engaged in
moving large rocks with crude tools, or carrying them by means
of a _mecapal_ for several kilometres. With the years, these children, prematurely turned into men, came to intensly detest all
kinds of forced labour. But there were other reasons for the peasants' opposition to the road construction. Some of these reasons had to do with the demands of many _corregidores_ wanting
the peasants not only to lend their working power indefinitely,
but also expected them to use communal funds for purchasing
materials, for paying craftsmen and foremen, henchmen who
were representatives of the Government. The peasants were also
opposed to working with the road construction because of arbitrary measures that hurt their interests; e.g. the petty official
of Huehuetenango who in 1866 required that the peasants paid
him during the entire period that the road construction continued in the region.

> _"The_ Juez Preventivo _is making himself a nuisance
> here",_ complained the peasants of Santa Eulalia to the
> President of the Republic, _"because ever since he arrived_

---

46. Ibid., folder No. 28595, from Fermin Enriquez to the Corregidor of Totonicapán, December 28, 1863.

213

> *in San Pedro Soloma he has said, that we should pay*
> *six* pesos *every month, six* pesos *for every visit; and he*
> *ordered us to work on the church in the place where he*
> *is living, as if we did not have enough trouble in*
> *repairing our own. Also, when the* Señor Juez
> Preventivo *arrives for a visit, we have to support him,*
> *and we have to give him a laying hen for his midday*
> *meal, and another one for his evening meal. He*
> *demands an* almud *of corn, and hay for his mule, and*
> *on top of that a* Señora *servant of the* Señor Juez
> Preventivo *demands eggs, and that we pay the entire*
> *meal. He sends soldiers to every house in search of*
> aguardiente comiteco *but they never find any. And the*
> *soldiers stay here in the village, asking for fire wood*
> *and water and food, and we must do whatever they ask.*
> *If there are any who do not obey the working orders,*
> *they must pay a fine of fifty* pesos. *But,* Señor, *from*
> *whence will we take the fifty* pesos *when we are so*
> *poor?"*[47]

The complaints from the community members lead to an inquiry from superior authorities. In the course of the investigation, it became evident that the *"juez preventivo"* mentioned by the peasants, was the *comisionado politico,* a subordinate of the *corregidor* of Huehuetenango. The *corregidor* asked his subordinate whether the latter really had imposed fines of up to fifty *pesos* on peasants who would not work on the road construction from San Juan Ixcoy to Soloma where the *comisionado* lived.

> *"Yes, it is true", answered the* Comisionado Politico*", in*
> *order to scare them I threatened to impose a fine if they*
> *do not cooperate in a satisfactory way with regard to this*
> *work; however, fines have actually not been imposed*
> *upon them, despite the community members' repeated*
> *lack of fulfilling their duties in obedience to orders.*
> *About their paying six* pesos *a month since my arrival*
> *in Soloma: this disposition is not mine, but comes from*

---

47. Ibid., folder No. 28606, Community of Santa Eulalia to the President of the Republic of Guatemala, June 12, 1866.

_the authority that created the post I am holding. Santa
Eulalia and the other villages in the district pay
according to their circumstances a modest allowance of
thirty_ pesos _monthly, which is the salary of the
undersigned"._[48]

Other injustices towards the peasants that accompanied the
plantation economy's vigorous expansion and the road construction in the Highlands, come to light when we read a protest
presented by inhabitants of Huitán and Cabricán, in the jurisdiction of Quetzaltenango. This protest was directed to President Cerna in the beginning of 1870. The peasants said that
they had been working on roads since 1857 and that the situation was getting increasingly more miserable, since they had
large families with many children but no possibility of providing for them by attending to their crops, _"and now we are
making yet another road, the one from Concepción Chiquirichapa to the Costa Cuca ordered by a foreigner who has established
himself on the Coast, and the other trapicheros_*"._[49] The peasants stated that they were forced to work, lacking even appropriate tools to accomplish the heavy tasks that they were assigned, and that they had to rent tools using the small sums of
money they had set aside for buying food. The road was to be
constructed _"in a jungle full of hills, rocky ground and huge trees",_ conditions that left the workers completely exhausted, and
in addition to the hardships, they were not even paid their wages.
The _comuneros_ requested President Cerna to relieve them from
the new work they had been required by the _corregidor_ to
accomplish.[50]

_"When the minister of the Interior requested an
explanation from the_ corregidor _of Quezaltenango
regarding the_ comuneros' _complaint, he received the
following reply: The people of Huitán and Cabricán are_

---

48. Ibid., from the Comisionado politico of Soloma to the Corregidor of Huehuetenango, June 30, 1866.
* Sugar mill owners.
49. Ibid., folder No. 28627, Communities of Huitán and Cabricán to the resident of Guatemala, January 11, 1870.
50. Ibid.

215

founding their petition on the fact that the work at the Costa Cuca has been ordered by a foreigner who resides there, and by the trapicheros, *and that they have earlier been working on the road leading to Suchitepéquez. This last is true since all people in the province are supposed to engage in the road construction, but when it has been their turn to do said work they have always been unwilling, no matter what the public utility it may have. I would like to emphasize that this is the best time to properly carry out the project, partly because of the season and partly because the Indians of the communities mentioned earlier are not too busy with their ordinary occupations. If one would have to pay both for the labour expended on the road* and *the workers who have hitherto shown no opposition, it would be advisable to suspend the project because there are no economic resources and no alternative method is more feasible than the one presently in operation. Thus the investments made would be lost entirely, due to the groundless opposition of the two communities whose members I have attempted to convince — as I have with others — that the present work would be the last assignation. Not even repair work is expected of them, as opposed to previous years."[51]*

Opposition to forced labour on the projected Costa Cuca road came not only from *"two communities",* according to the *corregidor* of Quezaltenango. There were protests also from members of the San Martin Sacatepéquez community, which is situated on the planned road, to the President of the Republic, complaining that the *jefe politico* was forcing them to build a road that would only benefit the coffee landlords and other agricultural entrepreneurs.

"We, the alcaldes *and other* principales *and community members of San Martin Sacatepéquez village, in the*

---

51. Ibid., from the Corregidor of Quezaltenango to the M.I., February 19, 1870.

*jurisdiction of Quezaltenango province, now relate how
we were sent for by the* corregidor *of Quezaltenango on
the 23rd of January. He demanded that we open a new
road to the Costa Cuca, and those gentlemen who have
come to look and inspect are the* finca *owners on that
coast. The new road is to run through rugged country
with crags and great boulders. It would take at least ten
years, and they want us to level out three hills. The
levelling of one hill takes two years! The* ladinos *who
own* fincas *on this coast want an eight* vara *wide road.
Is it right that the people should be forced to build the
road, risking their lives in an unhealthy climate, while
God only knows how our families should be provided
for? So we appeal again to you* Exmo. Padre Presidente:
*while we gladly would widen the old road of our
forefathers, we cannot, even on pain of death, permit the
construction of this new road. God willing, heed us,*
Exmo. Padre Presidente. *The* señores finqueros *want
us Indians to open a road through a place untouched
since our Lord Jesus Crist created the world; Where
there are such huge trees, and hills full of boulders, and
they want the trees torn up by the roots, and therefore
the community does not want to do the work. The*
señores *who have their* fincas *on the coast want us to
build the road without paying us. This is advantageous
to them since they get a lot of money on the* cafetales.
Exmo. Padre Presidente, *we beg of you: give orders that
we may continue working on the old road; pity your
humble sons; please give orders that this new eight*
leguas   *road shall not be made; working for nothing
and wasting time. We want only justice".*[52]

The road to the Costa Cuca was considered an "absolute nec-
cessity" by the *finqueros*, who lobbied the government to agree

---

* 1 *legua* = 4,000 m
52. Ibid., folder No. 28630, dossier No. 543, from the Alcaldes, Principales y
Comun of San Martin Sacatepéquez to the President of Guatemala, February
10, 1871.

to its opening in March 1866, "concerning the fulfillment of this agreement: the *finqueros* continue to make frequent petitions to the *corregimiento*", as noted by the *corregidor* of Quezaltenango:

> *"Unfortunately some of the Indians under silly pretexts refuse to work on the road project, but there is no reason why they should be exempted in some way or other. To achieve success it would be desired that the Supreme Government itself took measures as regards the Indians, otherwise the project would meet with difficulties".*[53]

On another occasion, the same departmental official stated that in order to bring about the completion of the projected road to the Costa Cuca, he had presented himself before the community members of Concepción Chiquirichapa, the starting point of the project, and that the local authorities assured him of their cooperation in supplying *mandamiento* to carry out the project.

> *"Since all this proved false I deemed it neccessary to punish them",* expounded the corregidor *to the Minister of Interior,* "and therefore I arrested the alcalde *and the* secretario municipal, *since they exerted a major influence on the minds of the people. The day after these measures were taken, however, the Concepción Chiquirichapa* principales *declared that they were now ready to take on the road work on condition that the prisoners were released. Afterwards, they were reluctant to fulfil their promises, so I sent a military patrol to march to Concepción and demand that the community provide* jornaleros *to work on the road mentioned. They insolently refused and tried to incite public rebellion against the military patrol of only thirteen soldiers. The patrol officer, seeing the danger of the situation, managed to capture the rebellious ringleaders and imprisoned them. After what had happened, he would*

---

53. Ibid., from the Corregidor of Quezaltenango to the Minister of the Interior. February 18, 1871.

*of course not release them. Furthermore, the work
demanded of the Concepción inhabitants — who
seemed surprised at these orders — is in accordance
with the law prescribing that all the inhabitants of the
Republic are obliged to work three days a year on road
construction".*[(54)]

The imprisoned Indian authorities, *"from the first to the last",*
expressed clearly to the President why they were opposed to par-
ticipating in the construction of the proposed road project, revealing the true feelings of the people about commercial coffee growing, and the laws of the State:

*"The coffee growers want to open a road from
Quezaltenango to the Costa Cuca and this benefits only
themselves and the Señor who happens to be corregidor
of the province, Licenciado Don José Flamenco, who has
tried to force us all without exception to work in the
opening of the abovementioned road. There are a
thousand reasons why we should refuse to comply with
the arrangements. Firstly, in an agreement between our
ancestors and the authorities of Quezaltenango we were
solemnly promised never to be forced to work on road
constructions in exchange for the water from our
homelands that supplied the public water in
Quezaltenango. Secondly — though we grow corn and
cotton on the Costa Cuca we use only the footpaths,
carrying our pitiful harvest in baskets and have need of
neither carts nor roads. For this simple reason we refuse
to cooperate in working on the road project. As a result,
the corregidor imprisoned our alcalde primero, and put
the secretario in chains, and forced them to work on the
road. Finally we request to be neither forced nor
harassed to partake in the construction of a road of*

---

54. Ibid., folder No. 28630, from the Corregidor of Quezaltenango to M.G., March
4, 1871.

> *which we have no need, and that benefits only the*
> *capitalists of Quezalteango".*[55]

The reluctance of the peasants caused the Conservative authorities to resort to using paroled prisoners to carry out the work. They served their time doing road work instead and were paid one *real* a day, the idea being that the prisoners would feel like free men. There was no lack of people serving time in prison.[56]

Many peasants, having been paid in advance, subsequently to work on the coffee or sugar plantations and could only expect a prison sentence or forced labour if they did not repay their advance. When the peasants were not prepared to pay back the advances, or were caught cheating various *finqueros* at the same time, the least they could expect was being put in jail or sent down to do public work. In March 1871, for instance, the *corregimiento* secretary of Amatitlán wrote to the *alcalde* of one of the communities in the area informing him of complaints regarding

> *"various* jornaleros *who have received payment in*
> *advance but refuse to work despite warnings from the*
> *local authorithy at the* finca *owners' request. The* señor
> corregidor *has already alerted the* alcalde *to take*
> *suitable steps as regards the Governments' edicts, using*
> *the neccessary force to accomplish the task. If the*
> *peasants do not start working after the second warning,*
> *those unwilling may be put in prison for fraud and*
> *subsequently sentenced to a month of public work. In*
> *case these measures will prove ineffective due to*
> *sluggishness on the* alcaldes *part, he will be fined ten*
> pesos *at the landlords' request".*[57]

---

55. Ibid, dossier No. 53, from the Gobernador, Municipalidad and Principales of Concepción Chiquirichapa to the President of Guatemala, March 12, 1871.
56. Ibid., folder No. 28605, from the Corregidor of Amatitlán to the Minister of the Interior, February 7, 1866.
57. Ibid., folder No. 28629, dossier No. 9, from the Secretary of the Corregimiento of Amatitlán to the Alcalde of Santa Inés Petapa, March 17, 1871.

Despite the punishments, however, there were everywhere outbreaks of revolt against the socio-economic and political system of landownership, regardless of which party held government powers- Conservative or Liberal. This shows that the State has always been the Guatemalan peasantry's worst enemy and that of this they had long been aware. In August, 1871, the recently appointed _Jefe Politico_ of Chimaltenango reported a peasant who was inciting his _compañeros_ to disobey the local civilian authorities by neither repairing nor constructing roads, or working on the _ladino_ plantations:

> _"José Maria Coló is persuading the people of his class to disregard the municipal government, holding that they can be as independent as the_ ladinos. _He exhorts them not to engage in road construction. The_ señor corregidor _has seen the resulting neglect; so I warned Coló. The warning was not only for the formation of a union, but also to prevent the Indians from working for the_ ladinos. _If the Indians help out with their corn and wheat crops, our own agricultural ventures will suffer a great setback for lack of workers"._[58]

Also in 1871, the _principales_ of Santa Lucia Cotzumalguapa turned to the _jefe politico_ of Escuintla, complaining that _"the natives refuse to continue their obligatory services"._[59] The continuous transgressions of the law, committed against the peasants, had reached such extremes already in 1872 that the same _fiscal_ of the Government declared that the measures taken in order to force the country people contribute to the material progress of the country _"exceeded the laws of the land"._ The official gave as an example impositions suffered by the _municipalidad_ of Palin in Escuintla in having to do constant maintenance work of the _carretera_ to the port of San José that passed through the _poblado:_

---

58. Ibid., dossier No. 21, Francisco Galván to the Jefe Politico of Chimaltenango, August 9, 1871.
59. Ibid., folder No. 28628, dossier No. 229, from the Gobernador of Santa Lucia Cotzumalguapa to the Jefe Politico of Escuintla, December 1, 1871.

> *"Regrettably, the Indians are obliged to maintain the* calle carretera *passing through their* pueblo *in good repair, but the* fiscal *can not find any law that demands this. As a matter of fact, three days of road maintenance a year is all that can be demanded from any one, be he* Indian *or* ladino, *so other ways of achieving this must be found".*[60]

According to the same *fiscal* it was illegal to force those *jornaleros* not wanting to work for the *finqueros* to accept *habilitaciones*, punishing them with prison and forced labour as *deudores fraudulentos* if they tried to back out of the contract:

> *"The undersigned can find no law authorizing an official to declare someone guilty of felony who is not, punishing him with imprisonment and forced labour. The mere act of asking for money in advance and not paying it back on time, which is something that not only* jornaleros *do, but many other individuals, even the most distinguished of this Republic, is not legally considered fraud, and it is not reasonable to oppress the most needy class of people to such an extent. Neither would it seem a suitable measure to proclaim a law specifically directed towards a certain number of individuals."*[61]

The national State was established by the coffee growers in order to develop agrarian capitalism, unobstructed by obstacles of any kind. Thus land expropriation and forced labour of peasants constituted the main basis of the agrarian entrepreneurs' wealth. Consequently, the legal considerations by the liberal *fiscal* could not keep the *finquero* powerstructure from functioning. In fact, this order could only be hampered, modified and/or destroyed by those subjugated by the State. According to the Indian community members, they had no need for those

---

60. Ibid., folder No. 28606, dossier No. 52, from the Comunidad of Santa Eulalia to the President of Guatemala, June 12, 1866.
61. Ibid.

new *caminos* and *carreteras* that were indispensible to the *finqueros*, as they had a knowledge from immemorial times of how to "get to the place they wanted in the fastest way possible".[62] But the majority of the population, farming individual and common land before the introduction of coffee growing in Guatemala, became more and more overburdened with forced labour on the emerging plantations and on public works from the second part of the 19th Century.

On the *fincas*, besides tasks like the initial clearing away of forest and the properly agricultural work that followed, it was necessary to perform heavy construction works (buildings for the workers, the *finquero's* house, barns, etc.), country roads, and aqueducts for supplying water from nearby rivers to the *beneficios* where it served to keep the coffee processing machines running, later being led back into the waterways. In addition to building all kinds of houses for governmental use, like prisons and military fortifications, so called *compañias de zapadores* were formed. These were engaged in the making of roads, often in unhealthy jungle swamps, or in the *Tierra Fria* regions where old volcanic deposits hindered the progress.

Everywhere the peasants, often ill treated by *ladino* or foreign overseers, suffered humiliating and inhuman working conditions. Officially, the work was for men between eighteen and sixty years of age, but it was not unusual to see children in the *mandamientos* sent to do forced labour on *fincas* and road constructions.

A resident foreign physician, having once met *mandamiento* workers from the Highlands working on the Western Railway comments:

> *"The majority of these two hundred Indians, among which several boys of thirteen and fourteen years could be seen, were intelligent, and some of them had very beautiful heads. They came from Chichicastenango at an altitude of more than 2,000 meters, where the climate*

---

62. Ibid., folder No. 28606, from the Comunidad of Santa Eulalia to the President of Guatemala, June 12, 1866.

> *is cold but healthy, and malaria free. Some of these men*
> *happily chatting away with their mates around the fire,*
> *will possibly never return to their* pueblo *but instead die*
> *from the unbearable work of levelling ground in the*
> *lethal hot and humid climate of Champerico".*[63]

The *jornalero* regulations of 1877 stated that an indebted worker running away from a *finca* would be sentenced to do public works if he, when caught, refused to return to his old employer and did not pay his debt. The close relationship between the State and the *finqueros* was furthermore expressed in the stipulation that advance payment in the form of *habilitación* from a *finquero* to a worker in debt or already employed elsewhere, together with all fines imposed on "authorities, *patrones* or *jornaleros*" who did not follow the regulations, was to go to a so called *"fondo de caminos"*. These stipulations were found again in the *reglamento del servicio de trabajadores agricolas* of 1894. These new regulations, however, stipulated that those who could prove that they were plantation workers were exempted from duty on the *compañias de zapadores*, and also from military service. Others relieved from work duty and military service were land owning peasants, or those paying 15 *pesos* anually, and also literate Indians, ready to abandon their traditions and cultural heritage, thus making themselves into *ladinos*. *"Boletas de camino"* had to be carried by those exempted from the law, and shown on demand to policemen in the *pueblos* or to armed patrols led by *comisionados politicos* and patrolling roads and paths all over the country, asking whoever they met to produce his charter. Everyone who did not have the *"boletas"* (also called *"boletos"*) was arrested on the spot, lead to prison and forced to do public work. Usually, the *boletas* were paid by the owners of plantations whose workers were either tenant farmers or temporary labourers. In this manner the *finqueros* managed to tie to their estates peasants looking for "protection" from *"patrones"* in order to free themselves from the *"servicio de zapadores"*.

The lack of labourers increased competition amongst landow-

63. Otto Stoll: Op. cit., page 419.

ners who, by not paying *boletas,* could retain the workers on the estates. Often a visit to the next *pueblo* could mean arrest as many lower ranking police disregarded the *boletas.* If a certain number of people were wanted to make up a *cuadrilla* anyone, with or without a *boleta,* risked being taken. This practice, though illegal according to the *"ley de trabajadores",*[64] was circumvented by the authorities by appealing to the "patriotic feeling" of those pressed into public work.[65]

Also, the *finqueros* frequently neglected their duty to pay the *boletas* necessary to free their workmen from public road work and/or the charge for their exemption from military service, and other *"contribuciones"* prescribed by State laws. The idea being to blackmail the workers, for if they disobeyed the overseers, rioted or simply refused to work for personal reasons, they were turned over to the law, which entailed back payment of *boleta* dues, fines and, finally, the dreaded forced labour.[66]

The only way of escaping from the forced labour was to flee the country (to Mexico, Belize, Honduras or El Salvador), hide in the mountains or in gullies and ravines; or to choose an almost illegal existence as a fugitive from justice. Sometimes the fleeing peasants did not forget to demonstrate what the *"contribuciones"* had meant to them. Thus, for instance, the *jefe politico* of Petén reported that

> *"despite the fact that the Northern Railway Construction Act, whose collection I have directed with strength and determination, has been well received everywhere, respites having been granted when deemed necessary, and even exemption when vouched for by the alcaldes, there are many ignorant people who, claiming that they have no interest in or obligation to take out a railway option, flee into the English territory to avoid paying. In*

---

64. A.G.C.A., B1, M.D., folder No. 14860, from the Jefe Politico of Sacatepéquez to the M.D., October 14, 1895.
65. Ibid., folder No. 14846, from the Jefe Politico of Suchitepéquez to the M.D., June 9, 1893.
66. Ibid., folder No. 14852, from the Comisionado Politico of Santa Lucia Cotzumalguapa to the M.D., August 31, 1899.

the Indian pueblos, *the peasants on fleeing, impale their unpaid bonds on thorns in the trees...*"[67]

Many of the *cuadrilleros* sent to work on the routes of communication escaped as soon as an opportunity arose, making their capture almost impossible *"for they abandon their homes"*.[68] Those who did not abandon their homes only went there after dark, like thieves in the night.

"As regards the legal obligation to perform work on public roads", reported the jefe político *of Sacatepéquez to the minister of Development in 1895, "in practice there is a difficulty in that many pretend not to be at home when called on, or by spending only the night there. In this manner, the law is rendered powerless, and it is illusory to think that the road projects will get the necessary attention.*
Señor *ministro, I suggest that forceful measures be employed by this* jefatura *and the workshy arrested by the police from their very houses if neccessary, specially those in the* pueblo *of Ciudad Vieja".*[69]

The minister of Development considered that the authorities should abide by the law which allows house arrests only in *"delito"* cases but,

"there are other ways of detaining the offenders. Lack of a "boleto" on demand in the street would lead to immediate arrest and, on booking the offence, a date set for labour duty. Absence on designated day would then entail that they would be wanted for contempt of court..."[70]

---

67. Ibid., M.G.J., No. 28709, from the Jefe politico of Petén to the M.I., April 17, 1884.
68. Ibid., M.F., folder No. 14855, from A. Cordero to M.D., November 28, 1893.
69. Ibid., folder No. 14860, from the Jefe Politico of Sacatepéquez to the M.D., December 12, 1895.
70. Ibid., Note written in the margin of preceding dispatch.

Towards the end of the 19th century the severe lack of workers in forced labour caused the government to restrict the issue of _"boletos"_ to _colonos_ and _campesinos habilitados_ working on plantations.

> _"Every time one tries to supply farm hands for agricultural work", stated the_ Jefe Político _of Alta Verapaz in 1897, "one runs up against various difficulties. The Indians have always shown their reluctance for_ servicio de mandamientos _by running away and hiding in the mountains. The majority are dispersed in the mountains, almost living the lives of nomads; therefore it is very difficult to gather them together. These difficulties apart, the available farm hands not_ habilitados _is very limited. In the months of June and July, when_ boletos _exempting_ jornaleros, colonos _and_ enganchados _from services as_ zapadores, _some Indian landowners who did not have larger coffee or sugar plantations managed to take the_ jefatura _by surprise, getting_ boletas _for their farm hands, though they were in no real need of workmen since their agricultural activities are carried out on a comparatively small scale. The decision to reclaim the_ boletas _issued to Indians for health reasons, even when no disability was apparent, was due to insufficient medical examination at the time of issue. Many seemed well enough to work and reexamination should be carried out before exemption is granted. Keeping these circumstances in mind when trying to reach a harmonious solution to the mentioned difficulties, I have given orders that_ boletas _issued to farm hands working for Indian farmers shall be reclaimed since they can make arrangements of mutual help, as they do not have much work in progress; and that the workers are put at the disposal of the_ finqueros _who, because of the sizeable coffee harvest have a great need of them. This measure has caused annoyance among the Indian farmers, however, and I know that they will travel to the capital with complaints. Since I wish to avoid them_

227

> *surprising the* Señor General Presidente, *I hasten to
> forewarn you of the developments here. There are strong
> reasons for the measures taken, justified by the urgent
> need to protect the general interest of agriculture".*[71]

Provisional abolition of the mandamiento system

The disrepute over the practice of forced labour in Guatemala grew to be such that the Liberal Government of José María Reyna Barrios, Manuel Lisandro Barillas' successor, was obliged to promulgate a decree which abolished it provisonally in 1894. Most of the *finqueros* did not object to this measure, firstly because many of them had already secured the labour they requested in their plantations, but mainly because they knew they could still count on the municipal authorities, as they had in the past, to find the men they required. In fact, during the period of capitalist development in Guatemala, debt slavery was the form of forced labour best suited for preserving the existing economic, political and social structure, and the one which best guaranteed the ruling class overnight wealth. As illustrated by a North American historian, throughout the nineteenth century Latin America's most progressive political leaders *"did not tackle the problem of slavery, because of their close economic and political ties with the landowners".*[72]

> *"The problems presently facing the farm workers in this
> department oblige me to address Your Excellency to seek
> the following advice", wrote the Minister of Development
> to the* Jefe Político *of Quiché in May of 1894: "Most of
> these inhabitants are involved almost exclusively in
> growing corn, beans and wheat, both to meet their
> individual needs and those of others who are so poor
> that they don't have anywhere to plant, and to supply*

71. Ibid., folder No. 14864, from the Jefe Politico of Alta Verapaz to the M.D., November 9, 1897.
72. William Z. Foster, *"Esbozo de una Historia Pol i tica de las Americas".* Havana, 1965, vol. II, p. 175.

neighbouring departments which lack fertile land on which to produce these staples. But now it is difficult to farm these items since the Indians absolutely refuse to accept this type of work, even though they've been offered 4 reales to do work which was only paid 2 reales last year. The reason for their not wanting to accept work is Decree 471 which, as of March 15 of this year, abolished the practice of forced labour which had been authorized by Law to benefit private parties; and since most of the residents, primarily the wives and mothers of the men who have been recruited, have come to the office to demand the return of their men, I take it upon myself to consult with you, Your Excellency, so that you might tell me whether I may meet their requests. Please indicate the number of men I can release, and for how long, should this request be acceptable."[73]

Central authorities addressed other departmental *Jefes Políticos* in a similar fashion. This gives us an idea of the ploys used by the *finqueros* to circumvent the government decree. The *Jefe Político* of Alta Verapaz said that he had stopped supplying men to the landowners after learning of the decree which abolished this practice.

"However, subsequently I have received several requests to supply men to carry loads from one point to another which is the only way of transporting on windy roads. I have not yielded to these requests, and have respected that which is established in the said Decree; but I understand that without assistance from the authorities, the landowners, due to the Indians' reluctance, will not find voluntary labour and accordingly I am addressing you in order to tell me what I ought to do to assist these growers and merchants."[74]

---

73. A.G.C.A., B1, M.F., folder No. 14858, from the *Political Chief* of Quiché to the M.F., May 22, 1894.
74. Ibid., folder No. 14859, from the *Political Chief* of Alta Verapaz to the M.F., March 26, 1894.

The *Jefes Políticos* were advised not to meet the *finqueros* demands, but at the same time they were instructed to ensure that *"(neither) agriculture (nor) trade would suffer the grave consequences of extreme losses"* and not to stop the *habilitadores* working for the landowners from providing the growers covertly with *"men to have coffee plants to be pruned and coffee ripe for picking".*[75] Furthermore, all indebted workers were to be forced to work on the plantations.[76]

In 1895, peasants from the community of Santa María Cauqué refused to work on a *finca* on the Southern Plain, where they had worked for many years and were accused of owing money to the landowner. According to the *Jefe Político* of Escuintla, the peasants had been contracted for 4 years and not even that period of time had lapsed.

> *"All the excuses that these Indians use to get out of these contracts are absolutely false and inaccurate; to get to the bottom of this. I've taken all the reports from this* finca, *in addition to the account books, and there is nothing to suggest that Don Misael Garces is guilty of fraud. In an attempt to safeguard agriculture and keep the labourers from continually breaching their contracts, I have ordered the Indians in question to return to "*Los Cerritos*", until they have settled all their debts..."*[77]

The peasants not only detested forced labour but the forced recruitment conducted by the Government in order to secure labour for public works and roadworks. This service was called the *"servicio de zapadores"*. Because all those workers who were indebted to *finqueros* or who worked on the *fincas* as tenant farmers and paid their dues by working in road construction were exempt from the *"servicio de zapadores",* many *finqueros* took advantage of the peasants natural aversion to this service to make them look like debtors. Thus in direct competition with

---

75. Ibid., folder No. 14862, from the *Political Chief* of Quiché, to the M.F., April 13, 1894.
76. Ibid.
77. Ibid., folder No. 14861, from the Political Chief of Esquintla to the M.D., April 18, 1895.

the Central Government, the landowners managed to secure more labour for their *fincas.*

> *"I am including some information which many shed*
> *light on the fraudulent acts committed by some*
> finqueros, *in an effort to make a mockery of Labour*
> *Regulations and I shall proceed with haste to avoid*
> *fraud in contracts between employers and wage*
> *labourers", wrote the* Jefe Político *of Alta Verapaz in*
> *1894. "Up until now contracts have been made by*
> *employers and tenant farmers for more than fifteen and*
> *thirty* pesos, *to benefit from exceptions referred to in*
> *clauses 1 and 2, Article 32, including in those contracts,*
> *sums which the tenant farmers recognize as monies*
> *owed for rent due on land which they lease on the*
> *respective fincas, to grow basic grains, at the annual*
> *rate of a* peso *for every* cuerda. *These contracts have*
> *been authorized by a notary public, clearly with the aim*
> *of making them more binding; but it is worth noting*
> *that the debts they contract take since the peasants have*
> *not received in cash, as a wage advance, the sums*
> *expressed therein."*[78]

Several other landowners took advantage of the Indians' unwillingness to do their military service or to be recruited for roadworks, in order to request that they be exampted from these duties to tie them to their plantations. By consulting the archives, I have managed to confirm that many tenant farmers who ultimately became perpetual slaves, owed less than 15 *pesos.* This is also true of young men who had wages advanced to them and who were forced, *"en masse",* to surrender to the landowners of the coffee, sugar and banana plantations.[79] The Liberal Government distinguished between medium-scale and large-scale landowners, a distinction based not only on the size of their property but on the capitalist nature of their pursuits.

---

78. Ibid., folder No. 14859, from the Political Chief of Alta Verapaz to the M.D., June 28, 1894.
79. Ibid., folder No. 14860, Entry in the margin by M.F., report forwarded by the Political Chief of Sacatepéquez, September 8, 1895.

On October 8, 1897, faced with pressure from the mediums-cale producers who had problems finding workers due to the way in which the wealthy landowners had cornered the labour market the Central Government sent a memorandum to the *Jefes Políticos* which officially authorized them to restore forced labour *"for the coffee harvest".*

> *"Every time it's a question of supplying men to do farm work",* wrote the Jefe Político *of Alta Verapaz in response to the Government memorandum, "innumerable problems arise. The Indians have always performed forced labour against their will and have sought refuge in the mountains to avoid having to work in this way. Most of them live scattered in the mountains, leading almost nomadic lives; consequently, it's very difficult to gather them together. In addition to these inconveniences, the number of men who are not in debt and are available for work is very low. During the months of June and July, when passes were issued exempting the wage labourers and other men forced to work on the plantations from public works, etc., some Indian landowners without large-scale coffee or sugar cane plantations fooled the Jefatura Política and obtained passes for their men, without really requiring their services since they were not true agricultural entrepreneurs.*
> *An order was issued to collect passes distributed to Indians who were not visibly handicapped, and who had received them because of supposed illnesses. this had occurred because of the unscrupulous physician assigned to examine the Indians. This leads us to imagine that not all bearers of these passes are so deserving, since several Indians, because of their excellent state of health, do not appear incapable of working; they ought to be re-examined to determine whether they are truly worthy of such passes. With all this in mind, and because I would like to reconcile these difficulties, I have ordered that these passes be collected*

*from the young men working for autoctonous
landowners, to accommodate the* finqueros *who really
need assistance for their coffee harvest. This measure
has displeased the native landowners and I've heard
that they are planning to go to the Capital to complain
because of it. In an effort to keep them from doing so, I
am informing you of all this. The very need to protect
agriculture justifies such measures."*[80]

The *Jefe Político* who replaced the Liberal Santa Cruz in Alta
Verapaz was a great admirer of the enterprising spirit of the
foreign *finqueros* who had invaded the region which represented, in his words, *"a veritable test"* of the meaning of *"spirit of
association",* typical of the powerful landowners and of their infinite *"efforts"* to exploit the Indian peasantry.

*"This Department was created a little more than ten
years ago and since then its economic situation has been
developing in a laudable way; this undying enterprising
spirit, the vast number of* fincas *established, the
development of trade, the increase of wealth and general
well-being vouch for this..."*[81]

Just like the large landowners and the agricultural entrepreneurs, the functionary identified totally with capitalist values
and the high rate of profits to be gained from taking full advantage of the optimal conditions available in the country which
made men and land suitable to the cultivation of an export crop
such as coffee, a cash crop on the international market. Clearly
the *Jefe Político* had not considered the fact that in Alta Verapaz there would not be sufficient corn or other foodstuffs to sustain the working population, that the peasantry would grow to
truly enjoy improved living conditions as a result of an appropriate agrarian and economic policy which had objectives other
than that of enriching a minority composed of foreign colonists
and power hungry nationals, and that Guatemala would no lon-

---

80. Ibid., folder No. 14850, from the Political Chief of Alta Verapaz to the M.D.,
November 9, 1897.
81. Ibid., folder No. 14866, from the Political Chief of Alta Verapaz to the M.D.,
January 10, 1898.

ger grow and specialize in a single crop as it had during the colonial period for the sole benefit of an élite of capitalist *finqueros.* This is evident in to following:

> *"Agriculture is the patrimony of the majority of inhabitants in this Department. They are devoted to growing coffee on a large scale and the results are gratifying because this product is doing particularly well on the European market. Because of its superb quality and the significant number of businesses of this nature, Alta Verapaz is flourishing today. The principal nucleus of coffee fincas is in Cobán, Carchá, Senahú, San Cristóbal, Tucurú and Santa Cruz Verapaz... The yields from the coffee fincas, which are being picked at present, promise to be abundant. In order for the growers to be able to harvest the coffee without any difficulty,* the Jefatura *in my charge has ordered the local authorities to procure the necessary help and has forced unwilling labourers to fulfil their responsibilities, punishing those who fail to comply with Regulations. I must make one exception. The men furnished for the growers are not as efficient as we had hoped. This is due to the fact that 1) there are so many wage labourers and* enganchadores; *2) many Indians have paid the fine of fifteen pesos, so as to be exempt from having to perform* servicio de zapadores; *and 3) the number of wage labourers without advances is low. Therefore, since there are few men available, it is impossible to accomodate all the* finqueros, *because this problem is irreconcilable."*[82]

The Indian was an indispensable work object for the *Jefe Político* who had no qualms about subjecting him to brutal slavery in the name of capitalism. His community or individual work in the countryside or in domestic crafts went totally unnoticed. The *Jefe Politico's* reference to the latter confirms this phenomenon.

_____
82. Ibid.

> *"Their crafts are so rudimentary that they are hardly*
> *worthy of mention. The reasons why they have not deve-*
> *loped are particularly complicated. However, it would be*
> *valid to conclude that the absence of any sort of stimu-*
> *lus which produces benefits for the civilization, their*
> *limited needs and the depressed condition in which the*
> *Indian class live, are the principal causes of this stagna-*
> *tion. Life, which is defined as constant movement, lacks*
> *impetus here. There is no such thing as aspirations and*
> *no one has visions of a brighter future".[83]*

Working and living conditions on the *fincas* deteriorated for
the labourers once the entrepreneurs understood and became
aware that many peasants were obliged, by virtue of not wanting to perform public works or do their military service, to commit themselves permanently to the plantations. However, these selfsame working conditions, as abominable as they were, only
alienated the labourers further and impeded the development
of a plantation economy.

> *"The key obstacle to agricultural development is the pro-*
> *blem of securing labour", wrote Richard Sapper in*
> *1898. "The number of Indians living in Alta Verapaz is*
> *quite high (according to the 1893 census, 95,134 persons,*
> *that is 95% of the entire population). But because the*
> *very soil is so rich as to permit them to sustain themsel-*
> *ves quite easily, there is no great need to earn money*
> *from working on the plantations, and accordingly, the*
> *number of permanent labourers is much less than expec-*
> *ted. The people working on the plantations are essential-*
> *ly Indians living on land belonging to the landowner*
> *and who have the right to enjoy the land and the fruits*
> *of that land, to grow their corn and other crops, and to*
> *raise cattle in return for working on the plantation two*
> *to three weeks a month. In some places they earn wages*

83. Ibid.

> *equivalent to 2 to 3* reales *a day, in others as much as 4. Most Indians don't work on the plantations — or do so only occasionally — , but live on their own land or on land belonging to the State, and most of them manage to avoid paying the tribute exacted from them according to law because of the negligence of the municipal authorities. These Indians farm and raise livestock on a small scale and produce small amounts of coffee for sale in Alta Verapaz or the Department of Petén.''*[84]

Another *finquero* and German diplomat from the same period reiterated that the lack of workers on the coffee plantations contributed largely to the *drop in the quantity* of coffee exported in some regions of the country.[85]

> *"On the whole, the last coffee harvest was quite good",* stated the same *finquero referred to above, in 1901, "however, a third of the entire harvest was lost for lack of labourers to pick the coffee.''*[86]

Some entrepreneurs threatened the indebted labourers by transferring their debt to the Government if they fled the plantations or if they refused to perform the arduous tasks they were ordered to carry out. Roadworks or the construction of the railways on the Southern Plain was enough to frighten those most opposed to slaving on the *fincas.* Even those men delegated to secure labour were subject to the same penalty if they were unable to come up with enough men for the *fincas.*[87] But despite all this, the *finqueros* were unable to break the workers resistance to oppression and forced labour. In response to the inhumane treatment and the outrages inflicted on the rural labourers by the agricultural entrepreneurs on the rural labourers, the lat-

---

84. DZA Potsdam, A.A., No. 53906, R. Sapper to Voigts-Rhetz, June 30, 1898.
85. ibid., No. 53910, Schaeffer to Füursten zu Hohenlohe-Schillingsfüurst, October 25, 1897.
86. Ibid., No. 53911, Schaeffer to Füursten zu Hohenlohe-Schillingsfurst, May 1, 1901.
87. A.G.C.A., B1, M.D., folder No. 14861, from the Political Chief of Sololá to the M.F., May 16, 1895.

ter often fled worksites and sought refuge in the mountains, burnt coffee and sugar plantations, slaughtered cattle, and not infrequently, killed farm administrators and even _finqueros._

> _"I have tried to deal with the problems between the workers and the_ finqueros _of this Department as best I can", informed the_ Jefe Político _of Sololá in 1895, "but I haven't had any success with the tenant farmers and day labourers from the finca "Monte Carlo". No sooner do I solve one problem then another one arises concerning the inhumane way in which Herman Span treats his workers. But it's because they refuse to accept the work he gives them, which is normally twice what it ought to be, he jails them, fines them and in short, treats them worse than slaves. And when they seek justice, or call his attention to the matter, he disrespects the authorities, as he believes he is immune to criticism because he is a foreigner."[88]_

"There are so many conflicts between employers and employees every day here", related a rural authority in a note sent to the Minister of Development,

> _"and there are so many complaints and requests for the capture of fraudulent and truant young men, that they take up almost all of the Jefe Político's time, at the expense of other areas of public service which go unattended."[89]_

The conflicts between the _finqueros_ and the workers led to the creation of an _"Agricultural Tribunal"_ designed to resolve the problems on the plantations.[90] The _"Tribunal"_ however served little purpose because the Indians had no political rights whatsoever. This permitted the entrepreneurs, together with the Central Power, to continue their efforts to debilitate and break the rural labourers fighting spirit, but without any success.

This became evident in September of 1896, when the _Jefe Poli-_

---

88. Ibid., from the Political Chief of Sololá to the M.D., February 25, 1895.
89. Ibid.,
90. Ibid.,

tico of San Marcos informed his superiors in the Capital that on several fincas in his jurisdiction the day labourers and the tenant farmers had declared a strike and refused categorically to work if the entrepreneurs did not stop abusing them and instead improve their wages and their living conditions on the coffee plantations.

This case is unprecedented in Guatemala's agrarian history and reflects the existence of a strong sense of libertarianism amongst the peasantry who were subjected to forced labour. This provides evidence of the existence of a tremendous revolutionary potencial and of a capacity for organization, especially considering the early stage of the country's history of agrarian capitalism. The departmental functionary responsible for the report interpreted this episode in Guatemalan history in the same fashion:

> *"Since action of this kind is detrimental to agriculture and because strikes of this nature are not prescribed by law, I ask that you be so kind as to tell me what measures to take so that this situation does not recur, even though the Jefatura has already taken some steps in this direction".[91]*

The Minister's reply was reminiscent of the *"vagos de levita"*[*] or who constituted the liberal bureaucracy of 1871, whom from their ivory towers administered the affairs of the coffee Republic and the interests of the parasitic agrarian bourgeoisie of Guatemala:

> *"Instruct the Jefe Político, when these strikes break out on the fincas in his Department, to verify who in fact is at the bottom of this and punish the guilty party with*

---

91. Ibid., from the Political Chief of San Marcos to the M.D., September 30, 1896.
* On one occasion, more than 200 persons were arrested in Antigua on grounds of vagrancy because they did not carry their worker's notebook. According to the *Jefe Político* they were young rich little daddy's boys without work. The Jefe politico called them "vagos de levita" (vagrants in frock-coats).

one month's imprisonment and the task of having to perform public works".[92]

As we shall see further on, under the finqueros dictatorship *"one month's imprisonment and the task of having to perform public works"* meant the most violent form of death conceivable.

---

92. Ibid., Marginal note entered by the Minister of Development on the report from the Political Chief of San Marcos cited previously

CHAPTER IX

THE DISTRIBUTION OF THE COMMUNAL LAND

The disentailment of the Church's real estate and the conversion of the collective property in hands of the native communities into private property is considered a success of the Liberals — as it is said — real estate was in a state of abandonment, impeding the agricultural development of Guatemala. The *finqueros* thought that the land should be in private hands willing to invest. According to Solís,

> *"there had been many legislations during colonial times and thereafter, in order to facilitate the appropriation of lands by the inhabitants of the country, being the ruling idea of those laws to extinguish the uncultivated lands and give a guarantee to the owners (...) but science and the simple meditation were expressing the need of a radical reform in territorial property. The Economic Society — group from which so many definitely progressionist initiatives came — began to spread ideas which were to lead to said reform. There were private*

241

> *uncultivated lands of a specific extension, which had been acquired with irrefutable owners certificate; there existed so called ad-corpus; others were occupied by people who lacked any document which could prove the legitimacy of possession; the villages had their common public lands and many of them had communal land as well; great portions of land belonged to religious communities, to ecclesiastical institutions, other ones belonged to the native fraternities or to religious festivity foundations. Of all these various ways of owning the land, only one satisfied the needs of agriculture, and it was the property of determined extension, secured with indisputable owners certificate. The other ways of gaining possession put farming in an uncertain position thereby originating distrust from the capital, which tried to buy up real estate for agriculture. The communal land apparently belonged to everyone, but it was actually profited by only a few, and even these few could not cultivate but transitorily, because as perpetual farming was in danger it was not on land whose property was indisputable".[1]*

It was vital for the development of emerging capitalism to break the spine of the political power of the big landowners of colonial origin, particularly that of the Church. The fact that the peasant communities owned the lands most suitable for coffee cultivation, made the greedy coffee growers fix their attention on them.

The Liberals agricultural policy

In spite of the fact that the main conservative leaders had illegally taken possession of vast areas of rural land, the agrarian policy of the conservative government had tried to limit itself to the regulations of the old Laws of Indias, the official sale of

---

1) Ignacio Solís: Op.cit., Vol. III B, pp. 900-901.

land, which the Crown had returned to their former owners — the native peasants — not being permitted. As a result of this, a decree promulgated on January 10, 1852, abolished the resolution of Mariano Gálvez' liberal government, which allowed the alienation of the villages' common public land.[2]

Since then, it was stipulated that — in the case of an uncultivated piece of land being reported — and before executing any of it, the opinion of 3 to 5 impartial witnesses who knew of the reported land and could evaluate it was to be heard. The denunciation had to be done publicly, by placing placards during 9 days on the doors of the Municipality in whose jurisdiction the reported land was situated. Only after no claim was presented and agreement about what had been reported was reached by all the neighbours, the land could be sold or granted for rental in public auction.[3]

This resolution was in force till 1873. The lands which had been granted for rental, though implying perpetual usufruct of them and this usufruct being hereditary and even saleable under the condition of previous municipal consent, were not the property of the beneficiary. This constituted the greatest contradiction of the system of land-holding before the _fingueros_ came to power, and hence their displeasure. They wanted the ownership in order to speculate freely, either by selling the land when it acquired a higher price on the market, or by establishing a _finca_ for export cultivation. On one occassion, already, we have pointed out the forms of property existing in Guatemala before 1871, private property coming first (vast rural property of creoles, of the Church, of small and medium _fingueros_, and of agrarian contractors who wished to extend their lands at the expense of the communal lands); secondly, the property of the village communities; and finally, the State property.[4]

The rising bourgeoisie could very well have appropriated to itself the State lands, and in a progressionist manner, turn them into arable ones. It could also have expropriated the lands of the big conservative landowners and not only those of the Cler-

2) Recopilación de Leyes Agrarias de Guatemala, No. 394.
3) Ibid., No. 391.
4) J.C. Cambranes: "Desarrollo Económico...", p. 50.

gy, then distribute them among the small and medium independent producers. In this case, the bourgeoisie would have played a revolutionary part as well, which corresponded to the second stage of the bourgeoise revolution in Guatemala in the XIX century as, according to Foster,

> *"capitalism has always developed best in regions where the land is well distributed among small growers, and not in the hands of a handful of big landowners:"*[5]

Nevertheless, it was more advantageous and convenient for the *finqueros* to compromise with the old landowners at the expense of the clerical properties, which were soon *"disentailed"* and distributed among them, as well as to appropriate the communal lands. In this way, a new kind of vast rural property appeared, with a markedly capitalist character, which soon extended the production of goods for the external market. The beginning agrarian bourgeoisie found it necessary to become allied with the old conservative oligarchy and foreign capital, in order to be able to face the peasant masses, which it aimed to expropriate.

According to the documents we have gathered, we have verified that the conservative government — in spite of the pressure from the coffee growers — was not interested in having problems with the peasant communities, trying to steal their territorial properties. This was so particularly after their political power was seriously threatened by the guerrilla movement of Serapio Cruz, who was supported by the *finqueros* who would later take over the power. In these circumstances, still in the first half of 1871, the departamental Mayors used to check the "record books" of each Municipality during their periodical visits to the peasant communities, and check the names of the persons to whom land had been granted by emphyteusic rental. They also urged local authorities to collect the annual land-taxes from debtors.

---

5) William Z. Foster: Op.cit., Vol. II, p. 168.
6) A.G.C.A., B1, M.G.J., folder No. 28629, from the Corregidor of Amatitlán to M.G., April 4, 1871.

Many of the debtors refused to pay, pretending that the conservative authorities should recognize their right to the property.[7] It is possible that this refusal to pay — particularly by the medium and big coffee growers — was related to the _"agitation"_ that _"the question of relations between land and capital"_ had caused among the influential _finqueros_ of the Economic Society.

> _"Dr. Mariano Ospina (in several writs), Mr. Marco Aurelio Soto (who was beginning his public career), and other members of the Economic Society, in a brochure about territorial credit, agitated the questions related to the land as a very powerful instrument of production of public richness."_[8]

In spite of all these pressures, the last word of the conservative government was categorical:

> _"There is no common public land which belongs to any private person."_[9]

The agrarian policy of the ruling class changed by the arrival to Power of the Liberals. The ladino growers complained that "the difficulties which we have had to face have not been few, the Indians' local spirit being the main one; they always look suspiciously upon the one who tries to turn the lands they keep abandoned into productive ones."[10]

The _finqueros_ used to make _"advances"_ on communal lands under cultivation since they had succeeded in penetrating the municipal lands thereby extending their possessions, as has been described by Santa Cruz. Therefore, the villagers did not _"look favourably"_ upon the foreign invasion, and accentuated their _"local spirit"._

In a memo sent to Garcia Granados in 1872, the villagers of Santa Lucia Cotzumalguapa complained about the above men-

7) Ibid., folder No. 28629, dossier No. 9, from the Corregidor of Amatitlán to M.G., March 15, 1871.
8) Ignacio Solís: Op.cit., Vol. III B, p. 901.
9) A.G.C.A., B1, M.G.J., folder No. 28629, dossier No. 9, from the Corregidor of Amatitlán to M.G., March 15, 1871.
10). Ibid., folder No. 28631,dossier No. 48, Memorial of Manuel Oliveros and Manuel Pérez to M.G., February 28, 1871.

tioned Political Chief of Escuintla, who had obliged them to rent
the lands they had already cultivated.

> *"These lands"* — *said the villagers* — *"are the main
> riches we the poor have, because all our sown roots are
> in them, "*cacaguatales"*, banana- trees, coffee and other
> fruits and provisions, and even if these products were
> paid for, we are not willing to give them up, because
> even if we are paid in excess for our sown field, what
> they want to pay is of no use to us, because our sown
> fields* — *even two or three plants* — *are a mine to us,
> because money is nothing for the poor, while the sowings
> are perpetual".*[11]

The Political Chief of Escuintla, in rejecting the commoners
note, exposed that:

> *"There is a general tendency in that class to oppose the
> occupation of the land by other people, their main desire
> having always been that of owning a great amount of
> land, even if it were to remain uncultivated, as they
> think they would be damaged if somebody was to take it
> away from them."*[12]

The Provisional President, Miguel Garcia Granados, did not
only not solve the problem that had arisen to the peasants' satisfaction but, profiting by his coming to Power, he took possession of communal lands in Escuintla, which had previously been
usurped by Rafael Carrera. As the victims said:

> *"This land is covered with forests, with plenty of wood
> and other construction materials; it is irrigated by
> various gorges and has irrigated fields, in such a
> suitable way for the desired purpose. It could happen
> that General Garcia Granados opposes its return,
> aducing the right of earlier possession, in which case*

---

11) Ibid., folder No. 28635, Memorial of the community members of Santa Lucía
Cotzumalguapa to the Provisional President of Guatemala, June 18, 1872.
12) Ibid., from the Political Chief of Escuintla to M.G., July 2, 1872.

> *one has to take into consideration that this man has*
> *kept and keeps, without any right or certificate,*
> *properties that have been usurped from a privileged*
> *class, and that he has neither reduced his right in the*
> *due occassion, and from which can be deduced that*
> *attention must not be paid to him for any reason".[13]*

Immediately after the Liberals came to power, it was impossible to carry out the expropriation of the communal lands as the *finqueros* required. The cause for this delay is to be found in the existing contradictions within the winning factions, one of which was very much interested in obtaining political supremacy over the defeated Conservatives — particularly over the Church, instigator and financier of the armed movement that broke out in the East and South of the country in 1871, in opposition to the liberal government — and over its own co-religionists. As we have already pointed out in another publication, the Liberals in power did not constitute a unity of interests and criterion. Besides the personal contradiction existing between Garcia Granados and Barrios for the conciliating attitude that the former adopted before the Conservatives, from the very first moment a struggle began between the two for the leadership of the liberal movement and the control of the administrative apparatus which had recently been conquered. These contradictions were to be partially solved by the expulsion of Miguel Garcia and the predominance of the Western *finqueros'* supremacy, the most agressive liberal fraction and the economically strongest in 1873.[14]

The liberal government, with Barrios as its leader, tried to gain the support of the conservative landowners in the east through political and economical allowances. So — for instance — when on one occasion people without land from the village of

---

13) Ibid., folder No. 28662, from the Municipalidad, Gobernador and Común of the people of Escuintla to M.G., August 11, 1877.
14) Federico Hernádez de León: "El Libro de las Efemérides", Guatemala, 1935, Vol. I, pp. 368-369. The autor gives a list of the members of the Constituent Assembly of 1876, where the names of the Liberals José Francisco Quezada, Martin Barrundia, Lorenzo Montúfar, José Antonio Salazar and Angel María Arroyo stand out among many landlords.

Sanarate appeared, in the North East of the city of Guatemala, and claimed land as common public lands — because they did not possess any — it became known that the whole village lived on a vast rural property which was owned by an old conservative. On the one hand, the government wanted to obtain the support of the peasants in the East in its struggle against the insurrection of the Clergy, giving *"everything that was just to the villages",* but on the other hand, it was not interested in increasing the landowners' uneasiness.

> *"The landowners do not give licences to the peasants in order to allow them to sow", the peasants said, "but subject them to the taxes they impose on them, besides the hiring fee (...); the owners being different in this area, the neighbours are not allowed to get fire-wood or logs for daily use (...) usually when work begins here, we use stubble that the landowners have given us in order to sow, keeping the grains of primary necessity in case of not finding where to sow (...), those who do not fulfil the impositions of the landowners are dismissed without having opportunity to claim their work, even if they have paid the rent fee (...); the inhabitants have to pay separate tax for each field in order to be allowed to sow; on the contrary, they have to leave the land or stubble (...); the landowners fence their properties so that the few waterholes for the cattle existing in the region stay within...*
> *Finally, there are many reasons which lead the people to demand the common public land from the government; that if not listened to, the misery will increase, because the inhabitants do not have any land to devote themselves to agriculture with the certainty of not being moved"*[15]

After confirming that the proprietors in the East possessed

---

15) A.G.C.A., B1, M.G.J., folder No. 28635, from the people of Sanarate to the Provisional President of Guatemala, April 18, 1872.

hundreds of "caballerías" (land measure), the authorities decided to investigate what _"the prudently presumable disposition
of the owners, in the event of an expropriation regarded as of public utility"_ was; and added to the instructions sent to the Political Chief, that

> _"it would be important to get information about whether
> there exist or not any uncultivated lands in this part of
> the Republic; and if that Municipality can find the
> means to indemnify in cash, in case the expropriation is
> estimated as indispensable."[16]_

When the departamental chief replied that the village had
no land at its disposal, and that the only _"remedy which could
be called heroic, was the expropriation which the well-being of the
whole village demanded"[17]_, the Prosecutor recommended the
Government Minister that _"before adopting the painful expedi-
ent the Political Leadership of the Department points out — and
which is in itself rather difficult"_ he should ask to buy

> _"some land from the neighbours of Sanarate, who
> possess too much of it, such as the Morales family, who
> — besides the private ones they have — are the owners
> of the farm called "Los Llanos", which is of more than
> one hundred "caballerías"...[18]_

The latifundia - minifundia binomy

The purchase of land from the big landowners — during the
1870's — and its distribution among the Eastern poor peasants,
was aimed at _"pleasing the sublevated mountain people"[19]_, at
the same time as it supplied the traditional farmers with finan-

---

16) Ibid., from the Government Prosecutor to the Political Chief of Santa Rosa,
May 23, 1872.
17) Ibid., from the Political Chief of Santa Rosa to M.G., June 17, 1872.
18) Ibid., from the Government Prosecutor to M.G., June 19, 1872.
19) Ignacio Solís: Op.cit., Vol. V, p. 1147.

cial resources for their transformation into a new kind of *finqueros*, without making any attempt to modify the interrelation between the big and the small production units. This phenomenon must be fully understood, because the secret of Guatemala's modern agricultural development lies here. The small peasant, usufructuary or owner of a small piece of land for sustenance cultivation, would make up the labour force for the capitalist sector of the agriculture from the second half of the XIX century. It was due to this that the Government did not completely expropriate the big conservative landowners, but just bought part of their lands when the circumstances permitted it. Following this same policy,

> *"the distribution of some uncultivated lands and the acquisition of others which were of private property, in order to grant them to some of the poor villages which — not having common land — lacked that resource to sow"[20]*,

This became a practice became present, not as an act of social justice, but rather as a well meditated plan to institutionally promote the binomial vast mini rural properties in the country, to the big *finqueros* satisfaction. This can be easily understood in the text which J. Rufino Barrios read before the Constituent Assembly in 1876:

> *"... trying to promote the enlargement of this Capital City's population, and simultaneously favouring a considerable number of poor people, I decided on the distribution of small pieces of land of the South-suburbs where a great number of buildings animate those places which were abandoned, without utility to anybody up to now"[21]*

In July 1873, the government proclaimed that the coffee-State was the owner of *"about two thousand "caballerías" on the Cuca Coast, which was the most fertile spot of the Republic"*. Here, fin-

---

20) Ibid.
21) Fragment of the Presidential Message read by J. Rufino Barrios before the Constituent Assembly, September 11, 1876. See Ignacio Solís, Ibid.

cas had already been established, _"without paying the value of the land to the Treasury"_; many others being uncultivated,

> _"because it is ignored that they are uncultivated and due to the delaying procedures which are needed to report them; the Nation being able to use them, with the positive utility agriculture and commerce could attain, once these lands are cultivated by those who require them today"; (as) "giving proportional and equally divided pieces of land to the growers who want them, agriculture — which at the moment is the real richness of the country, will be greatly improved"_.[22]

Replying to the petition of the Political Chief of Quezaltenango — who wanted to grant all those lands for rental — it was declared that _"it was preferable that they be granted in property, and not in emphiteusical rental"_, because _"those who have settled fincas on the Cuca Coast must be favoured, as they are the ones who have made the value of those lands known and have been the first to fight against the difficulties which are related with the foundation of real estate in unknown places"_; a decree was issued and thereby the sale of the lands of the Cuca Coast and El Palmar was decided, without taking into consideration the fact that they were already occupied by the commoners of the region. According to the mentioned decree, it was possible to sell pieces of land of one to five "caballerías" for the price of five hundred pesos each "caballería", payable in annual amounts of one hundred pesos. The fact that the first one hundred pesos must be paid when the purchase application was approved, as well as the fact that the price of the lands was not less than five hundred pesos, eliminated from the very beginning the possibility that a man-without-land became a landowner, and the distribution of the rural land remained among the rich _finqueros_.

> _"Those who own fincas on the above mentioned uncultivated lands"_, the second article of the decree on

---

22) Recopilación de Leyes Agrarias de Guatemala: Op.cit., p. 85.

> *agricultural despoiling read, "will buy their property,*
> *paying two hundred pesos cash for each cultivated*
> *"caballería" and for other uncultivated land, in the*
> *terms of the precedent article".*[23]

This implied that the *finqueros* were allowed to own uncultivated land, which contradicted the affirmation that the solici-
tants would cultivate them *"bringing positive utility to agriculture.*
— An official document proved that the lands of the Cuca Coast
and El Palmar were not uncultivated: on October 30, 1873, the
Political Chief of Quetzaltenango asked where he could get the
funds in order to pay the land-surveyor who was to measure the
lands of the commons of Santa María de Jesús and El Palmar.
The Political Chief was the rich *finquero* Juan Aparicio, who
a little later would become near relative to J. Rufino Barrios,
when he married Francisca Aparicio. According to the *finqueros,* by *"cultivated lands"* one should understand the coffee, sugar-
cane, fodder and cocoa plantations only[24]; thus the landless
were left aside and the agrarian despoiling of the inhabitants
of the Cuca Coast were made official.
*"The Indian community of Santa Lucía Cotzumalguapa beg not
to grant lands for rental, because the natives are being left without enough sowing land which is of their patrimony",* the Political
Chief of Escuintla wrote to the Government Ministry in a note
sent on august 13, 1873; adding that the decision about the selling of *"uncultivated land"* on the Cuca Coast gave rise to agitation and intranquility in the Indian villages.

> *"The landinos try to purchase the lands for their*
> *plantations",* the mentioned *Political Chief of Escuintla*
> *stated, "because they are convinced that richness is*
> *agriculture; the native try to keep them and do not agree*
> *in taking away the lands from the communal dominion,*
> *no matter how great their portions are; and this is the*

---

23) Ibid.
24) Ibid., p. 86.

_cause of the lack of harmony between both classes, and
the consequent displeasure. In Santa Lucía, a great part
of the common public land has been granted to the
ladino class, and what before was uncultivated land has
been transformed into beautiful and productive fincas,
where people can go to work in order to get what they
need... and what is more, there is hope for progress in
this benefical transformation of the Indians..."_[(25)]

The commoners of the South Coast accelerated the cultivation of their lands, thereby trying to avoid the invasion of their
uncultivated lands by strangers. This measure was nevertheless taken too late, because the Central Power, which had already decided the expropriation, decided to _"indemnify those who
had sowings"_ in the most fertile and suitable lands for coffee
cultivation, transporting the peasants to _"other areas"_ of the region, in most of the cases small villages which were near to already productive fincas.[(27)]

_"Many Indians — desperate by the misery — are today wan-
derers because they have nowhere to sow,"_ complained the commoners of San Raymundo, Department of Guatemala, to the President.

_"As a result of our village's Municipality's rental of
around four "caballerías" to Mr. José María Escamilla
and about three to Mrs. Cándida Orrego, besides a
similar quantity to Mrs. Rosa Paredes, we are left
without a hectare of land to cultivate, which is the cause
of the poverty we have been used to for years. We have
survived thanks to the hard work of our harrow, but if
the rentals of the lands which are occupied by Escamilla
and Orrego are extended every seven years — as it
happens now — we will never have anywhere we can
sow maize, kidney bean, and other articles of basic
necessity."_[(28)]

25) A.G.C.A., B1, M.G.J., folder No. 28639, from the Political Chief of Escuintla
to M.G., August 13, 1873.
26) Ibid., from the Municipalidad of Escuintla to the Political Chief of Escuintla, October 19, 1872.
27) Ibid., from the Government Prosecutor to M.G., March 7, 1873.
28) Ibid., from the people of San Raymundo to the Presidente of Guatemala,
November 7, 1873.

Already at the end of 1872, the Political Chief of Sacatepéqu-ez referred to the fact that the areas of his jurisdiction only produced to their municipalities, the amount of four hundred and twenty pesos and four *'reales'* a year, as hiring-fee, "due to having granted the land by emphyteusic rental when the cultivation of cochineal fig-trees started, for a tax of two, three and four *'reales'* each *'cuerda'* (land measure), according to their quality — dry, humid and irrigable — and the established tax not being easily paid, a fact causing serious difficulties in the present poor circumstances caused by the decline of the cochineal. Previously the transfer due right increased the production of the common lands, while it gave the direct dominion owner the faculty of recovering the land which was being transferred to others. However, due to its supression — was consent requested for the sale of said common public land on the following basis and conditions: 1st., those which were granted for two *'reales'* per *'cuerda',* consisting of 637,98 *'cuerdas',* i.e. 102,08 hectares, to be sold at the price of one hundred pesos each hectare; 2nd., those which were sold for three *'reales'* each *'cuerda',* consisting of 536,53 *'cuerdas',* i.e. 83,84 hectares, to be sold at the price of one hundred and fifty pesos; 3rd., those which were sold for four *'reales'* each *'cuerda'* amounting to 120,06, i.e. 19,20 hectares, at two hundred pesos each; and 4th., that all these sales be done by public auction."[29]

Concent was also required for the sale of 8,87 'caballerías' which belonged to the same common public lands,

> *"that under the name of* "El Astillero", *Messrs. Nicolás Larrave, father Maríano Romá, Manuel Quiñones and Pedro Arrechea have — granted for rental — between Ciudad Vieja, Dueñas and Alotenango, paying the insignificant sum of thirty pesos in annual tax. By selling* "El Astillero" *to the present users at five hundred pesos each* 'caballería' — *which they are at the least worth — the total capital produced will be of $*

---

29) Ibid., folder No. 28641, dossier No. 59, from the Political Chief of Sacatepé-quez to M.G., October 10, 1872.

*4.435,00, which added to the half percent, will result in
a premium of $ 266,10."[30]*

In 1874, the commission of Mayors of the Municipality of Antigua, when refering to the sale of common public lands in Sacatepéquez, pointed out that

> *"it is true that today the development of a new branch of
> cultivation, such as coffee is, starts and that during the
> current year this village will produce about twelve
> thousand quintals. But it must be observed that the
> fincas which have produced this quantity are the
> property of a few owners — some neighbours of the
> Capital City among them. As a result of this, the
> benefits are not yet noticeable for the majority of these
> inhabitants, who while hoping for a better future, are
> eagerly dedicated to the transformation of their
> cochineal fig-tree fields into coffee plantations".[31]*

The abolition of the emphyteusical contracts and the shaping
of all the conditions for the capitalist territorial ownership did
not depend — as we have already seen — on an agrarian
reform where it was contemplated that it was the peasant who
had the right to the land. On the contrary a redistribution of
land was investigated, which corresponded to the new conditions of agricultural development, aimed at production for the
external market. From this point of view, it must be clearly stated that the liberal authorities did not favour an agrarian reform
which democratically divided the territorial property, but rather tried to solve the agricultural question according to
their interests, those of a class on the rise, engaged in economic
expansion which would strengthen capital. The reformist liberal project was interesting because it initially — i.e. until 1876
— went along the same bureaucratic path which had been used
by the Conservatives: the Municipalities and the Political Depar-

---

30) Ibid.
31) Ibid., Report of the Municipalidad of Antigua Guatemala to the Political
chief of Sacatepéquez, April 22, 1874.

tamental Headquarters had the faculty of disposing of the communal lands, with the condition of a previous consultation and that consent was given by the government Ministry. The official distribution of the communal lands only established and deepened even more the unequal conditions in the land property structure which had been favoured during the Thirty Years Dictatorship, by granting communal lands for rental to private hands.

The invasion of the communal lands

The landowners had decided, before 1871, to take possession of those communal lands, whose property title-deeds they considered *"old and illegal bits of paper"*[32], and that of the *"informal day-labourers",* peasants who agreed to just do maize-field work, *"from which they neither prospered nor let the growers contribute to public richness"*[33]. In the beginning, the expropriation which had to be accomplished was simulated, as the despoiling of the communal lands on the Cuca Coast awoke a strong feeling of resentment against the liberal government in the peasants, which could at any time turn into a rebellion of great proportions.[34] The policy adopted by the Liberals was that of continuing the accelerated distribution of the emphyteusic rentals, creating, in this way, favourable conditions for a future conversion of all these communal lands which had been rented out to private individuals, into *"national"* uncultivated common lands. *"The President declared on his visit to this Department, his wish that the coffee cultivation be generalized in these villages",* said the Political Chief of Suchitepéquez, in a report which was adressed to the Government Ministry in the middle of 1875.

> *"As I wish, then to fulfil the healthy wish of the President, I have planned to grant some uncultivated*

---

32) Ibid., folder No. 28639, from the Political Chief of Escuintla to M.G., September 17, 1873.
33) Ibid., folder No. 28648, from Gonzalo Calvillo to M.G., January 25, 1875.
34) DZA Potsdam, A.A., No. 52610, Doeding to Bismarck, August 13, 1873.

*land in the village of Samayac for rental that is
certainly suitable for the mentioned objectives. This
measure would not only lead to the development of
agriculture in this part of the Republic, but it would
profit the in the improvement of conditions in the village
of Samayac and that of its estates, always maintaining
the possession of most of the lower land, which is
sufficient for the annual sowings of the natives. Several
persons interested in coffee-cultivation, have already
presented their request to the Headquarter...'*[35]

The *"allowances"* of Barrios' lands led to the mass-invasion
of the communal estates in different parts of the Republic; the
combat groups threatening the peasants and destroying the
maize-fields and those of other nutritional products in to subs-
titute them with coffe-plantations.[36]

The Political Chiefs did not cease to encourage these invasions by different means, pointing out *"the immense portions of
land that some villages possess"*.

*"It is a pity to see such great areas of uncultivated lands
in the hands of the natives, who neither cultivate them
nor let them be cultivated"*, remarked the Political Chief
of Chimaltenango, *"there is no doubt that the
exploitation of these lands would bring the Republic
positive profit. In order to achieve this, it would just be
necessary that the land tax included all parts of the
common public land that exceed the square "legua" (3,5
miles). Among the villages that own big fields, we find
San Martín Jilotepeque, Tecpán, Comalapa, Patzún,
Acatenango, Yepocapa and Chimaltenango. The
prosperous state of the first four are is evident, and due
to the emphyteusic rental of the land the villages do not
need the communal sowing; even the villages of Itzapa*

---

35) A.G.C.A., B1, M.G.J., folder No. 28648, from the Political Chief of Suchitepéquez to M.G.J., May 24, 1875.
36) Ibid., from the Political Chief of Chiquimula to M.G., October 25, 1875.

and Parramos, which possess no more than small areas for the whole community, are in a far better position than that of Acatenango, Yepocapa and Chimaltenango; this due to the same transfers which bring positive profit and the agricultural negotiations".[37]

The Political Chief added in the same report that:

"For some years now, the harvest has been bad in this Department, and the last year it was a little more fruitless not knowing today for what reason, because it has been observed that land which has been well prepared and opportunely attended to did not produce what was expected. Although I believe that, in general, the harvest is not obtained for the lack of convenient work due to the day-labourers laxity. I have no doubt that in so important a matter, the Supreme Government will issue an agrarian law which will put an end to so many misfortunes inflicted on agriculture by the disorder of the day-labourers."[38]

In September 1874, the Political Chief of Huetenango referred to the fact that the Department which was under his administration was featured by a great variety of land, suitable for any kind of cultivation.

"Actually", affirmed the official, "there are animals and fruits from every zone in the Department, construction wood of all kinds and very good results are obtained when cultivating plants as those that require high temperatures, as well as those that require warmth. Thus, maize, kidney beans, wheat, cotton, cocoa, grapes, barley, linseed, potatoes, red pepper (chili), vanilla, sarsaparrilla, coffee of a very superior quality, sugar

---

37) Ibid., folder No. 28650, from the Political Chief of Chimaltenango to M.G., March 10, 1875.
38) Ibid.

cane, juniper (known as "huite"), all sorts of vegetables, fibrous and medicinal plants, palms for weaving and many others which it would take too long to ennumerate are produced. As coffee is the product which is cultivated in the country and the kind produced in the Department is so superior that it could even turn out to be a specialty on the foreign markets. Many measures have been issued in order to establish plant nurseries which the advantageous government Resolution of May 10, 1875 directs, which authorizing the necessary distribution of public funds in order to sow 10 quintals of seed in each Department. Thus when the plant nurseries are ready to be transplanted they can be distributed freer of charge to those persons who cannot obtain them under normal circumstances. These measures have not been totally accomplished as all the funds were assigned to the expenses of the last war. In spite of the advantageous conditions and of the fact that the cultivation of just one of those agricultural products could secure the Department welfare and the future of many families who today live in misery, the neighbours being notably negligent hardly devote themselves to the cultivation of most basic crops such as maize, kidney beans, coffee and sugar cane. They do so but on such a small scale, that the products are not sufficient for the ordinary consumption of the Department itself. Such a pernicious negligence proves two things: one, which is common for the whole Republic, but more pronounced in the Department, is the lack of capital and spirit of enterprise and this cannot be repaired but with the course of time; and the other, is the isolated position of this part of the Republic and the lack of roads for communication with the parts and the main centers of consumption."[39]

39) Ibid., folder No. 28653, from the Political Chief of Huehuetenango to M.G., June 30, 1876.

The collective land property and relative isolation in which the peasants of Huehuetenango found themselves, before the rural landscape was transformed due to capital penetration in the region, was beneficial to the working population. The existing subsistence economy fully satisfied its needs and the misery which the Political Chief saw, was explained by the scarce currency circulation which existed in the Department, as regional products did not count with an infrastructure that would permit their transport to other markets in the country. Nevertheless, for the peasantry the preservation of its status of relative independence and its communal land were more important than the participation in an agrarian development which involved its incorporation to the forced work systems that ruled then and its submission to servitude for the benefit of a few owners who were eager for land and riches. The rural economy transformation which was being accomplished in other regions of Guatmala, thanks to the existance of *"capital and enterprise"*, was not exactly an edifying example for the land-labouring mass, and the authorities pretended not to see this. In a memo adressed to J. Rufino Barrios at this time, the Principal and the community of Escuintla reported that the departamental Political Chief had granted a contractor a piece of land that they used for their subsistence cultivating, after their traditional properties had been granted mainly to persons interested in commercial cultivation.

"Far from us, Mr. President", observed the peasants with dignity and respect, "is the idea to oppose the orders which have been issued by the Superiors and if today we wish to gain the attention of our President, it is for the following reasons: due to the various necessities that Escuintla has had, its neighbours have taken the opportunity to apropriate its land and have limited the area to such an extent that the natives cannot find anywhere for their annual sowings. Stripped of the immense land that is today part of the property of the "San Jorge", "El Chupadero" and other landed property, during the past administration the village's

_properties have been reduced to a limited number which
are part of the other lands that have been granted for
rental in their major part. The common public land has
been reduced to the land-area named "Los Rastrojales",
of about one "caballería", and to twenty one hectares in
the "Cerro de Paja", where Don Antolin Navarro today
pretends to be granted ten. The native community has
not been selfish: it has granted what was left for rental
and on their vast common public lands valuable farms
that produce great sums for the municipal funds are
seen. And if we today come and beg the President to
revoke that order, it is based on the limited land that is
required, which is not more than twenty-one hectares
that would be reduced to eleven if those which are
requested by Navarro were granted..."[40]_

The elimination of the emphiteutic rent

The development of capitalism in the agriculture of
Guatemala needed to eliminate the land-ownership which was
ruled by the regulations that dated from the colonial period,
particularly the emphyteusic granting for rental, which — as
the Liberals used to say — had permitted such big extensions
of land to be distributed among medium and big growers.
However it hindered them, to transfer them freely, and in this
way limited the investments because an official
acknowledgement of the lands "direct dominion" was missing.
The decree 170, of January 8, 1877, considered in the first place,

_"that the emphyteusic granting for rental contract, as for
its ancient origin, as well as for the special conditions
on which it is based, is an institution that is not in
harmony with the economic principles of this epoch.
Thus it is convenient to proceed with the recovery of the
direct dominion of the land that is today owned
following the conditions of the above contract."[41]_

---

40) Ibid., folder No. 28656, from the Gobernador and the people of the Villa of
Escuintla to the President of Guatemala, September 27, 1876.
41) Recopilación de Leyes Agrarias de Guatemala. See Decree No. 170.

What Solís has called the liberal *"land reform"*[42], i.e. the conversion of the communal lands into bourgeois property, through the decree 170, was a change in the property relations in favour of the ladino land-owners and of the finqueros. They were interested in the coffee-plantations which ruined the big mass of commoners, who overnight lost their owners rights, seeing themselves dragged into forced, waged labour and other forms of precapitalistic exploitation.

If the emerging bourgeoisie of Guatemala pretended to be consequent with the reform process in which it had got involved since 1871, it should in the first place, have attacked the personal dependence and the other forms of servitude to which the peasants were submitted by the landlords of colonial origin. However, what was more convenient to their interests as a "class" was to strip the peasantry of its land and establish the bourgeois land-property on this basis. In this way it was allowed, from then on, to sell and purchase lands without any obstacles of any kind to those foreigners who wished to make their debut as coffee-growers. In the case of Alta Verapaz, the sale of lands was promoted which included the peasants who had untill then lived and worked on them, as part of the inventory of the agrarian enterprise under constitution.

> *"As I consider it opportune to give some explanations on decree 170, in which the recovery of the representative value of the direct dominion of the rented land is advised"*, said a circular letter sent from the government Minister to all departamental Political Chiefs, *"the President of the Republic has arranged for me to adress you for this purpose so you, in turn, do the same with the Municipalities of that jurisdiction. It can certainly be easily stated that the mentioned provision is very convenient both for the interests of those who paid annuity and those of the Municipalities. Actually, the favourable redemption that is established will allow the former to dispose of the lands acquiring in this way the*

---

42) Ignacio Solís: Op.cit., Vol. V, p. 1173.

ownership. Moreover, the expiry dates which are fixed to pay the whole redeemable value, allow the persons concerned to accomplish their obligation without any high expense. In order to make the mentioned assertion clearer I shall give some examples as to the three methods of calculating the redeemable capital, according to article nr. 2 of the quoted decree. Supposing that in the case of an allowance made prior to the year 1840, a person who owns land pays twenty pesos in rent: according to the law those twenty pesos are the product of a yearly profit of a sum placed at 5 %, in which case he will have to pay four hundred pesos for the complete redemption of his land.

Yet, if the allowance is made later than the year 1840 and prior to 1860, and the owner pays the same rent of twenty pesos that according to the law is the 8 % annual interest of a sum, it will turn out that the land is worth two hundred and fifty pesos. Now, supposing that the allowance is made later that 1860 and that the person pays the above mentioned annual ground rent, calculating it then as the 10 % yearly interest of a sum, it would result in the land being worth the sum of two hundred pesos. As the entire value, we will act according to article nr. 5, i.e. in six payments one every three months except for the first one which will be due on the last day of next February; which means the total value will be divided in six equal parts. The mentioned redemption then, could not have been done easier and fairer, as it is favourable to the Municipalities as well, because thanks to it they will obtain profit from all their lands and not, as it is today, that many lands are properties which do not pay any rent at all. Also because they will not have to take care of the costly collection of taxes of the land, and thus in this way, instead of receiving a 3 % of the rent, they get a 4 % of the product obtained from the redemption."[43]

---

43) Recopilación de Leyes Agrarias de Guatemala. Circular to the Political Chiefs, January 15, 1877.

Solís points out that:

> *"The land law of 1837 fixed the base price for the
> auctions of uncultivated lands at twelve reales per
> 'caballería'. It frequently happened that the land was
> assigned to the person that had reported it, as a result
> of a lack of competition in the public auction, as poverty
> was so great in the country due to the lack of
> agricultural undertaking at that time In 1877, thanks
> to an incomparably better situation than the previous
> one that the land law could be changed, fixing the value
> of each 'caballería' of national land at fifty pesos and
> frequently on auction at request of the parts interested in
> purchasing them. Cases in which the disputation at the
> auctions increased the prices highly, were not
> strange."[44]*

Land speculation

As is indicated by Ignacio Solís, before the decree on annual
ground rent redemption of January 1877, the adjudication of
the uncultivated lands used to be done on the basis of 12 *Reales*
for each *'caballeria'* but as a Political Chief also said in 1874,
already then *"the value which nowadays the lands have got must
be taken into consideration"*, which meant that in reality the sale
was accomplished after the required lands were appraised by
"intelligent experts", who fixed a price according to the quality
and geographical situation of the lands.[45] In any case, it is
very possible that the purchase price depended above all on the
buyer's generosity towards the expert and the principal
departamental authority.

As from January 1877, the prise of the land varied from region
to region, according to the local conditions and the existing
demand. In the Quiché, for instance, the communal lands which
until February 1877 had still not been sold to private persons,

---

44) Ignacio Solís: Op.cit., Vol. V, p. 1174.
45) A.G.C.A., B1, M.G.J., folder No. 28646, from the Political Chief of Quiché
to M.G., July 10, 1874.

were divided into fields of ten thousand square "varas"(yards), the price being fixed at 2 pesos for each piece of land.[46]

In Sololá, at the same time, a _'caballería'_ could be bought for 86 pesos.[47] On February 24, 1877, the Political Chief of Chimaltenango complained about the fact that there was not a _"fixed rule"_ for the whole country which regulated _"the price of the 'caballería'",_ and that when this was done, the regional characteristic of the departments had to be taken into consideration, _"because the climates are many, the fields are many, and so are the sowings..."_[48] Probably in attention to this demand, the government in the agreement of April 4, 1877, fixed the price of 1 peso each hectare on broken land, 2 pesos on plain land, and 4 pesos on irrigable land.[49]

Stoll, nevertheless, foretells that by 1877, it was not possible to get a _'caballería'_ on the Cuca Coast for less than 500 pesos.[50]

> _"In a place denominated "Chuvá" there is a two_ 'caballería' _area which has no owner",_ a petitioner of _land informed the Political Chief of Quezaltenango, in the middle of 1878, "though the price of 200 pesos for each_ 'caballería' _has been decided by government decree, I am prepared to pay 400 pesos for each_ 'caballería'..."[51]

The Political Chief of Alta Verapaz told his superiors in August 1882 about the degree which speculating in land had reached in our country, a few years after the decree on annual ground rent recovery.

> _"Some people think that by the fact of reporting an uncultivated piece of land and their application being_

46) Ibid., folder No. 28658, from the Political Chief of Quiché to M.G., February 20, 1877.
47) Ibid., from the Political Chief of Sololá to M.G., February 1877.
48) Ibid., folder No. 28659, from the Political Chief of Chimaltenango to M.G., February 24, 1877.
49) Ibid., folder No. 28661, Antonio Colom to M.G., July 7, 1877.
50) Otto Stoll: Op.cit., p. 194.
51) A.G.C.A., B1, M.G.J., folder No. 28667, Rolando Robles to the Political Chief of Quezaltenango, May 7, 1878.

265

registered on file, they already have the right to the land, and sell it to someone else for a certain amount. A woman required a piece of land of 8 'caballerías' in order to breed cattle, and got the land through a resolution of this Ministry 22 months ago; up to now, she has no cattle and there is no possibility of her having it either. At that moment, another person reported the land; an audience was conceded to the first petitioner and she, instead of transacting and exposing some reason, offered the reporting right for sale to several persons. I do not know if she has sold it yet, but it might happen, and there could be other cases like this one..."[52]

In 1887 a foreign *finquero* reported that the land suitable for coffe cultivation were already very few on the Cuca Coast,

"in such a way that a greater expansion of the plantations is not possible, the limit of coffee production being almost reached, with a total harvest of 52.975,135 pounds in 1886."[53]

According to Franz Sarg, important capital investment in real estate had been done in 1889, the value of *"coffee plantations, as well as that of uncultivated lands though suitable for coffee cultivation"* having increased *"enormously, as much as the demand".*[54] In the middle of 1889 Sarg wrote to Bismarck that

"the permanent high prices of coffee has produced a fast and vivid speculation in all the productive districts, and this speculation has brought about more advantages to the plantation owners than to the speculators, who were talked into investing mostly in land purchase, paying excessive prices and then were

---

52) Ibid., folder No. 28690, from the Political Chief of Alta Verapaz to M.G., August 27, 1882.
53) DZA Potsdam, A.A., No. 57917, Boy to A.A., December 15, 1887.
54) Ibid., No. 53910, F. Sarg to Bismarck, May 6, 1889.

*glad of being able to get rid of them without having
made the expected profit, but without having lost
either.*[55]

The same Franz Sarg considered that, in 1893, there still existed good soils in Guatemala, and in sufficient extension to devote
them to coffee cultivation; which *"although being in firm hands,
can be acquired in exchange for corresponding payment".*[56] A
few years later, when the prices of coffee declined on the world
markets, the price of the land also fell. A foreigner maintained
firmly that this price *"has declined almost to ground-level because
of the bad prices of coffee".*[57] The decrease in the price of coffee
ruined many coffee growers who had pawned their future
sowings with foreign tradesmen and great foreign plantation
owners, and this situation was taken advantage of by the latter
in order to get more properties, concentrating more power in
lands and farms.[58]

In 1900, 159 German plantations in Guatemala covered an
area of 5.592,25 *'caballerías'* and the German *finqueros* were cornering more and more land.[59] Monopolizing of land by foreigners began already in the 1870's and not in the period which
followed the 1897 depression, as an author points out. Never-

---

55) Ibid.
56) Ibid., F. Sarg to A.A., September 6, 1893.
57) Ibid., No. 53911, Paul Schaeffer to Fürsten zu Hohenlohe-Schillingsfürst,
August 2, 1899.
58) Guillermo Náñez Falcón: *"Erwin Paul Dieseldorff, German Entrepreneur
in the Alta Verapaz of Guatemala, 1889-1937."* Unpublished disertation. Tulane University, New Orleans: 1970, pp. 50-94. Nánez refers, for instance, that
Dieseldorff acquired more than 100,000 acres of land between 1890 and 1937
(1 caballería = 111,51 acres). The biggest properties were *"Seacté"* (1890), *"Chi-
achal"* (1891), *"Chajcar"* (1893), *"Sepac-Ulpán"* (1893), *"Santa Margarita"* (1894),
"Paijá" (1896), *"Panzal"* and *"El Salto"* (before 1899), *"Raxpec"* (1899), *"Santa
Cecilia"* (1900), *"Cubilgüitz"* and *"Las Amazonas"* (1901), *"Chamcarel"* and
"Sachicagua de Secol" (1902), *"San Diego Yalpemech"* (1903), *"Chichochoc"*
(1904), *"Chicaíć"* (1905), *"Pocolá"* and *"Río Frío"* (1907), *"Sachamach", "Tzi-
majil", "Raxahá"* and *"Chiquijí"* (from 1924, after Dieseldorff came back from
Germany, when World War I finished). In 1964, E.P. Dieseldorff's granddaugh-
ters inherited 314 rural and urban fincas, which covered an undetermined extension.
59) F.C. von Erckert: *"Die wirtschaftlichen Interessen Deutschlands in Guatemala".* In: *"Beiträge zur Kolonialpolitik und Kolonialwirtschaft",* III, Berlin:
1901-1902, p. 226.

theless, already at the beginning of the XX century, the land concentration and speculation among foreginers reached such proportions that Richard Sapper informed the German Chancellery, that the government of Guatemala was doing its very best to control *"the continually increasing German land ownership in the country, by means of the systematical delay of the measurements and entitlements of the lands which are for sales"*.[69]

> *"The documents that the President of the Republic has to sign remain in his study untouched for months and years",* Sapper reported, *"until the person interested in the lands looses his patience and gives up his intentions of acquiring them. It may happen, too, that due to a supposed formal mistake, the period of legal adjudication expires and the solicitant looses his rights."*[61]

The peasant resistence to agrarian expropriation

Land expropriation was not passively accepted by the communities. Already before the decree on the redemption of land granted for rental, the small and medium ladino growers who had succeeded in gaining access to the lands of the native communities, complained about the evident hostility of the village people who, in many cases, prevented them from cultivating the land shares they had rented.

> *"We know the advantages of living in peace with the Indians, in only one family, removing eternal disagreements which bother the authorities so much",* exposed some ladinos who were settled in Santo Tomás Chichicastenango *"but without the land to sow basic grains and unjustly deprived of an unquestionable right, which we legally have to cultivate the previously mentioned lands and thereby satisfy our most essential*

---

60) DZA Potsdam, A.A., No. 53916, Richard Sapper to A.A., July 10, 1901.
61) Ibid.

*needs, we have been obliged to resort to the Political
Chief's protection."*[62]

In March 1877, the ladinos residing in Santo Tomás Chichicastenango bought ten *'caballerías'* which belonged to the communal lands and were uncultivated. Nevertheless, the Indian
peasants prevented them from taking possession of the land,
threatening them with violence, if they did not leave the village.

> *"Nothing can hold back the natives from taking our
> lands from us the ladinos now said, "the sowing period
> is coming and the natives have ploughed our lands to
> sow them themselves, without taking notice of our right
> and throwing us out, leaving our families to face hunger
> and misery, as a consequence of not having anything to
> sow. The ladinos have the same right as the natives to
> used the communal lands, and we do not want to repeat
> that it is neither just nor convenient to tolerate that the
> natives overpower the ladinos, and prevent the latter
> from using the land which is not of private
> property..."*[63]

In 1884, another ladino said that the indian peasants of the
Quiché

> *"oppose every reporting of land shares, arguing that
> these are the village's common public lands, which is
> untrue, because these lands have been uncultivated for
> many years and nobody takes care of them. Besides, Mr.
> Minister, the 8 small 'caballerías of land which I report
> — without any property encumbrance — are
> insignificant in comparison with the immense quantity
> of common public land. I believe my petition to be just
> as well as advantageous to the village itself, because my*

---

62) A.G.C.A., B1, M.G.J., folder No. 28652, dossier No. 21, Julian Alfaro and
companions to the Political Chief of Quiché, May 15, 1875.
63) Ibid., folder No. 28663, Apolonio Pérez and other neighbours of Santo Tomás
Chichicastenango to M.G., March 20, 1877.

> *work will stimulate other neighbours to cultivate that*
> *great extension of land, not in use today...*[64]

The Political Chief of Escuintla considered in 1885 that it was
very difficult to accomplish the distribution of lands in his jurisdiction, because of the tenacity with which the natives defen-
ded the territorial integrity of their communities and proposed
the agrarian despoiling to cease,

> *"because it is most natural to believe that the natives*
> *will not voluntarily consent to being deprived of a piece*
> *of land which they — if not today — could make use*
> *of soon, considering the increase of the agricultural*
> *activity and which will be greater every day."*[65]

Many of the peasant communities adressed the President,
asking for the decree on redemption of the annual ground rent
to be reconsidered.[66]

> *"Our poverty is notorious", some native peasants who*
> *had been deprived of their lands pointed out to the*
> *Government Minister in 1879, "we cannot leave our*
> *work and see our hopes disappear", claiming that "the*
> *fields which have been unfairly expropriated have to be*
> *returned to the natives and the miserable price paid by*
> *the person who now have these lands will be*
> *returned..."*[67]

The rejection of the natives towards the expropriation was
shown, in some cases, by misterious fires that burnt down coffe-
trees, coffee utilities and even the temporary worker's houses.[68] On other occasions, groups of villagers appeared in the

64) Ibid., folder No. 28709, Salomé Mejía to M.G., January 3, 1884.
65) Ibid., folder No. 28722, from the Political Chief of Escuintla to M.G., October 1, 1885.
66) Ibid., folder No. 28723, A. Díaz Durán to M.G., January 23, 1886.
67) Ibid., folder No. 28672, Community members of Chimaltenango to M.G.,
October 7, 1879.
68) Ibid., folder No. 28659, from the Political Chief of San Marcos to M.G., November 23, 1877.

fields, threatening the owners and the entrusted staff of the plantations with "machetes" (cane knives) and sticks.[69]

There are plenty of reports from departamental authorities where the _"lack of public spirit"_ of the peasantry is mentioned; the _"reasonably great difficulty to fight against the stubborn resistance of the Indians"_; the _"rebellious character"_ of the natives, _"that has imprinted their bad social position"_; as well as, and this is the most frequent, _"great problems"_ among the peasants due to the expropriations.[70]

In Every case the central government recommended to behave in a _"prudent way"_ and take care of the complaints and petitions of the dissatisfied commoners _"in the best way possible"_ in order to avoid clashes with those who were taking possession of the communal lands.[71] The opposition to the liberal dictatorships' arbitrarinesses did not confine itself to the countryside. J. Rufino Barrio's dictatorial regime had dealt for many years with imprisonment, whipping and assassination of opposers.

> _"Information that reached me confidentially", said the German General Consul to his Chancellor, on November 5, 1877, "showed signs of a revolt due for the past month or the beginning of the present one. The first of November the plan was revealed to the President, who consequently, made a lot of arrests, trying to discover the guilty persons and the revolution plot by the inhuman flagellation of the suspects. These acts of fierce torture are accomplished daily, partly under the direction of the Chief of the State in his private residence; partly by his bailiffs in the quarters. It is deeply regrettable that the foreign representatives do not have any means at their disposal to make the observation of the general rules concerning the natural rights to be valid and to lead the actual dictator of Guatemala from his continuous_

---

69) Ibid., M.J. Kelly to M.G., October 3, 1877.
70) Ibid., folder No. 28670, José Saborío to M.G., October 7, 1879.
71) Ibid., folder No. 28659, Circular to the Political Chiefs, September 11, 1877.

> *irregular instinctive outbursts towards human behaviour."*[72]

The peasants resistence to the expropriation was curbed by the landlords dictatorship in two ways. On one hand, the military and police barracks on the countryside were reinforced with "militiamen", in order to intimidate and suppress the commoners through the use of force, when the circumstances required it. On the other hand, and this may perhaps have been the most common, the regime devoted itself to distributing to some communities lands that belonged to other ones, in that way involving the different communities in interregional enmities and long judicatory disputes. When the native communities were big and neither the armed forces nor the dividing tactic could be used against them — as in the case of Santa Catarina Ixtahuacán and Nahualá, in Sololá — the dictatorship resorted to more subtle and conciliatory measures, as that of forbidding strangers to purchase land, but demanding that the sons of the village buy them, often at conventional prices, as the aim was to break the union and communitarian spirit of the rural population.[73]

The concessions of land to the communities

J. Rufino Barrios knew Guatemala's countryside quite well not only because of his rural origin and his guerrilla incursions before coming to power, but also because as dictator he used to ride through the whole country (except for the Petén) followed by his officers, protegés bailiffs.

As we have already seen, in 1875 Barrios personally took care of the distribution of communal lands as a first step towards their future expropriation and on condition that the granted lands would be sown with coffee. A circular letter sent to the departamental Political Chiefs instructed them to sow great are-

72) DZA Potsdam, A.A., No. 12436, Bergen to Bülow, November 5, 1877.
73) A.G.C.A., B1, M.G.J., folder No. 28793, from the Political Chief of Sololá to M.G., August 9, 1890.

as of land with coffee which they had to distribute to those who required it.

The decree that declared the communal lands of the Cuca Coast as uncultivated was meant to test the reaction of the native peasantry towards the measure of agricultural redistribution in the country. In order to calm down the communities that had been deprived of their lands, the dictatorship hastened to _"give"_ to the male members of the expropriated village a determined number of _'caballerías'_ in fileds for ther personal sowing.

The measure did not always obtain the peasants approval. The community of El Palmar, for instance, was given 12 _'caballerías'_ which, according to the male members of the village, were _"insufficient to supply all neighbours with the land they needed for their livelihood"._

> _"The village particularly feels", said the inhabitants, "a more urgent need, as there is lack of mountains, which do not exist in the area that has been granted, as this is composed only of cotton lands and fields that have already been tilled."_[74]

Before the protest by El Palmar's peasants, the government saw itself compelled to hand over two more _'caballerías'_ of land to the community, situated on a nearby mountain, where they could obtain fire and construction wood. These forestal resources which were commonly used by the peasants were known as 'astilleros'. "Astilleros", lands for the cattle posture which were provided with water holes and lands to be sown were constantly requested of the government by many impoverished communities, in Los Altos and in the East. On some occasions the petitions received attention and were favourably solved, particularly where the dictatorship had a political interest in appeasing a region, as was the case of many communities in the East, where after 1871 the Conservatives succeeded in maintaining their old influence. It is also possible that the initial redistribution of the communal lands was due to the landowners pressure and the Liberals' development projects.

---

74) Ibid., folder No. 28652, dossier No. 78, Bernardo de León to M.G., July 14, 1875.

The first official despoiling of communitarian lands to cede them to others, occurred in 1873, when Barrios agreed to grant 50 'caballerías' for rental — which belonged to the Chimaltenango community — to the neighbours of the Zaragoza community. Of these lands that had been expropriated, almost ten 'caballerías' were given to some foreign contractors who assumed the compromise to sow vineyards, teach the Zaragoza villagers to breed pultry and 'half-vara long' fish, introduce agricultural machinery, teach the young peasants of the region agricultural techniques and establish a colony of European emigrants. The mentioned contractors did not accomplish any cne of their promises devoting themselves to coffee-cultivation and requiring villagers in concession for their plantations. The lands snatched away from the community of Chimaltenango were, as the expropriated villagers said, the *"flattest and most beautiful"* communal properties *"of the village"*, where the neighbours kept their new seeding.[76]

In September 1874, the Municipality and Principals of Las Dueñas community manifested to President Barrios their needs of cultivable land and their *"current sad situation"*, as a consequence of the earthquake that the 3rd of that month had hit the area. The villagers said to be:

> *"tormented and continuously grieved by the disgraces that threaten us, as we are so close to the source which produced that terrible event. For this same reason, we consider that the land of Cerro del Tigre, the sole common public land we possess has become useless, which was from where we got the livelihood for our families."*

The villagers of Dueñas adressed the President after the Political chief of Sacatepéquez had not sent a memorandum to the superior authorities from them,

> *"With the security that we are adressing the common Father to all the Republic's villages, who enjoys to take*

75) Ibid.
76) Ibid., folder No. 28715, from the Political Chief of Chimaltenango to M.G., September 26, 1885.

*care of and solve everybody's needs". "We, then", said the
peasants, "impelled by necessity to secure the livelihood
for our families and get saved from the risk that
threatens us, of drowning in a flood, ask and beg to be
given common land — which we do not have; referring
to that which lies on the other side of the Guacalate
river, close to our village, known by the name of "del
Valle", property of Doña Jesús Nájera; the "Llano de
Alotenango" which Don Nicolás has by emphyteusic
allowance and a hundred hectares of Don Pedro
Arrechea's property, at the foot of the Agua volcano,
known by the name of Montanez...[77]*

The peasants requested the lands which, a few years earlier,
had almost been sold by the Municipal corporation of Antigua,
probably without consulting the real owners.

*"In the trouble which we find ourselves", referred the
peasants of Dueñas to the President, "we have not been
allowed to take out from the fields the construction tools
for the building of the provisional houses which serve as
municipality, church and convent; we are demanded
half a real for each load of wood or anything else and
this is a burden for the village. Therefore, we ask and
beg the President to be kind enough to act according
with our requests, taking into consideration that it is the
right time for the preparation of the land for the sowing
of basic grains, scarcity of which threatens us for the
year to come. What we implore is a favour and what we
ask for is justice."[78]*

The Municipality of Antigua received instructions from the
Ministry of Interior about

"giving the unhappy neighbours of the ruined village of

---

77) Ibid., folder No. 28646, Municipalidad and Principales of Dueñas to the President of Guatemala, September 21, 1874.
78) Ibid.

Dueñas the possible help they so much need,
endeavouring to move the village to the "Llano del
Astillero", and try to obtain by every possible means the
present owners consent."[79]

The Government arranged for the community of Dueñas to receive the lands for rental. Nevertheless, the Municipality of Antigua, whose members were ladino owners, arranged to protect its neighbours' interests against the peasants request:

"At the moment this land belongs to Don Nicolás Larra-
ve", replied the Municipality to the Political Chief of
Sacatepéquez, "to whom it has been given in emphyteu-
sic rental. He is, therefore, in this concept the owner of
this useful dominion he has possessed as up till now,
punctually paying the yearly rent of thirty pesos that,
since the time of the allowance had been fixed for the
nine 'caballerías' of which this land consists. For this
reason, the Municipality cannot dispose of it as it would
like, in order to grant them land to attain the objective
they are requested. The removal of the owner, whatever
the reason might be, only seems to be possible by com-
mission of the Supreme Government."[80]

Under the pressure of the peasants who refused to reconstruct their houses, destroyed by the earthquake, *"waiting for what the Supreme Government will decide, because they may incur in useless expenses that may have to be abandoned"*[81], the Political Chief had an interview with Larrave, who in exchange for the "Llano del Astillero" asked for other land of the same extension and fertility as indemnification.[82]

---

79) Ibid., from the Minister of Interior to the Political Chief of Šacatepéquez, November 13, 1874.
80) Ibid., Municipalidad of Antigua Guatemala to the Political Chief of Sacatepéquez, November 13, 1874.
81) Pablo Cancinos to the Political Chief of Sacatepéquez, November 10, 1874.
82) Ibid., from the Political Chief of Sacatepéquez to M.G., November 17, 1874.

*"For the village of Dueñas"; wrote the Political Chief of
Sacatepéquez to the Minister of Interior, in December
1874, "which has been reduced to a regrettable state by
the earthquake of September 3rd, one of the most urgent
needs was the lack of land to sow on, as the "Cerro del
Tigre" had been spoiled because of the deep cracks in it.
In order to restore the common land it requested the
allowance of the land of El Astillero, El Valle and
Montanez, all private properties, free from the action
that is proposed. In order to issue the report that has
been requested of me, I inspected the mentioned village
and found the church, the convent, the municipality,
schools and all tile houses and several straw huts,
completely destroyed. The most terrible loss was the
aqueduct which gave drinking water to the population;
they are now left without this element and without any
hope of recovering it. That water came from the
Calderas hills by cement canals from "La Estancia",
which is a quarter of a 'legua' away, and from there it
was carried through pipelines to the public fountains
and several village houses. A great part of the arcade
fell with the earthquake, the water spread out at a great
distance, and the village was left without any water and
depended on that of the Portal river which was
unhealthy and difficult to carry.*

*The earth tremors are constant and keep the inhabitants
continually worried and make rebuilding impossible,
even if sufficient pecuniary resources were available of
which they really lack. Being aware of this situation
and studying a way to solve it, as the ancient hill "El
Tigre" is the origin of the tremors, and the strength of
them is not foreseeable, I thought it necessary for the
village to move. The "Llano del Astillero", which is
situated by Ciudad Vieja towards the Southern part, at
the border of Escuintla road, half a 'legua' away and
composed of four 'caballerías', appeared to me as the
most suitable place for the village, far away from that*

277

*danger and on the straight road to Escuintla with
which trade relations are carried on, the same relations
as with Ciudad Vieja, having drinking water at a few
blocks distance and the possibility of carrying it.
The inhabitants of Dueñas are peaceful, industrious,tidy,
devoted to planting and sowing and these qualities
should form a good-looking population and bring
comfort to them without preventing the right to cultivate
their lands in Dueñas. This sole suggestion, with the
suitable explanation to those neighbours, was generally
accepted with affability. Some of them were unwilling to
move even though they were convinced of the dangers,
showing attachment to this threatening place, but as
they are only a few, it was fair to satisfy their wishes. I
only had to get the land of "Llano del Astillero" and
asked the Municipality of Antigua, owner of the direct
dominion, who knows the needs of the village, and is
prepared to solve them. He stated that they did not have
anything against its allotment, but for Don Nicolás
Larrave who owned it in emphyteusic rental and who
said that he did not have anything against ceding the
uncultivated part of the Astillero land emphyteusically
on condition that he got an equal area in any other spot
as compensation. As regards the uncultivated land he
had mentioned and which had been reported at the
Fuego volcano heights that is almost inaccessible, the
sowing would cause great floods as experience has
shown, and I suppose it would be useless and
pernicious for them. I am informed by several persons
that near the common land of Alotenango there is an
uncultivated area where the village of Aguatepeque was
earlier situated — which bears this name — and
which after the necessary explanations could be divided
between the practically contiguous villages of Ciudad
Vieja and Dueñas, in order to satisfy the needs of both.
In this way the calamituous situation of the latter
village could be improved. From the above I gather that*

> *the moving of the village of Dueñas to the place*
> *indicated is necessary and useful because it saves it*
> *from danger and it will enjoy water, lands, position and*
> *climate which will make its condition favourable. It can*
> *be said the land of El Astillero, which is rather large,*
> *has been granted."*[83]

The land tenancy system and the complexity of the sate bure-aucratic apparatus which the problem of the community of Due-ñas reveals, becomes even more complicated if we add that Nico-lás Larrave, a rich neighbour of La Antigua, had sublet the lands of El Astillero to the community of Alotenango, though he had declared the contrary.[84] Larrave, and other influential ladinos of Antigua, took advantage of the improvement of cochineal cul-tivation in the region, receiving in emphyteusic rental commu-nal lands close to the colonial city, part of which he sublet in small exploitation unities to other neighbours of Antigua and commoners of Alotenango. When he got the rent in agricultu-ral products, he sold them. In this way it is possible to find dif-ferent forms of soil exploitation and of land rental in the period previous to the expansion of coffee cultivation in central Gua-temala.

The socioeconomic and political structure which existed in our country during the 2nd. half of the nineteenth century, favou-red continued peasant exploitation by the parasitic colonial oli-garchy, enriched by the new people in power in 1871. The pea-sants — in their struggle for the land and their survival — were more the victims of the ruling class greed than of the natu-ral catastrophes.

The poverty situation and lack of land of the peasantry, which grew worse by the increasing monopolization of land by the *fin-queros*, obliged the liberal government to make some conces-

---

83) Ibid., from the Political Chief of Sacatepéquez to M.G., December 15, 1874.
84) Ibid., Simeón Azurdia to the Political Chief of Sacatepéquez, September 21, 1874.

sions, which in most cases were presented as *"gifts* from *"the common Father of all the people",* consisting of land shares which had been snatched from communities or from rich owners who did not make use of them. The demagogy of J. Rufino Barrios' dictatorship reached such a degree that the words *"Freedom and Reform"* were used as emblem, these slogans were used by the Liberals in their attempts to preserve the internal order and secure the labour they needed for the coffee farms.

In the beginning of 1874, Barrios gave instructions to the Political Chief of Sololá to deprive the community of San Lucas Tolimán of one hundred *'caballerías'* which were to be distributed among the neighbours of Sololá *"who aimed to grow coffee or sugar cane",*[85] and in October of the same year the dictator made the rich *finquero* Ernesto Klee a *'caballería'* to be distributed among the members of a community, whose lands were insufficient to satisfy their needs of food and cultivation. This was the way in which the régime used to show a supposed interest in the peasants' future, at the same time not hesitating in robbing those same peasants which it pretended to be protecting, of hundreds of *'caballerías'* of good land in order to distribute them among the coffee impresarios. This was the real meaning of their *"freedom"* and their *"reform".*

Each time a community was expropriated, any opposition to the robbery was silenced by coercion and violence. Nevertheless, the owners' lands were never intervened without their consent, and in most cases they got a high compensation. In this way, the régime showed that it was a *finqueros* dictatorship, classist, and not a one-man's. J. Rufino Barrios was only the head of the dictatorship, the dictator on duty; the foreign and ladino agricultural contractors were behind him.

> *"In conformity with the President's wishes, I presented myself at eight o'clock in the morning at the place where the measurement of the land the government bought*

---

85) Ibid., folder No. 28643, from the Political Chief of Sololá to M.G., February 5, 1874.

_from Mr. Ernesto Klee was going to take place. This
would increase the common public land of the
"Concepción Las Lomas village, the landsurveyor
officially informed his superiors. "And since the two
neighbouring villages "Concepción" and "Ciudad
Vieja" were called yesterday, I believed I would meet
them there. But that was not the case, because the
village of "Concepción Las Lomas" did not present itself
until ten o'clock in the morning, telling me that they
were not satisfied with the 'caballerías" of land, that
they protested and would protest against the measuring
I was going to do. Although it was true that the ditch
where we were, was the meridional limit of Mr. Klee's
lands and the lands of "Concepción" were the
septentrional one, this village was, notwithstanding,
already the owner of the land which now is being
measured. The President of the Republic had given
them all that part of Mr. Klee's lands as a gift, even the
ditch which is the limit of his sugar-cane fields; and
that for this same reason, they said that they would be
satisfied with the expressed 'caballerías", if it would be
from the ditch by the sugar-cane field to the North.
However they would protest against any other
measurement. I explained to them that the Agreement of
the Government pointed out the place where a
'caballerías" of land was to be segregated; that,
according to their pretensions, the land they bought
would include not only the sugar-cane field and offices
of the sugar mills, but the main houses of the farm too,
and that for this reason it was not possible for me or the
Government to take into consideration such a reckless
pretension. In spite of everything, they insisted on
protesting against what had been decided by the
Government, repeating that the President of the
Republic had given them as a gift all Mr. Klee's fields
which were situated between the limit of their common
public land and the sugar-cane fields of that farm. Thus_

281

> *they protested as they did, against every measurements*
> *done on those lands, which were theirs according to the*
> *President. As I understood it would be worthless to try*
> *to do the measuring which had been decided by the*
> *Government, and that only the Government could decide*
> *what is convenient for the tranquility of that village and*
> *respecting Mr. Klee's property, I have returned today*
> *from that place at half past eleven, in order to inform*
> *the Government about what has happened..."*[86]

Mr. Klee's inclination — the great old exporter Carl Friedrich Rudolf's son — to consent to the acquisition by some villagers of a *'caballería"* of his land, and possibly a little more, was due to one reason: Klee was interested in the concession by the Government of one hundred *'caballerías'* which belonged to the community of Pochuta, in Chimaltenango, which were considered of optimal quality for coffee cultivation.[87]

> *"I have pointed out to the natives the improvements the*
> *population will obtain", said the Political Chief of*
> *Chimaltenango to the Minister of Interior concerning*
> *Mr. Klee's petition. "The convenience and other*
> *favourable circumstances that the emphyteusic rental*
> *bring with them ought to be understood. They should*
> *know that two hundred or more 'caballerías' which are*
> *uncultivated today do not bring them any good."*[88]

The Minister's answer was to order the carrying through of the communal petitioners file,

> *"according to the law existing on the subject and that*
> *the land shares are to be of one to two 'caballerías', and*
> *that if the persons who get them do not make the plant*

---

86) Ibid., José B. Vasconcelos to M.G., November 23, 1874.
87) Ibid., folder No. 28647, from the Political Chief of Chimaltenango to M.G., October 29, 1875.
88) Ibid.

> *nursery during the first year and do not cultivate*
> *during the second, they will lose the right to those*
> *lands."*[89]

The official statement granting *"one to two caballerías"* to each petitioner was a formula aimed at concealing the concentration of land into a few hads. Actually, any impresario could get hundreds of *'caballerías'* just by bribing the authorities, or gaining the favour of the dictator on duty. In December 1875, more than sixty *'caballerías'* of land in the community of Pochuta had been distributed, and as the government revealed: *"the measuring and distribution of the rest can continue..."*[90]

In 1879, when the Political Chief of Chimaltenango referred to the practice of redemption of the annual ground rent in his jurisdiction, he exposed the dissatisfaction which existed among the Chimaltenango population owing to the fifty *'caballerías'* they had lost when the Government supposedly granted them to the community of Zaragoza, whose inhabitants, according to the Political Chief, had not yet begun to cultivate them.

> *"In Chimaltenango there is not enough land to grant, to*
> *those who eagerly request it daily and who do not own a*
> *foot of land",* the previously mentioned Political Chief
> *protested in his note to the Ministry of Interior. "The*
> *natives of this City applied to the President in order to*
> *ask for twenty* 'caballerías' *of the ones granted to the*
> *Zaragoza people. I think that ten* 'caballerías' *would be*
> *enough for the number of inhabitants of Zaragoza and*
> *their indolence; forty could be taken from them,*
> *including those of the natives, in order to distribute them*
> *here, with land shares no bigger than one* 'caballería',
> *and with their produce, create a special fund for the*
> *necessity expenses of the village. Those who have been*
> *favoured by this donation have not been able to profit on*

---

89) Ibid., from the Minister of Interior to the Political Chief of Chimaltenango, November 3, 1875.
90) Ibid., December 17, 1875.

> *this concession in any way, neither in general nor in*
> *particular. They are indolent people by nature, and*
> *many of them make a living on what is not theirs, in*
> *such a way that the land-shares remain uncultivated or*
> *in the power of those who have been favoured by the*
> *concession. While in Chimaltenango, agriculture will*
> *not only be improved, as many of those who today lack*
> *land will get it, but its funds will be increased and they*
> *will obtain improvements that they will*
> *acknowledge..."*[91]

The best way for the favoured villagers to "show gratitude" to the Government for the land donation, was to voluntarily enlist in the Army. These soldiers were faithful to, and firm defenders of the system. In 1878, for instance, the community of San José Nacahuil, in the Department of Guatemala, received twelve *'caballerías'* which belonged to the community of San Antonio Las Flores. Many of those who had been favoured became militia men, and were later used as riot-militia against the unsatisfied and rebellious peasants. In fact, the rebel communities were generally deprived of their lands in order to favour the rival neighbouring communities.

> *"We were the victims of a lamentable rivalry", said a*
> *spokesman for the inhabitants of San José Nacahuil in*
> *a memo adressed to the Government Minister soon after*
> *having received the mentioned twelve* 'caballerías'
> *which belonged to San Antonio Las Flores, "plundered,*
> *whipped and ill-treated in the most cruel way... the*
> *independence we enjoy today makes us happy..."*[92]

A rural authority of that period pointed out the hostility which existed between various communities, owing to that some of them had better cultivating lands, plenty of water, or were rich

---

91) Ibid., folder No. 28670, from the Political Chief of Chimaltenango to M.G., October 27, 1879.
92) Ibid., folder No. 28666, Manuel Reyes to M.G., February 21, 1878.

communities thanks to the industrious character of their inhabitants. The Political Chief of Guatemala complained about the lack of harmony between the communities in his jurisdiction, and believed that the most convenient way to put an end to this rivalry was by _"the incorporation"_ of the smaller communities into the bigger villages.

> _"The real cause of the hostility of San José Nacahuil towards San Antonio Las Flores is — in my opinion — "_, said the mentioned Political Chief of Guatemala, _"the fact that there have been attempts to actually separate these two, by nature united, villages. One has high lands, suitable for maize, and the other has low lands, from which they can take advantage exploiting some other industries. Consequently some will be eager to profit on the fruitful lands to sow maize, and others will be eager to profit on the advantages which the low lands offer..."_[93]

"The free concessions of public common lands which General Barrios has granted have caused quite a lot of animation in the villages", the official sources of the time said,[94] without mentioning — of course — that the villages which had been plundered did not have any reason to celebrate. Still at present, almost 100 years after J. Rufino Barrios' death, the neighbours of San Pedro Sacatepéquez, San Marcos, cannot stand hearing the old tyrant's name, and are very proud of the fact that the central park of the village is one of the few in Guatemala which is not adorned with his bronze statue. Each time a bust of Barrios has been place in the park, anonymous hands have pulled it down: the male members of the village have not forgotten that Barrios _"granted"_ another community 80 'caballerías' which belonged to them, and that he tried to change their Indian nature by decree.

On some occassions, Barrios' generosity reached the extreme of depriving three communities from their lands, in order to

---

93) Ibid., from the Political Chief of Guatemala to M.G., February 22, 1878.
94) Ibid., folder No. 28719, Gregorio Romero to M.G., October 6, 1885.

donate them to one distant community. This was the case when
he expropriated the commons of Pamaxán in the communities
of San Pedro La Laguna, San Juan La Laguna and Santiago
Atitlán, in order to grant them to the Municipality of Totonicapán; this land *formed* — as an official of Sololá would sadly say
afterwards — *a unity in the Southern part of this Department*".[95] There exist documents which tell about peasants
"who have been thrown out from their huts", about abuses which
were committed by intruders to whom the liberal authorities
have *"granted"* lands which *"since time immemorial were the exclusive property of the inhabitants of this village, through legal purchase from the King of Spain, as it stand in the titles in force";*
and the occupation of communal lands under cultivation by
strangers. Barrios' reputation of being generous with what was
not his was so well known, that when visiting a village, more
than one asked him for a piece of land, taking the risk of being
beaten in public if the tyrant was not in a good mood. Barrios
on many occasions wrote a note on the spot, considered as an
"indisputable" title-deed. All the gifts and land donations granted by Barrios, were officially acknowledged by the governors
who succeeded him in the Presidential post. Not at all strange,
if one considered that they too had been favoured by the decea-
sed dictator.

> *"Considering",* said the decree nr. 352, issued by
> *Manuel Lisandro Barillas, Barrios successor, on
> September 19, 1885, "that badly disposed persons are
> spreading rumours in some of the villages that the
> present administration aims at depriving the neighbours
> of public lands or commons acquired thanks to the
> concessions done by General J. Rufino Barrios; that
> though the formalities of the legislation in force for these
> concessions have not been carried out, they have
> produced benefical results in favour of the poor class;
> that, besides, the present owners have cultivated the*

95) Ibid., folder No. 28670, Francisco Alfaro to M.G., November 28, 1879.

*land-shares and have built living quarters and that the
present administration aims at giving the same
protection to the underprivileged and wishes to
transform them into owners. Thus they will have the
absolute security that they will never be hindered or
bothered at all in the possession and free disposal of
what they have got. All the free concessions of public
lands, commons or communal land which have been
granted by General Barrios, are acknowledged, being in
favour of private persons of collectively, or benefitial to
municipalities, villages or valleys."[96]*

In spite of the attempt to assign social contents to the land
concessions made by J. Rufino Barrios, it is not very difficult
to understand the political objective that the liberal authorities were striving for. Even after the tyrant's death, militia men
from the community of Olintepeque, Quetzaltenango, requested six *'caballerías'* from the common public lands of the community of San Andrés Xecul, as a reward for having participated in the campaign for Central American Unity in February
1885, where Barrios lost his life. The attention paid to this kind
of petitions meant more than the simple *"protection of the underprivileged"* as the Liberals pretended to make believe.[97]
Barrios' passion for coffee cultivation could make him — as happened more than once — grant land *"on condition that they be
sown with coffee"*. This used to happen particularly when the
places were suitable for coffee cultivation but too mountainous
for an impresario to transform them into cultivable lands.
Nevertheless, after the peasants who had been favoured by the
donations had cleared the mountain, the foreign speculators and
impresarios made their offers for the already prepared shares
to incorporate them to the plantation economy. We have found
documents which concretely refer to *"poor people"* who sold their
lands — which they had received as gifts — *"to other persons
at very low prices"*. This kind of transactions reached such a level

---

96) Recopilación de Leyes Agrarias de Guatemala, p. 120.
97) A.G.C.A., B1, M.G.J., folder No. 28712, from the Political Chief of Quezaltenango to M.G., October 29, 1885.

that the government itself became obliged to forbid the sale of land which had been granted freely, for a period of ten years after the donation.[98]

In all cases concerning free land concessions to the members of any one community, the economic factor was also present, consisting in securing the *finqueros* temporal labour who had a place where to sow their surviving cultivation. In other words, while the Liberals promoted the development of middle-class ownership, creating great capitalistic vast rural properties, they also promoted the development of small rural properties among the poor peasants. *"The breaking-up of property in small land-shares",* it was said in a circular letter of February 19th, 1877, adressed to the Political Chiefs by the government Minister, was very important *"to make the land-shares more productive, which being owned and cultivated collectively, only satisfy transitory needs"*.[99]

"It was procured that the areas were of small extension" affirms Ignacio Solís, *"in order to increase the crop."*[100]

The resolution of breaking up the communal lands led the rural authorities to determine the extension of the commons, which was considered as indispensable for the fire-wood fields and for the cultivation of the communal maize fields, officially stipulating that these lands would not be for sale.[101] Stating for all the communities that ownership of common public land of a square *'legua'*[102], many of them could keep from five to eight *'caballerias'*[103], *while a few obtained up to 46 'caballerías'*, as long as these lands were not suitable for coffee cultivation. Such was the case of the community of Canillá, in the Quiché,

98) Ibid., folder No. 28716, Juan Grajeda to M.G., December 4, 1885.
99) Recopilación de Leyes Agrarias de Guatemala, pp. 95-96. Circular of the Government of Guatemala to the Political Chiefs, February 19, 1877.
100) Ignacio Solís: Op.cit., Vol. V, p. 1173.
101) Recopilación de Leyes..., Circular of February 19, 1877.
102) A.G.C.A., B1, M.G.J., folder No. 28659, from the Political Chief of Sacatepéquez to M.G., October 22, 1877.
103) Ibid., folder No. 28660, from the Political Chief of Escuintla to M.G., March 18, 1877.

which the Government allowed to keep the mentioned quantity of _'caballerías'_.

> _"The land is mostly broken", informed the official land-_
> _surveyor, "and only suitable for maize sowing and cattle_
> _breeding..."_[(104)]

The land-surveyors, associated with the Political Chiefs and
agricultural impresarios, were those who actually determined
the land area which was considered convenient to grant to the
communities, ordering the expropriation of the best and most
accesible lands. The fact that the rural authorities were the ones
who many times decided the area of land that each community
was to keep, led to many arbitrary acts, doing as they pleased
according to their personal interests. So, for instance, on one
occasion when a community protested before the Central
Government, because they disagreed with the low number of
'caballerías' the Political chief had assigned to them, the Government's answer clearly reflects the arrogance of the _finquero_ in
power: _"in my opinion the area I offered you is more than sufficient for the inhabitants of that village."_[(105)]
The Political chief was Manuel Lisandro Barillas, and in
giving this answer he knew very well that what he meant: a
few days later, he registered to his own name the farm "Pensa-
miento", on the Cuca Coast, which included the lands that had
been taken from the referred community, whose inhabitants
became integrated to the labour force of the new coffee plantation.[(106)]

The purchase of land by the communities

Some medium and large sized communities, which thanks to
their industriousness had succeeded in gathering enough

---

104) Ibid., folder No. 28667, R. González to the President of Guatemala, February 6, 1878.
105) Ibid., folder No. 28665, Manuel L. Barillas to the President of Guatemala,
February 6, 1878.
106) Indice de los Expedientes... op.cit., No. 9, Quezaltenango, 1878. p. 166.

money, bought great areas of land. The municipality of Santo
Tomás Chichicastenango, for instance, could buy more than 30
'caballerías'.[107] The communities of Santa Catarina Ixtahuacán and Nahualá also bought denaries of *'caballerías'* valued at
thousands of pesos, and the community of Santiago Atitlán
bought a total of 35 *'caballerías'* from a private person.[108] Another 35 *'caballerías'* were acquired by a community of Huehuetenango from another one, paying 60 pesos for each *'caballería'*[109]

The land purchases by the natives seemed to be done after a
collect had been effected in the community, the land shares then
being distributed according to each villager's personal contribution.

> *"The natives of this village — three thousand of them
> — voluntarily agreed to complete up to thirty thousand
> pesos in order to buy the farm "Molino de Argueta",
> with the purpose of distributing fields in proportion to
> each ones contribution", the Political Chief of
> Totonicapán informed his superiors in 1883.*
> *"Consequently, a new native district of this village will
> be formed on that land. Considering the character of
> these Indians the difficulties which will arise between
> them and the authorities of Sololá, regarding the
> exercise of jurisdiction can be understood, once the lands
> is in that Department, and its new
> inhabitants live in this neighbourhood. The conflict
> would be the same or maybe greater between the two
> municipalities of both Chief towns, regarding the
> neighbours of Argueta, one moment offering the council
> posts, the next bringing them under municipal
> jurisdiction and claiming that they fulfil the duties
> expected of a neighbour. On the other hand, the Indians*

---

107) A.G.C.A., B1, M.G.J., folder No. 28704, from the Political Chief of Quiché
to M.G., February 12, 1884.
108) Ibid., folder No. 28658, from the Political Chief of Sololá to M.G., February
19, 1877.
109) Ibid., folder No. 28664, from the Political Chief of Huehuetenango to M.G.,
June 8, 1878.

> _who are going to settle down on those lands would not
> agree to submitting to the authorities of Sololá, because
> they originate from this municipality, and this fact
> would frequently disturb the order and good harmony
> among these people. For that reason, this Headquarters
> considers as conventient to separate the land area of
> Argueta from the Department of Sololá and join this
> area to that of Totonicapań, as a part of the city's
> land."_[(110)]

We have seen the same procedure of fund collection inside the community for the buying of lands in the Department of Alta Verapaz.

When the members of the community were ladinos, each one acquired the land which he could afford to pay for, though the rule here seems to be that each ladino tried to obtain the greatest possible quantity of land, even if he did not plan to cultivate it. This is not so strange, if we think that the profit and speculation spirit was more developed among the "mestizos" than among the natives.

> _"From the sixty eight_ 'caballerías', _three hectares and
> five thousand and five hundred and eighty six square
> 'varas' of land very suitable for coffee growing, owned by
> the community of San Juan Ostuncalco, twelve
> 'caballerías' and twenty eight hectares have been
> distributed among thirteen neighbours",_ the official
> land-surveyor informed the Political Chief of
> Quezaltenango in 1878, in whose jurisdiction the
> mentioned community was. _"But the majority of them
> will not be able to pay the value of the land to the
> Supreme Government, and much less improve a branch
> of agriculture as important as coffee cultivation; because
> up to now, they neither could nor can pay the cost of the
> measurings. Due to this, the fields granted to the
> neighbours of San Juan Ostuncalco, and which_

110) Ibid., folder No. 28702, from the Political Chief of Totonicapán to M.G., March 5, 1883.

> *represent an inexhaustible element of the national*
> *wealth, will remain in useless hands for their*
> *exploitations, and the benefical dispositions of the*
> *Supreme Government in favour of coffee cultivation will*
> *become effectless".*[111]

According to the circular letter which was sent by the Government to the Political Chiefs on February 19, 1877,

> *"the community land redemption act is not obligatory*
> *for the municipalities who ought to sell to the persons*
> *who are settled in the same region. The area of the land*
> *shares is to be fixed by the respective Political*
> *Headquarters, taking into account the number of*
> *inhabitants and the extension of the land shares."*[112]

This resolution was interpreted at each ones advantage or simply not taken into account by most of the rural authorities, in some cases under pressure of the local powerful owners, who were very interested in enlarging their possessions by getting the best of the communal lands. Many peasants, nevertheless, rejected until the very last moment the agrarian plunder that the *"annual ground rent redemption"* and forced land purchase implied.

> *"The Department of Santa Rosa is exclusively*
> *agricultural", stated its Political chief in 1884, "though*
> *the major part of human industrial knowledge has not*
> *yet developed among the inhabitants of these*
> *underdeveloped villages. This in spite of the fact that the*
> *agricultural nations are quite deficient as well,*
> *agriculture has already had progressive development*
> *both because the movement is general and because*

---

111) Ibid., folder No. 28665, Luis Wolfran to the Political Chief of Quezaltenango, January 18, 1878.
112) Recopilación de Leyes..., p. 96. Circular of the Government of Guatemala to the Political Chiefs, February 19, 1877.

cultivation is made with elaborate effort and enconic dedication. This due to the fact that the natives of Sinacatán, Nancinta, and particularly Guazacapán, have always been against giving up their common public lands and have not allowed others to give up a palm of this very fertile region, which they never cultivated themselves because of their natural indolence. Only basic grains were cultivated, and this in such a reduced scale that it was normally not enough for the consumption of those regions. When the natives' resistance and destructive repugnancy towards the communal lands redemption was finally overcome, the reporting began, and in a short time, those lands — uncultivated for so many years — started to show signs of industry. All kinds of cultivations, — between five and six hundred — have definitely not yet been carried through, nor have the land owners had the time necessary to start carrying out serious work. Up to now, two great advantages have been achieved as a result of the disappearance of the Indians' resistence: the first is the powerful impulse given to agriculture, which is the origin and source of every one's as well as the country's improvement and wealth; and the other is the income to the Nations coffer which will very soon be coming from the uncultivated lands. Among the most extensive areas of plantation are found the vast and well cultivated pasture-lands, which are still being cultivated, along the entire coast. This land is suitable for the breeding of all kinds of cattle as well as the pasture of young bulls destined for slaughter. I have said that all kinds of plantations are being made, and this is actually the case. The indigo plant which although not completely unknown to this department, has not been cultivated at all for a long time. This is being sown on a regular scale in the municipal district of Barberena, by the Avila gentlemen, from the Capital City. Tobacco is being cultivated in nearly the whole Department, but in Barberena, where the best quality is produced, it is sown

293

*in greater proportions. The number of plants cultivated
last year was not less than 1.000.000. In
Mataquescuintla, San Rafael, Jumaytepeque and
Casillas, wheat, barley, maize, kidney bean, potato, yucca
and sugar-cane are grown with good results. Coffee is
grown both in Barberena and in this Chief town. But
going back to the villages on the coast, I want to
mention particularly the rubber tree, cocoa, balsam and
vanilla, which are being grown with great success.
Perhaps in Guazacapán, Chiquimulilla and in the other
locations on the Pacifica Coast, cocoa has been
cultivated for a very long time, but if that was so, its
existence can only be presumed by the many and robust
plants of this kind which are usually found in the more
uncultivated and remote jungles of the vast public lands.
Even though the exuberant forests spontaneously showed
that they produced such a valuable product, it was not
until approximately thirteen years ago that Messrs.
Leonardo Lazo and Francisco Maldonado actually
started to cultivate this, and recently, other people have
started preparing considerable plant nurseries, which
will be transplanted in a few months time. Rubber trees,
vanilla and balsam — as I said — are already being
carefully cultivated. The growers are not concentrating
on just one product, thus agricultural industry will from
now on be broader and have a more secure and positive
profit. Though the coffee growers were last year
discouraged by the fall in price of this product on the
foreign markets, they recently began considering growing
it with renewed vigour, thanks to the latest news
regarding the price improvement on Europe's and North
America's markets. New large-scale plantations are now
developing. There is no doubt that the redemption of
common public land has brought and is bringing many
advances to agriculture, because once those lands have
been transformed into private property, they are looked
upon by their owners with interest and with the
attention which originates in the need for survival and*

294

*the stimulation of giving the greatest possible value to
that which is one's own. Considering that this
Headquarters is convinced that this is true, it has not
neglected any means of putting pressure on the people
until it has triumphed over the Indians' stubbornness
with which they resisted to redempt and profitably sow
all the lands within the jurisdiction."*[113]

According to the public official of the liberal régime, it was
incorrect to say that the lands could be redeemable, if they were
not already occupied:

*"Redeemable is the representative capital, and the effect,
the property consolidation, i.e. the concentration of the
direct and the useful dominion of land in one person's
hands. The expression "redeemable land" is not right
here, and according to decree 170, the fields which
corresponded to the common public land of a village,
and were in possession of a private person at the date of
the decree, paying or not the allowance which is called
rent by emphyteusically granted rental, and which was
paid to the owner's exclusive dominion, fulfilling the
requisites the same decree demands, were redeemable.
Any land which belongs to the community or to any
other common public property of a village, and which is
not owned by any private person previous to the same
decree, is not redeemable, following the same
expression."*[114]

The decree on annual ground rent redemption of January 8,
1877, was actually the legal instrument with which the ruling
class deprived the Indian communities of their lands, in spite
of all the Government's recommendations, expressed in circu-

---

113) A.G.C.A., B1, M.G.J., folder No. 28710, from the Political Chief of Santa
Rosa to M.G., June 7, 1884.
114) Ibid., folder No. 28683, from the Government Prosecutor to the Political
Chief of Chimaltenango, July 13, 1881.

lar letters to the Political Chiefs, and of the liberal jurists theoretical considerations. Guatemala's recent agrarian history shows us that the *finqueros*, after coming to power in 1871, considered that the time had come to apropriate the people's possessions, and making the peasants lands their own by "laws" which were only a legal framework to their stratagems. The *finqueros* voracity showed no limits; they not only appropriated the best lands for coffee cultivation, but also every piece of land which could yield them any profit (as the lands used for cattle breeding and other cultivations in Santa Rosa), forests with precious woods, rivers and water sources. The liberals retorically declared that everyone who occupied communal land, or who had the intention of undertaking coffee cultivation, could buy the land property title he needed, on the condition that it was not an area larger than two *'caballerías'*. In practice we have seen that forced expropriation and agrarian property redistribution (incorrectly called *"land reform"* due to the misunderstanding of the progressive character of the mentioned concept) was made through means which were very characteristic of the country's new masters and according to the new conquerors' logic: on the one hand, obligating the commoners to *"buy"* small land shares which they legally owned; and on the other hand, they made *"denunciations"* of great territorial extensions, which in many cases included their inhabitants. In this way, the new vast rural properties were born in modern Guatemala, which differ from the colonial ones in so much that the lands are destined to the development of capitalistic agricultural enterprises, as big-scale coffee plantations.

According to liberal lawyers, the annual ground rent redemption should be applied to the common public lands, *"or to those that belong to the community with any other title"*.[115] The acquisition of any other state property should be carried out according to the decree of November 2nd, 1837, of the liberal Mariano Gálvez' government, which considered as uncultivated all fields which had been *"realengas"* during the spanish domination period, and — as the above mentioned decree stated: *"have*

---

115) Ibid., from the Government Prosecutor to the Political Chief of Chiquimula, March 6, 1881.

not been sold to private persons, villages or corporations, being property of the State.[116] This resolution in force, allowed the finqueros to appropriate many communal lands, limits of which were unclear, the titledeed *"illegible",* or simply had disappeard as if by magic. These lands, reported by the mighty were not put on public auction, the excuse being that the person who could purchase them by official favour, was an impresario who would improve coffee cultivation, *"which will have a positive influence on agriculture and commerce."*[117]

The development of bourgeois land property

For the liberal authorities, the "secret" of the welfare and the development of the villages lay in the division of the territorial property; *"as land and work are the sources of public wealth",* said the Liberals, *"it is natural that the more territorial properties a country has, the more it flurishes."*

The liberal government revealed that from 1864 to 1871, 1040 *'caballerías'* had been distributed to only 16 persons, while from 1871 to 1879, 1539 *'caballerías'* had been distributed among 128 owners; which gave an average of 64 to 12 *'caballerías'* per person, respectively.

> *"In the last period",* it was declared, *"not only an incomparably larger number of title-deeds had been set free, but also the property has been notoriously divided, because before 1871, a title-deed which consisted of less than a hundred 'caballerías' was rare. The current administration, which faced great difficulties many times, has tried by every means within its power to give an impulse to agriculture, making the purchase of lands easier, and this is how the beautiful areas of the Cuca Coast and Alta Verapaz have to a great extent been*

---

116) Recopilación de Leyes..., pp. 70-72. Decree of November 2, 1837.
117) A.G.C.A., B1, M.G.J., folder No. 28672, Ignacio Montenegro to M.G., November 7, 1885.

> *turned into productive plantations, there where it was*
> *impossible for the active finquero to penetrate earlier. No*
> *doubt the wealth of a country comes from that of the*
> *private ones and as the facts which have been given*
> *show an important sum in favour of the latter, due to*
> *the property division, it goes to show that in this sense*
> *the Republic has sensibly prospered and, even though*
> *this involves greater activity for the Political chiefs and*
> *other officials who are in charge of the carrying through*
> *of the requests on uncultivated land, we believe that*
> *passivity in so important a matter could be both*
> *harmful and unforgivable. Besides the Government in*
> *trying to decrease the quantity of areas to be given in*
> *ownership, has aimed at getting all possible utility*
> *through cultivation, because otherwise great country*
> *estates are created which do not produce, or resemble the*
> *feudal dominions."*[118]

The results of the land distribution project could not yet be seen by 1879, and what is said by the liberal spokesman must be understood only in the sense that there existed enough clearness as regards the orientation that the plantation economy in development should be given. The immediate effect of agricultural plunder was, however, far from responding to the Guatemalan people's interests. In many regions of the country the inhabitants to parcel out their lands, in spite of the dictatorship's propaganda; in others, the peasants could definitely not pay up to 500 pesos for good cultivable lands or 260 pesos for *"useless lands"*, that a Political Chief engaged himself in getting acceptance for to be able to distribute the most fertile land shares among his friends.[119] Inhabitants of Quezaltepeque, in Chiquimula, complained about the fact that the lands there were supposed to be given for the cultivating of their nourishment were only good for grazing.[120] In Chimaltenango, the lands

---

118) See Ignacio Solís: Op.cit., Vol. V, pp. 1174-1176.
119) A.G.C.A., B1, M.G.J., folder No. 28660, from the Political Chief of Chiquimula to M.G., September 27, 1877.
120) Ibid., folder No. 28670, from the Neighbours of Quezaltepeque to M.G., September 25, 1877.

sold to the peasants did not excede 30 hectares, most of the purchase petitions being refused by the authorities.

"*Carry on to sell to the highest bidder", the Government attorney suggested once in a note adressed to the Government Minister, "the following plots: two, requested by Francisco Argueta, fo 10 and 9 hectares; one which consists of six and a quarter hectares of the two required by Lucas Tuc; two of the four to which Alejo Blán alludes, some previous explanation being required on this point because it was not clear in the report from the San Martín Municipality; one of the two hectares, of the two Juan Balán mentions; one of one hectare, of the two about which Manuel Jesús Tic speaks; three, of the four which Francisco Tomás wants; the one of fourteen hectares to which José Tuyúc refers to; the one of thirty hectares which Tomás Tuyúc would like to acquire; one of ten hectares, of the two which Toribio Tuyúc requires; one of fourteen hectares, of the two which Bernardo Tum is asking for; one of five hectares, of the two which José Maria Tum mentions; that of one and half hectares which Martin Tum requests; that of eight hectares which Juan José Quelex mentions; that of one and three quarter hectares which Ramón Velazco mentions; one of two hectares of the two which are mentioned in the writ from José Higinio Puy; one of three hectares, of the two which Alejandro Mejia speaks; the two plots which Martin Morején wants; the four requested by Pablo Mutzuts; one of three hectares, of the four which José Cas is asking for; one of three which Secundino Batres is asking for; one which consists of three hectares of the six that Andrés Coyoy is interested in; and one of four hectares, of the three which are related to Ramón Coyoy's statement.*"[121]

---

121) Ibid., folder No. 28690, from the Government Prosecutor to M.G., August 30, 1878.

We do not know on what basis the land to be put on auction were selected by the attorney and what made him not pay any attention to the other 160 requests of purchase that were enclosed with those mentioned by him, although knowing about the corruption that has ruled among the high officials of the coffee State, it would not have been strange if the favoured petitioners acknowledged with anticipation his good offices. In San Marcos, two hundred villagers had been left completely without land; when they requested ten *'caballerías'* in order to cultivate their daily needs, a local authority told them that there was no land available.[122] In this department the peasants obtained only small plots, while the impresarios were owners of great areas of land. J. Rufino Barrios and other members of his big family took possession of more than 500 *'caballerías'* suitable for coffee cultivation, and established *fincas* that later on would become property of German consortiums, as *"El Porvenir"* and *"Santo Domingo",* in San Pablo.[123]

The Political Chief of the Department said that of the peasants from Totonicapán who had bought land in the Sololá jurisdiction:

> *"the increased number of contributors to the purchase of that land will make the plots so small, that they will only measure between three to five* 'cuerdas' *each".[124]*

In the Alta Verapaz, it was decided to give each peasant without land *"between one and ten 'cuerdas"",* while the foreign impresarios kept three quarters of the best lands suitable for coffee-cultivation.[125]

> *"He who wanted to establish a* finca*", wrote a German who settled down in Alta Verapaz years later, "had first of all to find a set of lands which not only had the right*

122) Ibid., folder No. 28710, from the Síndico 1° of the Municipalidad of San Marcos to the Political Chief of San Marcos, March 24, 1878.
123) DZA Potsdam, A.A., No. 12436, Bergen a Bülow, November 8, 1879.
124) A.G.C.A. B1, M.G.J., folder No. 28702, from the Political Chief of Totonicapán to M.G., March 5, 1883.
125) Ibid., folder No. 28704, from the Political Chief of Alta Verapaz to M.G., February 19, 1883.

*climate and soil, but also an Indian village from which
he could get the necessary labour-force. Without labour-
force close to the land, the enterprise had not a
chance."*[126]

The appropriation of both lands and men committed by the
coffee growers in Alta Verapaz reached such a degree, that already in 1885 the Political Chief verified that men disappeared
from the village overnight, escaping from the coffee growers who,
not being satisfied with snatching away their lands, also pretended to enslave them and oblige them to clear ground and set
up modern plantations in the middle of the jungle.

*"There has been a considerable decrease in the number
of inhabitants", said the Political Chief to the
Government Minister confidentially, "because the sites in
the village which still belong to the municipality have
been turned into properties."*[127]

The native peasants did not stop complaining about the arbitrarinesses which were committed against them by the local and
foreign impresarios:

*"We, the signers, neighbours of the "Guaxac" village, of
the San Miguel Tucurú jurisdiction, department of Alta
Verapaz", they wrote on one of many occasions, "before
the President of the Republic and with our deepest
respect, come to explain that, tired of so much plunder,
of so much hostility towards us, a humble race, we once
more request the protection of the First Magistrate of the
Nation. We do not ask for absolutely anything which
goes against our laws, we do not ask for punishment of
our cruel exploiters; we only came to ask you for the
honest accomplishment of justice, venerable sovereign of
the Universe. A lot has already happened, Mr. President,
the moment has already come for the First Leader to*

---

126) Adrian Roesch: "Allerlei aus der Alta Verapaz". Stuttgart, 1934, p. 34.
127) A.G.C.A., B1, M.G.J., folder No. 28721, from the Political Chief of Alta Verapaz to M.G., November 26, 1885.

> *protect us and hide us from such calamities committed*
> *by some disreputable persons, who not being satisfied*
> *with getting rich at our expense, want to take from us*
> *what we most need, our and our sons' future: a piece of*
> *land."[128]*

In 1886, a foreign impresario said that he had been given 500 *'caballerías'* by the Liberal government, and this gives us an idea of the degree of submission towards the foreigners and disrespect for the villages properties, that the country's authorities had reached. Obviously, the Liberals did not hesitate to give such quantities of lands to one person only while they snatched properties from the peasants, if we take into account that already in 1877, J. Rufino Barrios himself said to the German representative in Guatemala that for him *"100 foreign families were worth as much as 20.000 indians".*[130] This attitude, however, was an old one among the liberal guatemalan leaders: in 1834, President Mariano Gálvez gave the Department of Verapaz to an English colonization company. Said Department did not only include the Alta and Baja Verapaz, but also El Petén and half of Izabal, plus the District and Port of Santo Tomás, with a total area of 6.422.100 hectares of land. Gálvez himself also granted almost the whole of the Eastern Republic, hundreds of thousands of hectares, to the English impresarios Marcial Bennett and Charles A. Meany, pioneers of coffee cultivation in Guatemala.[131] Fortunately for the country, both projects failed to a great extent due to the peasants' armed resistence.

Besides their inclination of granting what was not theirs, the Liberal leaders themselves tried to take the greatest advantage of their come to power, by becoming rich or enlarging their family fortunes even more. The names of J. Rufino Barrios, Miguel Garcia Granados, Herculano Afre, Manuel Lisandro Barillas, Francisco Lainfiesta, Juan Aparicio, José María

---

128) Ibid., folder No. 29025, Community members of Guaxac to the President of Guatemala, June 13, 1900.
129) Ibid., folder No. 28723, J.G. Anderson to M.G., March 10, 1886.
130) DZA Potsdam, A.A., No. 12436, Bergen a Bülow, November 15, 1877.
131) Enrique del Cid: "Llegada de los primeros alemanes a Guatemala, como consequencia de la colonización belga." Guatemala, mimeo., 1969, pp. 1-3.

Samayoa and those of many Liberals, appear among the main individual usurpers of communal lands. Some of these thefts of land were brought to light when the protagonists disappeared from the political scene. The major part of the usurpations, however, have remained as a *"family secret"* from a beautiful epoch that has continued till our days, very favourable for taking possession of the national and popular properties in an easy manner and often *"legal".* This provides a Mine of investigations for our historians to come.

> The Political Chief of Sacatepéquez referred to the Government Minister in 1878 that "the Municipality of Magdalena claims sixteen 'caballerías' of land which Don José María Samayoa took from this villages public land, in order to enlarge his property called Bárcenas", Later the outstanding impresario was disgraced, "the need of those lands for these as residents was being unquestionable."[132]

In 1874, in the same jurisdiction of Sacatepéquez, the Political Chief of the Department pointed out that the Municipality of San Felipe did not have any funds to build a school for the peasants' children because *"the community did not have any public land for the villagers to sow".* The inhabitants considered that the *"lands of Candelaria would serve their purpose",* but that the same *"belong to Don José María Samayoa".*[133] A neighbour of Antigua Guatemala complained to Barrios in 1878, saying that the Political Chief of Sacatepéquez *"was falsely claiming previous possession of different plots close to my plantation"* and was bribing the minor authorities *"to give him the property documents".*

> "He has done the same in the Chief City of the Department", the grower informed Barrios, "and it is evident to the whole village that when he created large

132) A.G.C.A., B1, M.G.J., folder No. 28664, from the Political Chief of Sacatepéquez to M.G., January 19, 1878.
133) Ibid., from the Political Chief of Sacatepéquez to M.G., December 4, 1874.

303

> *kidney bean plantations he plundered many old and
> unhappy native owners."*[134]

What the residents of Antigua said during the rural lands expropriation process which accompanied the formation of the modern plantation economy in Guatemala can be considered as typical. Many new landlords appropriated land that was much larger than what they used to declare, so that on many occassions, they exceeded more than five times the lands they purchased according to government stipulations.[135] Yet this phenomenon was not at all unusual and was simply part of the *"rules of the game"* of the peasant expropriation, openly accepted by the dictatorship. During the period of Spanish domination, the so called *"land composition"* was a practice that permitted an owner, in exchange of the corresponding payment, to take legal possession of all those lands he illegally occupied, not considering purchases or donations he received. Starting in 1871, the custom of requesting *"suplemental title deeds"* in order to legalize the theft of lands through another form of *"composition",* i.e. through the payment, often symbolic, of the value of the lands that had been usurped from the peasants. The protection that the authorities gave the expansionist owners was so ample, that when the peasants who were to be despoiled tried to get on with their traditional farming, the landlord resorted to the use of physical violence against them, without any fear of being punished.

In reply to a complaint from the peasants of Barberena about the agricultural plunder and violent acts to which they were submitted by a foreign *finquero*, the government attorney supported the *finquero* calling the peasants' attempt to recover their lands as *"invasion".* Nevertheless, he confidentially wrote to the Government Minister that

> *"unfortunately, the question of lands, that is day to day
> reaching alarming proportions in that part of the*

---

134) Ibid., folder No. 28665, Rafael Escobar to the President of Guatemala, September 21, 1878.
135) Ibid., folder No. 28683, from the Government Prosecutor to M.G., January 13, 1881.

*Department, are not only connected with Mr. Evans'
property. The villages of Zapote and Naranjo complain
about land plundering. As the Government has directly
intervened in almost all affairs of Corral de Piedra and
Barberena, this office has abstained from intervening in
those matters, which in the end can have unpleasant
consequences".*[(136)]

For many Liberals, the culmination of the annual ground rent
redemption deserved to be called *"surprising"*, because already
in 1885 it was believed that *"the useful lands were unavailable"*,
after the multiple denunciations and purchases made since the
1860's.

*"Enthusiasm still credits the land that was despised
before", affirmed a Political chief in 1885, "demonstrates
the great advantage that the private property
signifies."*[(137)]

In 1889, E. P. Dieseldorff referred that in Alta Verapaz it was
already very difficult to find uncultivated lands that were not
already in the hands of private owners or denounced by
them.[(138)] In the same year of 1889, E.P. Dieseldorff referred to
the case of a foreigner who came to Alta Verapaz with empty
hands, and some time later was given *"a donation consisting of
200 'caballerías' of land by the government that were actually
worth approximately 600.000 mark."*

"The land here is rapidly increasing in value", wrote Dieseldorff, *"even if one can still buy cheap lands from the Government
in some places, which will be impossible within a couple of
years".*[(139)]

"The general situation of the Departments is peaceful",

---

136) Ibid., folder No. 28643, from the Government Prosecutor to M.G., August
5, 1874.
137) Ibid., folder No. 28715, from the Political Chief of Chimaltenango to M.G.,
February 2, 1885.
138) E.P.D. archives: Box 2, folder 28, E.P. Dieseldorff to Hanna Dieseldorff,
May 4, 1889.
139) Ibid., Box 2, folder 27, E.P. Dieseldorff to Hanna Dieseldorff, April 27, 1889.

*affirmed an official of the Liberal Government in 1884
with great satisfaction, "a real lively atmosphere in
those villages has developed enthusiasm for work and
industry in each and every one. The impulse of the
administrative action favoured improvement and
progress in multiple manifestations, the correction of
abuses, the widening of agricultural activity and
property division have also been procured. Unstable
property whose origin had to be searched for through
the activity of the Chief of the nation, who through his
initiative of continual visits to the departments and his
love for everything that was connected with the interests
of the Fatherland, carried out improvements. The
division of the territorial property has been a factor for
development, thanks to the different agreements issued
by the Executive. All the large uncultivated lands on the
Cuca Coast are there, within sight of everybody,
transformed by hard work into sources of agricultural
richness, into productive plantations that increase
society's capital,
that give work to thousands of hands. These lands were
earlier inactive and paralized, and to thousands of
families who not so long ago were decimated by
abandonment and misery there are the valuable fincas
which in the name of progress suddenly sprouted in
what once were but barren deserts of Alta Verapaz.
These are the valuable estates where coffee, sugar-cane,
cocoa and other fruits which are cultivated on our fertile
soil and on which our commerce and industry rest. All
this means that the villages rapidly advance along the
path of their own welfare, and the faith is strengthened
in those who in order to assist the progress of
Guatemala, only expected to see the principles of our
Revolution supported with all patriotic abnegation, turn
into glorious reality".[140]*

---

140) A.G.C.A., B1, M.G.J., folder No. 28718, José Vicente Martínez to M.G., April 2, 1884.

E. P. Dieseldorff considered that he who wished to initiate a coffee plantation had to invest an initial sum of not less than 150.000 mark, revealing in a letter to his mother, in 1889, the enthusiasm that existed among the rich foreigners who came to the country in order to become finqueros.

> "I have decided to devote myself to the coffee-trade", Dieseldorff then wrote, "i.e., to become a plantation owner. The great advantage of this kind of trade is that it is excellent for the health and that one can always have free time during long periods without too much loss. Besides, coffee cultivation pays off more than any other kind of trade, if one invests correctly and administrates well. The most correct is to buy a plantation that has already been completed to three quarters, as there exist a lot of them, and cheap at this time. One can do a lot with one of these plantations and the idea of having so much free time and moreover being able to administrate a new plantation fills me with enthusiasm. Therefore, my plan is to acquire a new farm, and find the way to by adjacent virgin lands from the Government. They do not cost much and they are an excellent source of richness."[141]

As a matter of fact, towards the end of the 1880's, the South-West of the country, the Orient and Alta Verapaz, had been turned into zones of large coffee-plantations, which were properties of national and foreign impresarios. Where coffee-cultivation did not give the benefits which were expected, the owners sold the plantations or left, trying to develop their agricultural undertaking somewhere else. In this last case, they kept their owners documents or their rights of notification and rented the lands to poor peasants that needed to cultivate basic grains. This is what happened, for instance, with San Felipe and its neighbourhood, the old community of the Department of Retalhuleu

---

141) E.P.D. archives: Box 2, folder 25, E.P. Dieseldorff to Hanna Dieseldorff, April 10, 1889.

that so stubbornly opposed the invasion of strangers and speculators, that in the end they succeeded in taking possession of
their lands, devoting themselves to coffee cultivation.

> *"San Felipe is the second town of the Department",*
> *confirmed a rural authority in 1885, "well situated and*
> *with a benefical climate, that had its summit during*
> *1870 to 1876 owing to the agricultural increase of coffee*
> *cultivation, which at that time gave excellent results,*
> *attracting the industrious immigration, thanks to whom*
> *there existed a regular commerce. The place is now in*
> *decline, in spite of the neighbour's efforts to raise*
> *commercial life which existed before, due to the fact that*
> *the coffee trees that gave life to it have reached old age*
> *without giving the opulen product of their exuberant*
> *epoch. This has caused most of them to be abandoned,*
> *their owners moving to other places, and the mentioned*
> *lands destined to the cultivation of the basic*
> *necessity grains."*[142]

The Political Chief of Chimaltenango, referring in the year
1900 to the private property development in his Department,
said that of the ancient communal lands, *"there is not one small
area which is not private property".*
As a result of this, the old commoners became tenants or were
obliged to emigrate to the coffee plantations along the coast,
as the few *'caballerías'* which remained in the hand of the departamental communities were insufficient for the growing of maize, kidney beans, and other food-stuff of traditional cultivation
in the region.[143] *"There exist between 15.000 and 20.000 fincas
in Quezaltenango, Totonicapán, Huehuetenango, Solalá and Quiché",* referred a Government official to the General Director of
Statistics, in 1893, pointing out that *"the owner documents rarely
specify the name of the farm, which is subject to change, according to the different owners."* Obviously, these were rural proper-

---

142) A.G.C.A., B1, M.G.J., folder No. 28711, from the Political Chief of Quezaltenango to M.G., September 3, 1885.
143) Ibid., M.F., folder No. 14882, from the Political Chief of Chimaltenango
to M.F., June 2, 1900.

ties, which are officially registered as _"rustic farms"_ even if reference was made to uncultivated land. The above mentioned official, however, pointed out that while the _finqueros used_ to measure their estates in _'caballerías', "the peasants measure their lands in 'cuerdas'_ of 24, 25 and 28 'varas'"[(144)]

The effects of the agrarian plunderage of the communities

In Huehuetenango, a Political Chief pointed out in 1879, that the land controversies between the communities, and between communities and private persons, _"are becoming greater every day":_

> _"That is why, in spite of its numerous population (38 villages) it produces so little agriculturally. It should yield fruit and considerable profit, but it is not so because the land controversies and lack of natives hinders work. The cereal crop is very scarce, and that of other fruits even more so, but the first mentioned — on which the population makes a living — is hardly enough to make it worthwhile. On some occasions, the scarcity is alarming, and particularly in the main city because its lands are so arid that nothing, absolutely nothing, can be obtained from them. All these causes are generating poverty."_

On that occasion the same public official said that due to the sale of communal lands, the villages were _"slowly"_ being left without lands for cultivation, which _"damaged the inhabitants seriously, who are faced with great poverty."_ [(146)]

Misery for many and well-being for a few was the coffee cultivation's main characteristic in Guatemala, from it beginnings until now. In Sololá, for instance, a Political Chief said in 1879, the coffee cultivation had transformed the Department into a

---

144) Ibid., folder No. 14846, Carlos Larrave to the General Director of Statistics, May 31, 1893.
145) Ibid., M.G.J., folder No. 28670, from the Political Chief of Huehuetenango to M.G., May 7, 1879.
146) Ibid.

"prosperous and progressive one"[147]. One hundred and thirty four farms had been created with the lands expropriated from the peasants, and a great number of their former owners had been converted into labourers by the *finqueros*. The communities of Santa Catarina Ixtahuacán and Nahualá were also pressured to give away part of their lands, after having enjoyed a special status for a long time, their inhabitants not being forced to serve according to mandate nor to sell off their lands. The reason for the Government's change in attitude was the capital's need to extend its activity, once the greater part of the lands suitable for coffee cultivation had been submitted to the impresario's dominion, and the other lands had been divided among small rural growers and poor peasants. Besides, the lands for the settlement of plantations, the finqueros needed to parcel up great areas of land for their corkers's use.

> *"Through the official newspaper, the news of the governmental Agreement of last February 22 has reached our communities", said the representative of the communities of Santa Catarina and Nahualá to the President of the Republic, in a memorandum dated March 26, 1889, "in which the expropriation of the lands of Parraché due to reason of public convenience and according to decree 170, issued in the General J. Rufino Barrios's time is ordered. In the same Agreement, the incultivated lands of Paná are to be broken up into plots which are to be gratuitously granted to the present owners who request them. We believe we have the right to them, as in spite of the referred decree, President Barrios let us continue keeping the lands of Parraché, considering the fact that we were one of the first villages in Tierra Blanca that acknowledged his as the legitimate Leader of the Republic. Even if it is true that the public wealth has been maintained and improved by the rising coffee plantations it is not less true that the necessary*

---

147) Ibid., folder No. 28659, from the Political Chief of Sololá to M.G., May 12, 1879.

*consumption-cereal cultivations' are not enough during
regular years to supply and provide the villages of the
Occident. This is shown by these last years' statistics, in
which are registered the quantity of maize, flour, etc.,
which have been imported from California and other
countries for prices which are beyond the reach of the
majority, and which is still a great hindrance even to
the actual coffee growers.'*[148]

The scarcity of food, growing every day, was intimately related to the rural expropriation of the communities, because earlier, the peasants had enough fields to rotate them according
to the needs of the soils which were submitted to the temporal
cultivation of maize, kidney-bean and other food-stuffs. The lack
of food in the country, which before the coffee cultivation used
to be of a local character and caused by long summer or rain
periods, or by the periodical calamity of grasshopper plagues,
became a national and permanent problem since the appropriation of the best cultivation lands by the impresarios. Since the
expropriated peasants were obliged to work permanently on the
plantations, to do military service, or to make or repair track
and roads, to put up telegraph poles or build railways, in order
to fulfil the coffee cultivation's needs neglected their maize fields
and sowings. It was so difficult for some rural authorities to see
this cause-effect relationship, that a Political Chief in Izabal sentenced all peasants who did not produce *"three winter maize
'almudes'* (measure of grain, about 4,625 liters), one kidney-bean
'almud' and another of rice" to prison, due to the *"frequent scarcity of first necessity grains"* existing in the Department.[149] The
Political Chief of the Quiché, alarmed by the lack of food-stuffs
in his jurisdiction, ordered the peasants to *"leave that state of
prostration"* in which, according to him, they were, *"due only to
the lack of interest in work, because their lands were suitable for
potato and wheat sowing"*, requiring, besides, that they *"estab-*

---

148) Ibid., folder No. 28617, Community members of Santa Catarina Ixtahuacán and Nahualá to the President of Guatemala, March 26, 1889.
149) Ibid., folder No. 28709, from the Political Chief of Izabal to M.G., April 9,
1884.

*lish two ten 'cuerdas' plots each, to sow the indicated grains to spread these products".[150] In 1895, Guatemala's Political Lea-dership decided that all municipalities were to promote *"the sett-lement of coffee plantations on their barren lands, to benefit their common funds"*[151]; the Mayors replied that there was despe-rate need of food-stuffs. One of them, The Mayor of San Raymun-do, for instance, replied that the commoners could not fulfil the forced work on the roads,

> *"because they have to get maize for themselves and their families every day, not being able to condemn their families to poverty, nor neglect getting provisions which are gathered with great effort. The people are in a regretful situation due to the terrible grain scarcity."*[152]

The Political Chief of Jutiapa also complained in 1895 about the scarce development of fruit production for the working peop-le's consumption,

> *"because the lands which are near to the village are completely arid, and there is a lack of labour, due to the fact that many have moved to the neighbouring Republic of El Salvador to avoid doing the military service".*[153]

Zacapá's villages were also *"in a pitiful state"* at that time, because of the scarcity of food-stuffs. The departamental Politi-cal Chief said, referring to this, that

> *"for this reason it is expected that basic grains, which are at present very expensive, will reach such high prices that they will not be available for the common people. In*

---

150) Ibid., folder No. 28713, from the Political Chief of Quiché to M.G., Agust 9, 1885.
151) Ibid., M.F., folder No. 14860, Circular of the Political Chief of Guatemala to the Municipalidades of Guatemala, July 1, 1895.
152) Ibid., from the Alcalde of San Raymundo to the Political Chief of Guate-mala, August 23, 1895.
153) Ibid., folder No. 14861, from the Political Chief of Jutiapa to M.F., May 8, 1895.

_order to avoid scarcity, it is necessary to make the
sowing of the few irrigable fields which exist in the
Department obligatory. This Headquarter will prompt
an accord stating that every individual who possesses
irrigable lands is obliged to cultivate them with maize
and kidney-beans during the corresponding month, for
the harvest to be gathered later. The land-owner who
cannot or does not want to sow the mentioned lands
must grant them to somebody else to cultivate them
during the summer, paying a reasonable hiring fee. The
land-owner who refuses to cultivate or grant the lands to
others will be fined with five pesos for each hectare, sum
which will be destined to a special fund which the
municipalities will have, in order to cultivate on their
own the reluctant owner's lands. It will also be
convenient to oblige the natives of Acasaguastlán,
Magdalena and San Agustin — who manufacture
palm hats — to sow maize in the mountains instead of
carrying on with their occupation for the time being.
Each one shall receive a hectare of land, knowing that
they will succeed with the harvest, if sowing at the
beginning of the next month.
In order to guarantee the effectiveness of this measure,
the non-fulfilment of it could be punishable with two
months service in the Sappers Battalion, though the
referred natives are mostly soldiers."[154]_

Food-stuffs became scarce in the South-West of the country as
well, particularly in Retalhuleu[155], and in Escuintla, where
(towards the end of the century) the best lands of the Department had been converted into pasture lands by the cattle bree-
ders who had succeeded in concentrating the former communal lands into their hands.[156] In the year 1900, in a circular
letter sent by the Promotion Minister to the Political Chiefs,

---

154) Ibid., from the Political Chief of Zacapa to M.F., August 21, 1895.
155) ibid., folder No. 14850, from the Political Chief of Retalhuleu to M.F., May
8, 1897.
156) Ibid., from the Political Chief of Escuintla to M.F., July 11, 1897.

the high public official regretted that *"the basic articles produced in many departments were not enough to supply their jurisdictions' populations"*, and ordered the departamental authorities to dictate *"active regulations for the growers to sow the referred products in a greater quantity and in this way avoid their scarcity"*.[157] Among the arrangements made by the representatives of the Central Power to achieve a greater maize and kidney-bean production, the hiring of the farmer's uncultivated lands to the peasants *"who do not own lands"* was to be of priority. To hire land to poor peasants, in exchange for part of the harvest or work services, was an ancient practice in Guatemala. Nevertheless, since the rural redistribution in 1877, the number of tenants increased as never before.

> *"As has always been the custom on the coast"*, declared a landowner of Escuintla in the middle of 1880, *"this year I rented out lands for maize growing as I have done before; agreeing with the tenants a 'cuartilla' of thirty bands of maize for each 'cuerda' of twenty trusses they sowed. (Cuartilla = grain measure) I have more than eighty tenants, and thirteen of them presented themselves at the Headquarters of Escuintla, asking that I should be obliged to accept only one maize 'fanega' (grain measure) from each of them; to which the Political Chief, Mr. Luis Beteta agreed and with this precedent, the others will not be willing to hand me out the same quantity."*[158]

In 1882, the Political Chief of Zacapa informed that many persons in the region were *"semi-nomad"* peasants, living wherever they *"sow their maize"*, and that owing to the fact that they lack lands to settle down on permanently,

> *"when maize which they sow is finished, they move somewhere else the next year, to clear virgin woodlands,*

---

157) ibid., folder No. 14879, from the Political Chief of Chiquimula to M.F., April 26, 1900.
158) Ibid, M.G.J., folder No. 28676, Tomás Balcárcel to M.G., July 13, 1880.

> _cutting away cedars, mahogany trees, and all kinds of_
> _valuable woods which are abundant in this_
> _jurisdiction's uncultivated lands"._[(159)]

The Political Chief of Zacapa proposed that the peasants be obliged to have a permanent residence, hiring uncultivated lands to them to sow on. [(160)] The government attorney agreed with the Departamental Chief's proposal, on condition that the person who wanted to sow on lands declared as uncultivated, had first to get the corresponding municipality's permission, paying two pesos _"per rural year, if the area to be cultivated is no larger than ten thousand square meters"._ The tenant would pay twenty-five cents more for each one thousand square meters he got. Permission to sow on uncultivated lands did not have to be granted for areas of less than ten thousand square meters. According to the Attorney these land allowances did not mean that the peasants who sowed them were to be favoured if they reported them in order to acquire them through purchase, _"nor can these allowance be invoked to oppose the definitive appropriation of a land-share, whatever the title-deed"._[(161)] Actually, the objective was to get the peasants to keep on clearing virgin lands, which then were appropriated by the _finqueros,_ the peasants remaining within the limits as _"tenants"._

> _"Those who live on farms, commonly known as tenants",_
> _said a liberal attorney in 1866, "are always obliged to_
> _do the work the masters or his representatives order,_
> _except during sowing, clearing and harvesting time, of_
> _basic grains. They shall accept the wages which have_
> _been established at the farms they live on; they will not_
> _be allowed to build houses, enclosures, or work on their_
> _own, without the owner's written permission, who will_
> _always have the right to destroy any work done without_
> _these requisites."_[(162)]

---

159) Ibid., folder No. 28694, from the Political Chief of Zacapa to M.G., August 23, 1882.
160) Ibid.
161) Ibid., from the Government Prosecutor to M.G., September 7, 1882.
162) ibid., folder No. 28723, from the Government Prosecutor to M.G., July 12, 1886.

The lack of cultivated lands led to the peasant communities' gradual dissolution, particularly in the East of the country, and obliged their members to become dependent on the local landowners; in the capacity of *"tenant labourers".* Many landowners engaged in settling *"labourers-farms",* where labourers with debts who often were hired, and even sold, to farmers who needed labour-force, were settled.

> *"Tonajuyú is not a village, as is said", wrote the Political Chief of Chimaltenango in 1896, "it is my land, which has been bought only in order to recruit labourers in debt to whom I — with no profit — supply rooms, fields for sowing and discretional exploitation; in this way securing them for the work on a farm I am establishing in Pochuta. Workers complain that I pay them miserable wages — three reales a day — and they call it miserable while most of the growers in the Department only pay one or two reales, and do not give any of the facilities I referred to above. They say I make them work more than the time agreed, which they suppose to be twice a year, fifteen days each time; when actually — as is stated in the worker's books — they should work, according to the law, at least three months a year, if they want to obtain the permit which releases them from working as sappers. They owe me great sums of money I have given them in advance for their needs and for their debts to different masters. Finally, I am accused of transferring them to another master when the truth is that I became Mr. Martin Robert's partner, who then took care of the administration of the farm because I could not. Even if I had sold the farm I would not have thereby violated the law, because when a farm is sold, all the workers are included in the operation.*
> *This is the kind of complaint which the workers daily accuse their masters of. Some of them are well-grounded, and I have tried to solve them with complete equity, considering the obligation I have of improving*

_agriculture. But I always feel sorry for the unfortunate
native race, though they are very used to deceit and
become an easy instrument of petty intrigues,
particularly against the public officials."_[163]

The peasants complaints were many, as the departamental
public official points out, and prove that the peasants never passively accepted the _finquero's_ arbitrarities, particularly as far
as the theft of land is concerned. By 1879, a rural authority confirmed the native peasant's tenacity in their claims for justice.
If they were denied what they asked for it was not unlikely that
serious conflict arose and, occasionally _"some victims among those who have liberated land"._[164] _"Our plebeian spirit is never
more disturbed than when questions about land arise"_, observed
another Political Chief in 1885.[165] This was also confirmed by
another rural authority at the end of the nineteenth century,
when the commoners of San Juan Ixcoy, Huehuetenango, revolted. This occurred after the native authorities signed a contract
with a foreign _finquero_ by means of which the finquero had given
13.000 pesos to the local authorities (municipality) as a loan,
so the municipality could pay the measurement of the land parcels for the peasants.

> _"In order to pay off the debt it had acquired", referred
> the Political chief of Huehuetenango to his superiors
> afterwards, "the Municipality obliged the Indians to
> work on Mr. Koch's farm, without previously giving
> them a single cent. Though this was reported to the
> Corporation upon the request of the interested parties
> and in order to settle this matter, nothing could be done
> because the revolt surged immediately."_[166]

---

163) Ibid., M.F., folder No. 14863, from the Political Chief of Chimaltenango
to M.F., August 27, 1896.
164) Ibid., M.G.F., folder No. 28670, from the Political Chief of Chimaltenango
to M.G., October 7, 1879.
165) ibid., folder No. 28722, from the Political Chief of Escuintla to M.G., October 1, 1885.
166) Ibid., M.F., folder No. 14876, from the Political Chief of Huehuetenango
to M.F., October 31, 1898.

The native insurrection, as has been common in Guatemala since the arrival of the Spanish conquerors, was crushed by fire and sword by the armed forces of the powerful, *"the chief troublemakers, that is to say, those who have been captured"*[x167] being jailed and murdered. In spite of the official repression, however, the authorities never succeeded in dissuading the native peasants resistence to the expropriation of their land, to abuses and other acts of violence committed against them by the *finqueros* and the system they had succeeded in establishing. Many years later, the written or verbal protests were to take the form of great social battles which would threaten the *finqueros* centennial dictatorship and their corrupt and rotten "coffee-State".

---

167) ibid.

EPILOGUE

The origin and first development stage of the modern cultivation economy of Guatemala, which we have studied in this volume, the capital, land and labour factors constituted the main resources the agrarian impresarios availed themselves of for capitalist accumulation.

For the *finquero*, the profits obtained by the annual coffee harvests were due to his work, the compensation for his contribution to the development of the agriculture and of the country. Notwithstanding we have seen how the development process of cultivation and marketing of coffee, the distribution and use of material richness coffee cultivation produced was highly contradictory and harmful for Guatemalan society in general and the peasantry in particular. To this we will refer in detail in the coming volume *"Coffee and Finqueros in Guatemala"*

In view of the economic situation of Guatemala during the first half of the XIX century, the development of capitalism in agriculture needed different political and social conditions to those existing in the country during the spanish domination. with the arrival of the first foreign investors in the 1820's, the rural life started a slow transformation process characterized by the conversion of the relations existing among the people involved in nutritional production, into relations which more and more circled around the power of capital and of the merchant spirit.

As from the second half of the XIX century, the activity of the agrarian impresarios concentrated on giving impulse to coffee cultivation, considered as the greatest primal source of richness. The successes of coffee-production and of the free enterprise system allowed the contradictions of the latter to be considered as secondary or deliberately hidden. The profits of capitalism were considered the new rule for measuring the value of men, being these what determined their position on the social ladder. As from 1871, at the same time as the liberals adapted the state structure to their political interests, on the economic field they concentrated in the expropriation of the peasants common public land and to establish forced labour on the plantations.

In this way, the great contradictions of the modern plantation economy sowed its roots deeply in Guatemalan society, which on the one hand enriched the agrarian impresarios, businessmen, and foreign bankers, the corrupt politicians and big Guatemalan *finqueros;* and on the other hand, it empoverished the rural working masses. It was the contradiction between the economic theory that capitalist production and a free trade system generated the best development method to follow, in opposition to the reality of the working and living conditions ruling in the plantations. This contradiction influenced, in several ways, the structures of class domination, existing still today in Guatemala.

In the economic field this domination drove the big agricultural exporters, who each time concentrated and at the same time centralized the best productive land and capital, to successfully claim the rationalization of the explotation of the rural workers. They also exacted an extraordinary tax and great profit from the small and medium *finqueros,* whose harvests they used to finance through the mortgage credits system. These small and medium proprietors who saw their profit reduced in the circulation sphere, i.e. in their commercial transactions with impresarios who practised usury, tried to recover from their reduced income through the over-exploitation of their tempo-

320

ral and permanent workers, reducing their minimum salary as much as possible, while extending the working hours and the work to be done. Towards the end of the XIX century this over-exploitation flared up, as the workers nominal salaries were not only reduced, but the wages were paid with devaluated paper money of scarce value. This was due to the fall of the coffee prices and the inflation which was generated by the issuing of paper money which did not have gold backing.

From the political point of view, functioning agrarian capitalism in Guatemala had direct consequences on the structure of domination and control of society by the _finqueros_. Each time the coffee State was hit by the impact of an international strong economic depression, the national political scenery was presented with a brutal figure invested with exceptional dictatorial power, behind which was hidden the insecurity of the dominating class. This is what happened in 1898 when the crisis of low coffee prices and the assassination of President José Maria Reyna Barrios made Manuel Estrada Cabrera appear. The same happened 30 years later when the world depression and the ruin of several finqueros admitted the enthronement of Jorge Ubico in 1930.

The crisis of low coffee prices was caused by a lack of control of production at international level, was also taken advantage of by the great agricultural exporters and money-lenders. They concentrated more land, when small and medium owners went broke for having their properties mortgaged. Theoretically, it was the coffee State's task to solve this cyclic problem that so seriously affected the medium rural class, which to a great extent formed the social basis of the system, and were employed as allies of the foreign capital in the subjugation and exploitation of the peasantry. The only possible solution of the problem was the definitive rupture of traditional mono cultivation and the diversification of the agrarian production. However, as a new contradiction of the system, the functioning of the coffee State was precisely based on the increase of the power of the finqueros and on the support these gave by paying their taxes after their annual profit. On this interdependence between the permanent political power and the temporal economic benefits of the agrarian impresarios, depended the conservation and

321

strength of the finqueros dictatorship, until 1897.

The subjective need of State intervention in the expropriation of communal land, the establishment of forced labour and the regulation of agrarian production was, in this way, adapted by the *finqueros* to the objective need of developing the productive structure of the plantation economy based on coffee growing.

The main mission of the coffee State was that of protecting the interests of the agrarian impresario sector of the dominant class and that of developing the middle-class power system in the Guatemalan society. The class struggles, as urban working class did not exist, occurred in the rural areas, where the peasantry of the communities opposed the expansion of the commercial coffee growing at the expense of their expropriated land. This was done through the reinforcement of the commanding system and the militarization of the working force on the *fincas*. The Liberals succeeded in controlling growing social agitation and in consolidating the power postions the plantation owners had established by means of capital, taking advantage of the organizational weakness and regional antagonism among the native peasantry. Like the Spanish colonialists, the foreign neo-colonialists and their national allies could only impose their will on the rural workers by effectual measures and extra-economic work compulsion. While the Liberals tried to decrease the importance of the contradictions which occurred between the *finqueros* and the peasantry, they made efforts to impede the development of their class consciousness, granting some communities special privileges and deepening their division. The propagandists of the *finqueros* dictatorships' spent their time praising the supposed benefical role of the enterprises in relation to the progress of the country, while they tried to strengthen the plantation economy as a basis for economic development, encouraging foreign capital investment in agriculture. The whole liberal economic theory was based on this principle. This influenced the ideology of the urban and rural middle strata, which allied to the dominating class opressed native peasantry. Notwithstanding, in spite of the Liberals' efforts to hide the fundamental contradiction of Guatemalan society, i.e. the fact that hundreds of thousands of peasants worked only to enrich a parasitic minority and to maintain an opressive coffee State, the economic and social stand-still of the country put this fact in evidence. This situation rapidly developed each time there was a reduction in the price of coffee on the international markets. In these critical periods it was revealed that the country's so called _"development"_ went in the opposite direction of the one propagated by the Liberals and that the State was full of internal contradictions. At the end of the 1890's, the whole economic and financial system of the coffee State was shaken by an inflation that had no precedent in the history of Guatemala, apparently with no force existing, capable of controlling the situation nor a Government willing to solve the problem. As a matter of fact, this problem started several years before the presidency of José Maria Reyna Barrios in 1892. He and his economic counselors, however, were enraptured by the high prices of coffee during the 1890's. They asked for loans from the banks established in the country, which they expected to cover by the issuing of paper money. They expected to get backing in gold from the fiscal earnings that the high prices of coffee would produce. The economic and financial crisis was accelerated by several circumstances, which are worth mentioning:

a) in spite of the high income obtained from the sale of coffee, a relatively small percentage of it remained in the country, in view of the fact that the production and marketing of the grain, monopolized the earnings, and was controlled by big enterprises in Hamburg;

b) the major part of the banks had exhausted their monetary means in coin due to excessive paper money emissions, and many small and medium plantation proprietors had already great difficulties in getting loans which allowed them to fulfil the harvest;

c) everywhere there existed money shortage, the general commercial movement being influenced by this;

d) a government decree in May 1897, introduced a forced rate on paper money issued by the banks, making the dollar rate rise 220% in relation to the Guatemalan peso;

e) the bank shares, as well as the value of agrarian property suffered an unexpected decline, which made many

323

finqueros and merchants, who worked basically on mortgage guarantess and who could not fulfil the incurred
compromises, go bankrupt. As a result, the import of foreign manufactures decreased, and consequently, the import
taxes which in 1897 were 2.600.000 pesos less than in
1896.

The bad financial situation of the country not only affected
the merchants and small and medium agrarian impresarios, but
also the whole population who saw the buying power of their
money reduced. This contributed to the breakout of violent
revolts in the West and East of the Republic in September 1897,
which could only be stifled by the Government by means of the
mobilization of strong military contingents. Due to the fact that
these uprisings coincided with the start of the coffee harvest,
a lot of the working force which was destined to the plantations
was rapidly recruited and transported to combat fields, for which
reason a great part of the harvest was lost, and with it, the possibility of more monetary imcome for the country.

On January 8, 1898, President Reyna Barrios was murdered,
his death made evident the deterioration process in which the
finqueros dictatorship found itself. His successor, the lawyer
Manuel Estrada Cabrera, continued the policy of administrative disorder and superfluors expenses, bureaucratic corruption
and deficient economic and financial planning of the previous
governments. His dictatorial government continued till 1920,
distinguishing itself for opening the doors of the country even
more to foreign capital, especially the German and North American capital, as well as for the support it offered the finqueros
to keep the peasantry in a permanent state of semi-slavery. The
coffee State, in fact, was not ready to face the crisis of the fall
in coffee prices on the international markets in 1898 and, as
a consequence, the State finances were completely ruined, remaining mortgaged for more than 25 years. In a determinate way,
the resolution of Estrada Cabrera's government to issue more
bank notes and 6 million in State shares contributed to this,
as he did not count with the respective backing in gold nor was
able to give any kind of guarantees. To the above has to be added
the measure, adopted by the liberals, of consolidating all the

State debts in only one, without taking into account the obligations incurred earlier with the creditors; as well as the prohibition of exporting silver coins in circulation. This made all silver mint money disappear, including the coins of low value. The
price of gold on the market rose even more and the Guatemalan peso in relation to the American dollar was devaluated by
500%; and the banks went bankrupt. The modern plantation
economy as a system had failed in Guatemala in 1898, most of
the peasantry finding itself without land and submitted to a
brutal opression system and exploitation by unscrupulous agrarian capitalists.

The bankrupcy of the country was total, and this can only be
seen in its real dimension taking into account that the major
part of the private property debts were in hands of Guatemalans. The slow but constant transference of this property into
the hands of Germans and other representatives of foreign capital was a consequence of the great speculations which followed
the favourable decades of the XIX century. Bank shares continued to decrease in value, to their nearly absolute lack of value.
To this can be added the fall in prices of coffee on the international markets; the devaluation of the cultivated land and of the
coffee plantations; the non-renewal of external credit to the
importers of manufactures, which resulted in making even the
smallest transaction practically impossible.

To say it in only one phrase, the whole country was already
in the hands of the big _finqueros_ and the international capital.
This is very clear in the year 1900, when the Guatemalan peso,
which in 1874 was equivalent to the American dollar, had a rate
of 8,50 pesos per dollar. The words of the German vice-Consul
of Alta Verapaz and prominent _finquero_ of the region, Richard
Sapper, are very aloquent in this respect;

> _"Although the strong descent of the coffee prices meant
> the arrival of difficult times for the_ finqueros... _it has
> not only been the owners of the coffee plantations who
> have suffered less under these extraordinary
> circumstances, but that even the rising exchange rate
> has supplied a certain advantage: in general, the
> workers wages were not increased, they continued to be_

paid in devaluated paper money as if it were silver coins. Through this, the production costs could be diminished considerably, which is very fortunate in view of the low level of the coffee prices, of the high freight rates which have to be paid in our region for the transportation of merchandise and agrarian products, and the high tax of 56 pesos per quintal of coffee to be exported that the Government demands according to a resolution of last year. In this way, the owners of coffee plantations in this region (three quarters of them being Germans) have been able to keep afloat during the bad times of low prices, without having to make major sacrifices". (Richard Sapper to Fürsten zu Hohenlohe-Schillingsfürst, DZA Potsdam, A.A., Folder No. 53916, July 2, 1901)

BIBLIOGRAPHY

I. Unpublished Sources

1. Archivo General de Centroamérica (A.G.C.A.), Guatemala City, Guatemala.
2. Deutches Zentralarchiv Abteilung Merseburg (DZA Merseburg), Merseburg, German Democratic Republic.
3. Deutsches Zentralarchiv Abteilung Potsdam (DZA Potsdam), Potsdam, German Democratic Republic.
4. Erwin Paul Dieseldorff Archives (E.P.D. Archives), Howard-Tilton Memorial Library, Special Collection Department, Tulane University, New Orleans, USA.

II. Published Sources and Contemporary Works

Acuña Ortega, Víctor Hugo, *Capital comercial y comercio exterior en América Central durante el siglo XVIII. Una contribución.* In: *"Estudios Sociales Centroamericanos",* San

327

José de Costa Rica, Mayo-Agosto de 1980, Año IX, No 26.

Apuntamientos sobre la agricultura y el comercio del Reyno de Guatemala. In: *"Economía de Guatemala en los siglos XVIII y XIX"*. Jorge Luján Muñoz, editor. Guatemala, 1974.

Bates, H.W., *Central America, the West Indies and South America*. Standford's Compendium of Geography and Travel. Based on Hellwald's *"Die Erde und ihre Völker"*. London, 1878.

Bernouilli, Gustav, *Briefe aus Guatemala*. In: *"Petermann's Geographische Mitteilungen"*, 1869 & 1870, Bände 15 & 16, Hefte XI & XII.

Reise in der Republik Guatemala. In: *"Petermann's Geographische Mitteilungen"*, 1874, Band 20, Heft VIII.

Burgess, Paul, *Justo Rufino Barrios: A Biography*. Quezaltenango, Guatemala, 1946. There is a Spanish version translated by Francis Gall och published i Guatemala City in 1971.

Cambranes, J.C., *Aspectos del desarrollo económico y social de Guatemala, a la luz de fuentes históricas alemanas, 1868-1885*. Published by the Instituto de Investigaciones Económicas y Sociales (IIES), Universidad de San Carlos de Guatemala, Guatemala, 1975.

El Imperialismo Alemán en Guatemala. El Tratado de Comercio de 1887. Published by the Instituto de Investigaciones Económicas y Sociales (IIES), Universidad de San Carlos de Guatemala, Guatemala, 1977.

Casal, Pío, Cardoso, Ciro F. Santana osv. *Reseña de la situación general de Guatemala*. Guatemala, 1981.

Chandler, David L., *Juan José de Aycinena. Conservador idealista de Guatemala del Siglo Diecinueve*. Unpublished Doctoral Thesis, Tulane University, New Orleans, 1972.

Del Cid Fernández, Enrique, *Bienes de la Familia Aparicio, y llegada de los primeros alemanes a Guatemala como consecuencia de la colonización belga*. Guatemala, 1969.

El Cultivo del Café en Guatemala. Published by the Instituto de Investigaciones Económicas y Sociales (IIES), Universidad de San Carlos de Guatemala, Guatemala, 1982.

Erckert, F.C. von, _Die wirtschaftlichen Interessen Deutschlands in Guatemala_. In: _"Beiträge zur Kolonialpolitik und Kolonialwirtschaft"_, III, Berlin, 1901-1902.

Foster, William Z., _Esbozo de una Historia Política de las Américas_. La Habana, 1965, 3 volumes.

Friede, Juan, _Bartolomé de las Casas: precursor del anticolonialismo_. Siglo veintiuno editor, s.a., 2a. edición, México,1976.

García Añoveros, Jesús María, _La realidad social de la Diócesis de Guatemala_. In: _"Mesoamérica"_,Antigua Guatemala, 1980, volume I.

Estructura Agraria y Poder Político en Guatemala: la Reforma Agraria de Arbenz. Unpublished Doctoral Thesis, Departamento de Historia de América de la Facultad de Geografía e Historia, Universidad Complutense de Madrid, 1982.

Hanke, Lewis, _Estudios sobre Bartolomé de las Casas y sobre la lucha por la justicia en la Conquista española de América_. Universidad Central de Caracas. 1968.

Hernández de León, Federico, _El Libro de las Efemérides_. Guatemala, 1935.

Holleran, Mary, _Church and State in Guatemala_. New York, Columbia University Press, 1949.

Innes, Frank C., _Plantations as Institutions Under Stress in the Caribbean Today:_ A Historical-Geographic Approach. In: _"NS/Canadian Journal of Latin American Studies"_;Vol. VI, No. 12, 1981.

Jones, Chester Lloyd, _Comunicaciones y Servicios Públicos en Guatemala_. In: _"Economía de Guatemala 1750-1940. Antología de Lecturas y Materiales"_. (Introduction & selection by Jorge Luján Muñoz), published by the Facultad de Humanidades, Universidad de San Carlos de Guatemala, 1980, vol. II.

Konetzke, Richard, *Colección de Documentos para la Historia de la Formación Social de Hispanoamérica, 1493-1810.* Published by the Consejo Superior de Investigaciones Científicas, Madrid, 1953.

América Latina, La época colonial. Historia Universal Siglo XXI editores, s.a., Madrid, 1971.

Le Goff, Jacques, *Mercaderes y Banqueros de la Edad Media.* Editorial Universitaria de Buenos Aires, 5a. edición, 1970.

MacLeod, Murdo J., *Spanish Central America. A Socioeconomic History, 1520-1720.* University of California Press, Berkeley- Los Angeles-London, 1973.

Martínez Peláez, Severo, *La Patria del Criollo. Ensayo de interpretación de la realidad colonial guatemalteca.* Editorial Universitaria Centroamericana, Sexta Edición, San José de Costa Rica, 1979.

Marx, Karl, *Grundrisse der Kritik der politischen Ökonomie.* Dietz Verlag, Berlin, 1953.

El Capital. Fondo de Cultura Económica, decimotercera reimpresión, México, 1978, vol I.

McCreery, David, *Desarrollo Económico y Política Nacional. El Ministerio de Fomento de Guatemala, 1871-1885.* (Translated by Stephen Webre). Published by the Centro de Investigaciones Regionales de Mesoamérica (CIRMA), Serie Monográfica No. 1, Antigua Guatemala,1981.

Miller, H.J., *La Iglesia Católica y el Estado en Guatemala, 1871-1885.* (Translated by Jorge Luján Muñoz). Published by the Universidad de San Carlos de Guatemala, Guatemala, 1976.

Nañez Falcón, Guillermo, *Erwin Paul Dieseldorff, German Entrepeneur in the Alta Verapaz of Guatemala, 1889-1937.* Unpublished Doctoral Thesis, Tulane University, New Orleans, 1970.

Naylor, Robert A., *British Commercial Relations with Central America, 1821-1851.* Unpublished Doctoral Thesis, Tulane University, New Orleans, 1958.

Nieto Arteta, Luis, *El café en la sociedad colombiana.* Bogotá, 1975.

Ots Capdequí, José María, *El régimen de la tierra en la América española durante el período colonial.* Universidad de Santo Domigo, Santo Domingo, República Dominicana, 1946.

Pérez de la Riva, Francisco, *El Café. Historia de su cultivo y explotación en Cuba.* La Habana, 1944.

Pérez de la Riva, Juan, *La contradicción fundamental de la sociedad colonial cubana: trabajo esclavo contra trabajo libre.* In: *"Economía y Desarrollo",* La Habana, Abril-Junio de 1970, No. 2.

Pinto Soria, Julio César, *Guatemala en la Década de la Independencia.* Editorial Universitaria, Guatemala, 1978.

Estructura agraria y asentamientos en la Capitanía General de Guatemala. Algunos apuntes históricos. Published by the Centro de Estudios Urbanos y Regionales (CEUR), Universidad de San Carlos de Guatemala, Guatemala, 1980.

Rodríguez, Juan J., *Desde cuándo se cultivó el café en Guatemala?* In: *"La República",* Guatemala, 31 de julio de 1900.

Roesch, Adrian, *Allerlei aus der alta Verapaz.* Stuttgart, 1934.

Rubio Sánchez, Manuel, *Historia del Añil o Xiquilite en Centro América.* San Salvador, El Salvador, 1976, II volume.

Historia del Comercio del Café en Guatemala. Siglos XVIII y XIX. In: *"Anales de la Sociedad de Geografía e Historia de Guate mala".* vols. L, LI & LII, Guatemala, 1977-1979.

Salazar, Ramón A., *Historia de Veintiún Años.* Guatemala, 1928.

Sarg, Franz, *Alte Erinnerungen an der Alta Verapaz.* In: *"Frey",* Stuttgart, 1939.

Scherzer, Karl von, *Las tribus indias de Guatemala,* (Translated by Evelin Paap). In: *"Mesoamérica",* Publication of the Centro de Investigaciones Regionales de Mesoamérica (CIRMA), Antigua Guatemala 1980, vol I.

Smith, Robert S., *La producción y el comercio de añil en el Reino de Guatemala.* In: *"Economía de Guatemala 1750-1940.*

Antología de Lecturas y Materiales". (Introduction & selection by Jorge Luján Muñoz), published by the Facultad de Humanidades, Universidad de San Carlos de Guatemala, Guatemala, 1980, vol I.

Solano, Francisco de, *Los Mayas del Siglo XVIII. Pervivencia y Transformación de la Sociedad Indígena guatemalteca durante la Administración Borbónica.* Ediciones Cultura Hispánica, Madrid, 1974.

Solís, Ignacio, *Memorias de la Casa de Moneda de Guatemala y del desarrollo económico del país. Contiene datos sobre la riqueza mineralógica de la América Cantral.* Published by the Ministerio de Finanzas, Guatemala, 1987-1979, 6 volumes.

Stoll, Otto, *Guatemala, Reisen und Schilderungen aus den Jahren 1878-1883.* Leipzig, 1886.

Torres Moss, Clodoveo, *La Propiedad Agraria en el Reino de Guatemala durante el Siglo XVI. La tierra, estímulo en las empresas de descubrimiento y conquista,* In: *"El Imparcial"* Guatemala, 28 de mayo de 1982.

Ukers, William H., *All Abut Coffe. New York, 1922.*

INSTITUTE OF LATIN AMERICAN STUDIES
University of Stockholm
Address: Box 6909, S-102 39 Stockholm, Sweden

Other titles of interest

MONOGRAPHS

1. MÖRNER, Magnus: La corona española y los
   foráneos en los pueblos de América. Stockholm
   1970, 445 pp, 7 maps.
2. KARLSSON, Weine: Manufacturing in Venezuela. Studies on Development and Location. Stockholm 1975, 240 pp, 32 maps.
3. MÖRNER, Magnus: El Perfil de la sociedad
   rural del Cuzco a fines de la Colonia. Lima 1978,
   187 pp.
4. El Sector Agrario en América Latina: estructura
   económica y cambio social. Papers from a Sympo-
   sium at Uppsala. Edited by M. Beatriz Albuquer-
   que and Mauricio Dias D., Stockholm
   1979, 188 pp.
5. ALBERTS, Tom: Agrarian Reform and Rural
   Poverty. A case Study of Peru. Lund-Stockholm
   1981, 306 pp.

6. ABRIL, Galo: The Role of Disaster Relief for Long-Term Development in LDCs — with special reference to Guatemala after the 1976 earthquake. Stockholm 1982, 264 pp.
7. BUZAGLO, Jorge D: Planning Alternative Development Strategies: Experiments on the Mexican Economy. Stockholm 1982, 271 pp.
8. Capitales, Empresarios y obreros europeos en América Latina. Actas del 6⁰ Congreso de AHILA Estocolmo, 25-28 de mayo de 1981. Stockholm 1983, 813 pp (2 vol).
9. Simón Bolívar 1783-1983. Imagen y presencia del Libertador en estudios y documentos suecos. Stockholm 1983, 88 pp.

PERIODICALS

1. Ibero Americana — Nordic Journal of Latin American Studies. Vol. 6 (1976).
2. Latinomericana. Series of acquisitions lists and documentation reports. No 1 (1977).

COMMUNICATIONS AND REPORTS

1. MÖRNER, Magnus: Tenant Labour in Andean South America since the Eighteenth Century. A preliminary report. Moscow 1970, 15 pp.

2. Estudios y documentos suecos sobre Cuba. Stockholm 1971, 87 pp. (Out of print).

Tryckt hos arbetskooperativet
Tryckop Grafiska Verkstäder,
ek. för. (Comunidad)
under kollektiva arbetsformer.
Stockholm, januari 1985.

Impreso en forma cooperativa
en los talleres gráficos de
Tryckop – Comunidad
Estocolmo, enero 1985.
Tel. 08/714 78 58.